Masterworks:
Architecture at the
Royal Academy of Arts

Masterworks:
Architecture at the
Royal Academy of Arts

Neil Bingham

Royal Academy of Arts

Royal Academy Publications
David Breuer
Beatrice Gullström
Carola Krueger
Sophie Oliver
Peter Sawbridge
Nick Tite

Design: Esterson Associates
Colour origination: DawkinsColour
Printed in Italy by Conti

British Library Cataloguing-in-Publication
Data

A catalogue record for this book is available
from the British Library

ISBN 978-1-905711-83-3

Distributed outside the United States and
Canada by Thames & Hudson Ltd, London

Distributed in the United States and
Canada by Harry N. Abrams, Inc.,
New York

*This book is dedicated to the memory of
my father.*

Acknowledgements
The task of researching and writing about each
of the Diploma Works by the architect-
Academicians, and giving a short historical
and contemporary study of the discipline of
architecture at the Royal Academy, has left
me owing a debt of thanks to many people.

First and foremost, I would like to extend my
appreciation to the Royal Academicians, and
especially of course to the architects. I have
had the honour of knowing many of them, and
it is with deep respect that I have written about
their designs. I thank those architects who
spoke and corresponded with me. I hope that
I have done justice to the work of all architect-
Academicians, past and present.

Among the staff of the Royal Academy,
I am extremely grateful to MaryAnne Stevens,
Director of Academic Affairs, for proposing
the commission, enthusiastically following
my research and making invaluable
suggestions to my text. Nick Savage, Head
of Collections and Library, is always ready
to engage in lively discussions on matters
architectural and academic; his critical
observations on my drafts have saved me from
no few embarrassing errors. Needless to say,
any remaining embarrassments are mine
alone. Helen Valentine, Head of Cataloguing
Project, offered her charming good guidance.

My colleagues in the Royal Academy Library
and Collections have all helped with my
studies with their customary spirit of dedicated
teamwork: Mark Pomeroy, Morgan Feely,
Pat Eaton, Annette Wickham, Adam
Waterton, Rachel Hewitt, Edwina Mulvany,
Linda Macpherson, Miranda Stead, Elizabeth
King, Andrew Potter, Cathy Dembsky, Tanya
Millard, Laura Valentine, Jennifer Camilleri
and Sue Graves. And, consulting to the Royal
Academy Collections, Catherine Rickman,
Sally Esdaile, Christina Mulvihill, Sara Stoll,
Sarah Beecham and Peter Schmitt.

In the preparation of this publication,
my grateful thanks go to Peter Sawbridge,
Managing Editor, who untangled my prose
with calm discretion. Also at the Royal
Academy, I would like to thank Dr Charles
Saumarez Smith, Nick Tite, Sophie Oliver
and Kate Goodwin.

Many friends have come to my rescue to
track down sources familiar to them. I would
like to thank Professor Dirk van den Heuvel
of Delft University of Technology, Dr Basile
Baudez of the Université de Paris-Sorbonne,
and Dr Andrew Hopkins of the Università
degli Studi dell'Aquila. Other historian friends
and colleagues who have been of invaluable
assistance include Tim Knox, Jill Lever,
Margaret Richardson, John Harris, Dr Elain
Harwood, Dr Frank Salmon, Dr David Watkin,
Dr Alan Powers, Dr Gavin Stamp,
Michael Hall, Dr John Martin Robinson,
Edward Denison, Oliver Bradbury, Frank Albo
and Harriet Sandvall.

The families of architects have been very
generous with information, including Ann
Davis-Thomas, daughter of Arthur J. Davis RA;
Ann Gage Smith, daughter of Charles Gage;
Olivia Thomson, daughter of Herbert
Worthington RA; Simon Houfe, grandson
of Sir Albert Richardson PRA; Dr Timothy
Brittain-Catlin, nephew of Leonard
Manasseh RA; Dinah Casson, daughter
of Sir Hugh Casson PRA; and Simon
Smithson, son of Alison and Peter Smithson.

Others who have kindly provided
information include Oliver Mahony, Ben
Bisek, Charles Pugh, Rik Nys, Nick Holmes,
Alan Mitchell, John Haworth, Hannah Fuller,
Michael Wilford, Sir Jack Zunz, Antonio de
Campos, Manon Janssens, Anna Barlow,
Victoria Bergman, Pat Holford, Bernadette
Ratigan and Susan Steyn.

A number of close friends kept my spirits up
during the writing of this book. I would like to
pass on my warm thanks to Luis Perel Ananda,
Peter Fuller, Neil Einarson, Zac Norman,
Jonathan Hoyle, Joan, Fraser and Kevin
Linklater, Charlie Mackeith and Madeleine
Adams, Kerry Taylor, and Amy Franck.
Neil Bingham

Illustrations
Page 2: detail of page 153
Page 5: detail of page 111
Page 8: detail of page 119
Pages 40–41: detail of page 51

Contents

President's Foreword

In 1768, at the founding of the Royal Academy of Arts, King George III sanctioned four disciplines. Architecture was represented by a select group of practitioners. Chief among them was Sir William Chambers, designer of New Somerset House on the Strand, erstwhile architectural tutor to the King, and Treasurer of the new institution. Chambers's involvement ensured that architecture figured at the centre of the Royal Academy's activities from the outset: it was taught in the Royal Academy Schools, represented by a Professor of Architecture, and shown at the Annual Exhibition. The roll of subsequent architect-Academicians came to include almost all the most eminent names in the profession.

A requirement of the Royal Academy's Instrument of Foundation was that all newly elected Royal Academicians be obliged to deposit in the institution's collections a representative example of their work. In exchange for this, a Diploma, signed by the reigning monarch, would confirm their status. The parade of illustrious architect-Academicians has ensured that the remarkable corpus of architectural drawings and models presented by them now recounts the story of British architecture and architectural representation from the late eighteenth century to the twenty first. The Royal Academy has played a pivotal role in this development.

The distinguished architectural historian and curator Dr Neil Bingham has astutely revealed these layered histories throughout this volume, at the same time bringing insight to each Diploma Work. As befits an institution established to 'encourage the arts of design', its architects' Diploma Works – beautifully delineated and often grand in scale – have the power to reveal confluences and crosscurrents within the arts.

This book, the first full catalogue of architecture in the Royal Academy's collection to have been published since the small handlist for the Diploma Galleries in 1939, has grown out of the Royal Academy's project to catalogue its collections, library and archive, a process initiated in 2000. As well as cataloguing, this has encompassed conservation, imaging and display on a dedicated website of all the institution's holdings.

Many trusts, foundations and individuals have provided important financial support to help us realise the Cataloguing Project. In the particular case of the architectural Diploma Works, we wish to acknowledge the exceptional generosity of the Eugene V. and Clare E. Thaw Charitable Trust, the American Associates of the Royal Academy Trust, and the John S. Cohen Foundation. They all share an understanding of the historical significance of these works and a profound appreciation of their intrinsic beauty. Together they have enabled us not only to preserve and study digitally these important works and to make them accessible virtually on the web, but also to publish them in this handsome book.

Sir Nicholas Grimshaw CBE PRA

Architecture at the Royal Academy of Arts

At the request of a group of distinguished artists, led in particular by the architect Sir William Chambers and the painter Benjamin West, King George III signed an 'Instrument of Foundation' on 10 December 1768 to create an entirely new kind of British institution for the promotion of the 'Arts of Design' in painting, sculpture and architecture. The King's new Royal Academy of Arts was, and continues to be, unique in being independent of the state, privately funded, and run by artists of merit, a self-perpetuating group of Royal Academicians, who alone are eligible to appoint new members to their strictly limited number.

Promotion of the arts was to be 'by instruction and by emulation',[1] chiefly through exhibition – the Royal Academy Summer Exhibition (known as the Annual Exhibition until 1869) – and training at the Royal Academy Schools. Although the Royal Academy was not the first society in London to offer artists the benefits of drawing from the life model and plaster casts, or to mount annual exhibitions where they might compete for public fame, the Royal Academy's combination of these activities was unique. Moreover, the Royal Academy Schools offered, for the first time, a systematic training of artists and architects as opposed to the practice of apprenticeship offered in individual artists' studios and architects' offices. Immediately upon its creation, the Royal Academy became the national powerhouse of design.

Every newly elected Royal Academician receives royal approbation in the form of an engraved Diploma, signed by the monarch, which sanctions the privilege of placing the initials 'RA' after his or her name (fig. 1). There is, however, one important requisite that the successful candidate is obliged to fulfil: having been elected by the General Assembly (the full body of Royal Academicians), the chosen artist is required to present, for approval, an example of his or her work to the Council (the governing body of the Royal Academy). In the early days, presentations had to be made before the Diploma was received; today there is

a grace period. In the picturesque language of Clause III of the Instrument of Foundation, the Academician-Elect 'shall not receive his Letter of Admission [the Diploma] 'til he hath deposited in the Royal Academy, to remain there, *a Picture, Bas-relief, or other specimen of his abilities*'. This accomplished piece of art, this masterwork, is thus known as a Diploma Work.

In 1768 the number of Royal Academicians was set at forty 'artists'. A few years later the Associateship order of the Royal Academy (ARA) was created as a stepping-stone to full membership.[2] Over the years the number of Royal Academicians was increased little by little until the dramatic increase of 1991, when the ARA category was abolished and all existing Associates were automatically elected as Royal Academicians. Today the number of Royal Academicians is fixed at eighty. Moreover, there is also a Senior order of Academicians consisting of all members over 75 years of age, as well as an Honorary order of other nationalities instituted in 1869 (see p. 244). Painters, by tradition, make up the largest class, today numbering approximately 40%, with a balance of about 25% sculptors, 20% architects and 15% engravers, printmakers and draughtsmen.

After nearly 250 years, the Royal Academy has accumulated a large and ever-growing collection of Diploma Works. By mid-2010, it possessed 532. Of these, 86 were by architect-Academicians, the earliest dating from 1786, when James Wyatt was the first elected architect to join the Foundation Members, who did not have to present Diploma Works. Fortunately, however, several are represented by later acquisitions. The aim of this book is to illustrate and discuss all architectural Diploma Works and the few supplementary examples by Foundation Members. Unfortunately, there are no works by George Dance the Younger (1741–1825) and John Gwynn (1713–1786), and in the modern period, Berthold Lubetkin (1901–1990), who died the year after his election as a Senior

1   RAA/PC/10, Annual Report, 1859, p. 6.
2   Associates had full use of the Academy, the right to have their works hung in the Summer Exhibition without having to have them accepted by the Selection Committee. ARAs had no voting rights and were ineligible to sit on Council, although they were asked to serve as Visitors in the Royal Academy Schools. They were not required to submit a Diploma Work. Seven architect-Associates did not become full Academicians although all were practitioners of

outstanding reputation (see p. 244). Some ARAs died before an opportunity arose for their elevation. Others, such as Joseph Bonomi, were dogged by controversy and rejected, mainly by the painter-Academicians (see Peter Meadows, *Joseph Bonomi, Architect, 1739–1808*, exh. cat., RIBA Heinz Gallery, London, May–June 1988).

Fig. 2
The Penguin Pool at London
Zoo in Regent's Park, an early
project from 1934 by the
Russian-born émigré architect
Berthold Lubetkin RA
(1901–1990), a pioneering
modernist. Photograph by
Morley von Sternberg, from the
collection of the Royal Institute
of British Architects, London.
Lubetkin is the only architect-
Academician who should have
submitted a Diploma Work but
was prevented by his death
soon after his election. In the
background are the concrete
walls and copper roof of the
Elephant and Rhinoceros
Pavilion designed by Sir Hugh
Casson PRA, who submitted a
drawing of this building as his
Diploma Work (see pp. 152–53).

Royal Academician in 1989, before depositing his Diploma Work (fig. 2).[3]

The Royal Academy's architectural Diploma Works are demonstration pieces by Britain's leading architects, as well as some all-but-forgotten figures.[4] Individually, each tells us much about the maker, the project and the time. As an historic collection, they offer the unique opportunity of following evolving methods of architectural representation for the purposes of presentation. Moreover, as Diploma Works are created within the highest tradition of an academic institution, they are the works of masters.

The Architectural Diploma Work as Masterwork

The presentation of a masterwork has a long tradition. During the Middle Ages, European cities controlled specialised trades, including those associated with art and building, through the formation of guilds. A long period of apprenticeship under a master of the guild culminated in the presentation of a masterpiece or masterwork (from the Latin *magister*, meaning 'teacher'), making the apprentice or the more experienced journeyman a master himself.

In the Renaissance, guilds came to be replaced by academies. No longer confined to manual skills, academies offered study in schools that imparted a broader cultural and historical approach. It is said that Plato, no less, created the first academy in the fourth century BC as a place for scholarly debate, named for its templed site near Athens which had, according to tradition, belonged to the hero Akademia. Renaissance thinkers were keenly interested in Neo-Platonism, a term which came to embrace knowledge of various schools of philosophy related to the Greek and Roman periods. In the arts, academies concentrated on the beauty and established design forms of classical antiquity. At its formation, the Royal Academy inherited and propagated this attachment to the ancient world.

Often, as indeed was the case with the Royal Academy, academic bodies were established under the patronage of royal or aristocratic figures. The most powerful academies of art and architecture arose in France in the seventeenth century under the absolute monarchy of Louis XIV. With the creation of the Académie Royale de Peinture et de Sculpture (Royal Academy of Painting and Sculpture) in 1648, the concept of a masterwork reappeared as the so-called *morceau de reception*, which is the closest parallel to the Royal Academy's Diploma Work. At the Académie Royale, the *agréé*, the artist who had been 'recognised', was given admittance only upon presentation of the *morceau de reception*, a practice that continued until the reorganisation of the Académie in 1793 during the French Revolution.[5]

A complementary academy for architects, the Académie Royale d'Architecture (Royal Academy of Architecture) was formed in 1671 at the instigation of Louis XIV's great minister of finance Jean-Baptiste Colbert. The architects, however, were not obliged to give an example of their work. Instead, their focus on masterworks was shifted to the architectural drawings made by students of the Académie's school in competition (*concours*) for the prestigious Prix de Rome, a scholarship that sent the winner to the Eternal City for three years to study the ancient monuments.

In Italy almost every major city-state had its own art academy. In Rome, the venerable Accademia di San Luca (St Luke's Academy), founded in 1593, held architectural drawing competitions (*concorsi*) that attracted many young hopefuls from abroad, including the Scottish architect Robert Mylne, who won the Silver Medal in 1758. Like all winning entries, Mylne's work was retained by the Accademia and is today to be found among its large and fascinating collection dating from the seventeenth to the early twentieth centuries.[6] Historically, as presentation pieces, architectural drawings for hypothetical

3 Other architects have died before depositing a Diploma Work, but works have been submitted by their families and colleagues and accepted by the Council of Royal Academy. The fine pair of drawings by Sir James Stirling for Channel 4 Headquarters, London, is an example (see pp. 202–03).

4 It is almost as interesting to note which architects were not Academicians. Robert Adam (1728–1798), for example, Chambers's rival as leading architect of the day, was conspicuously absent at the time of foundation; he was not looked upon with particular favour by King George III. However, Adam made a point of presenting to the Academy's library a copy of his *Ruins of the Palace of the Emperor Diocletian at Spalatro in Dalmatia* (1764). Adam was not the first eminent British architect not to become a Royal Academician. There are many reasons for this, beginning with the simple fact that there may not have been a place for the election of an architect-Academician at the appropriate time. Some architects did not wish to participate, or disapproved of the Academy's current attitude to architecture. A. W. N. Pugin (1812–1852), although not greatly interested, was encouraged by friends who were Academicians; when he failed to be elected, he was embarrassed because, he said, 'it is cause of a good deal of ridicule' (Rosemary Hill, *God's Architect: Pugin and the Building of Romantic Britain*, London, 2007, p. 417).

5 The collection of *morceau de reception* paintings and sculptures is now housed at the Ecole National Supérieure des Beaux-Arts, Paris, one of the five academies of the Institut de France and the successor of the mergers between the Académie Royale de Peinture et de Sculpture and the Académie Royale d'Architecture.

6 Robert Mylne made copies of his winning drawings; these are deposited on long-term loan at the Royal Academy. For a history and illustrations of architectural drawings in the Accademia di San Luca, see P. Marconi, A. Cipriani and E. Valeriani,

projects by students in French and Italian academies are analogous to the Royal Academy's Diploma Works by professionals for actual projects.

Drawings reigned supreme in the architectural Diploma Works until 1975. After this date, although the drawing has continued to dominate, it has been joined by the reproduction print, usually hand-coloured by the architect, as well as by architectural models, photographs, etchings, works in mixed media and, as is to be expected, computer-generated printed images, which are still, by convention, called 'drawings'.

Without doubt, drawing lies at the heart of design. The earliest acknowledged academy of art, created during the Renaissance in Florence in 1563, was the Accademia delle Arti del Disegno – the Academy of the Arts of 'Disegno', a term that can be translated as both design and drawing. Michelangelo was a founder-member; the architect Andrea Palladio joined shortly afterwards. And, two centuries later, the young William Chambers became a member, after having attended the first full-time study course in architecture at the Ecole des Arts in Paris, an offshoot of the Académie Royale d'Architecture. This was the academic route that prepared Chambers for his role as architectural tutor to the Prince of Wales, the future George III, beginning in the late 1750s; he instructed the prince for up to three mornings a week on how to draw the classical orders of architecture while setting his royal pupil exercises in designing classical buildings (fig. 3).[7] Architectural drawing brought patron and architect together in a partnership that was to blossom into the formation of the Royal Academy.

In the mid-eighteenth century, the title 'architect' was reserved for those few surveyors, master-masons or carpenters who built on a grand scale but also had the talent to design by drawing. Alternatively, an architect could be an artist, the ability to draw being the key. In the early seventeenth century, Inigo Jones (1573–1652) was a painter and stage designer as well as Surveyor to the King's Buildings. Sir Christopher Wren

(1632–1723) was a mathematician-scientist who became an architect by means of his knowledge of mechanics and draughtsmanship. Patronage was another means to acquire design and drawing abilities. Gentleman-architects often undertook the Grand Tour through Europe, a privilege open to aristocrats and wealthy commoners. Richard Boyle, 3rd Earl of Burlington (1694–1753), is a celebrated example. Having travelled to Italy on his Grand Tour he returned to England and gathered around him a talented group of artists and architects. The 'Burlington set' were to change the course of architectural history, formulating a new approach to design largely by studying their patron's collection of architectural drawings by Palladio and Inigo Jones, the first British architect to design in the fine classical style of the Renaissance. It is fitting that the Royal Academy's home today, only its third permanent address since 1768, should be Lord Burlington's town mansion on Piccadilly, which he remodelled in the Palladian style, positioning at the very heart of the building William Kent's roundel painting (fig. 4) showing the Muse of Architecture presenting a portrait of Inigo Jones while being shown an architectural drawing by a putto.[8]

Architectural drawings assert authority, even near-divine power, as Kent's allegory proposes. They are the arrows in the architect's quiver, the weapon for bolstering and elevating the status of architects above all contenders. At the time of the creation of the Royal Academy, the rise of a middle class and the Industrial Revolution were stimulating increased building activity and demanding new building types, forcing the construction trades into specialised professions. Many architects felt under threat, and their disquiet increased as surveyors and engineers began to organise their own professional bodies. The establishment of the Royal Academy, which could deliver training in drawing skills and regular exhibitions, ensured that the architect was able to exert influence not only over the manual trades of the builder, but also the functional skills of the

I Disegni di architetture dell'Archivo storico dell'Accademia di San Luca, Rome, 1974. The Accademia di San Luca recently began requesting that its current and new Academicians contribute a *pièce de reception*: two drawings from different periods of their careers. See Francesco Moschini (ed.), *L'Accademia Nazionale di San Luca: Per una collezione del disegno contemporaneo. Pittura, scultura, architettura*, exh. cat., Accademia di San Luca, Rome, 2009.

7   John Harris, *Sir William Chambers, Knight of the Polar Star*, London, 1970, pp. 18–31; Janine Barrier, 'Chambers in France and Italy,' in John Harris and Michael Snodin (eds), *Sir William Chambers, Architect to George III*, New Haven and London, 1996, pp. 19–33; the Hon. Lady Jane Roberts, 'Sir William Chambers and George III,' in Harris and Snodin, op. cit., pp. 40–54.

8   Today Kent's roundel painting *Architecture* is over the Great Staircase of Burlington House. The canvas is probably roughly in the position that Lord Burlington chose for it in about the early 1720s, inset in the ceiling of a small anteroom, which was destroyed when the architect Samuel Ware created the Regency staircase compartment in c. 1818 for Lord George Henry Cavendish.

engineer. This perceived need for the architect to chisel out a professional niche, and to maintain rank, is a strong theme that runs throughout the Academy's history. Architect-Academicians tend to be influential educators and formulators of the architectural educational system. The Royal Academy's foundation in 1768 has long been considered the introduction of the first model in the establishment of a professional role for the architect.[9] Gradually, step by step as time progressed, a number of architect-Academicians became part of a wider, organised lobbying group, which was boosted by the establishment of the Royal Institute of British Architects in 1834. Architects established rights for ever greater control not only in architecture but also in town planning and on broader issues of environmental and societal organisation.

Architect-Academicians, very importantly, maintain their professional status by encouraging dialogue between the various arts, especially painting and sculpture, in keeping with academic tradition. The Royal Academy promotes first and foremost, as its Instrument of Foundation states, the 'Arts of Design'. At the Royal Academy, irrespective of discipline, painters, sculptors and architects are all called 'artists'. Foundation Members did not register their artistic specialisation. In fact, no specific categories of membership were laid down in the Laws of the Royal Academy until 1917,[10] by which time professionalism had become more of the norm.

The principle of unity across the board, the symbiotic relationship between the arts within the Royal Academy, takes place most noticeably during the Summer Exhibition, when the Selection Committee, a group chosen from among the Royal Academicians, gathers to judge all entries for this open-submission exhibition. Architects review the work of artists, just as artists assess the work of architects. And, until relatively recently, at the full General Assembly that is held annually on or around 10 December, the anniversary of the Academy's foundation, all attending Royal Academicians would examine and vote upon the work done by students of the Royal Academy Schools in all classes; the day was then marked with a ceremony of awarding prizes, medals and travelling scholarships.

The Diploma Work was inextricably linked to the two major foundations upon which the Royal Academy was created: the Schools (education and achievement) and the Annual Exhibition (achievement and authority). Instruction for architecture students in the Royal Academy Schools comprised drawing and attending lectures, illustrated with drawings, by Royal Academy Professors. In the eighteenth and nineteenth centuries, only a few architectural models were shown in the Architecture Room of the Annual Exhibitions; it was the architectural drawing that demonstrated, for all to see, that its maker had cultivated a high sense of design and was therefore 'an architect'. In the Annual Exhibitions, high status was – and often still is – reserved for the most recent Diploma Works submitted by Royal Academicians.

9   Mark Crinson and Jules Lubbock, *Architecture: Art or Profession?*, Manchester, 1994, p. 8.

10   Nicholas Savage, 'Preface', *Royal Academy of Arts: Directory of Membership from the Foundation in 1768 to 1995 including Honorary Members*, Chippenham, 1996, p. vi.

Thus the architectural Diploma Work of the Royal Academy of Arts is at its most basic level, 'a specimen of ... abilities'; in its fuller sense, a Diploma Work should be among the finest examples of work that an architect can present, nothing less than a masterwork.

The Classical Academic Tradition, 1768–1840

The Foundation Members of the Royal Academy did not have to submit Diploma Works. They were already masters, appointed by royal command. The three principal architect-founders of the Royal Academy, Sir William Chambers, Thomas Sandby and George Dance the Younger were all eminent practitioners of their day. John Gwynn, as a fourth, would also have been considered to be working in the broadly defined field of architecture; in 1766 he had published, to great success, a work combining a massive town-planning scheme for London with a plea for the 'study of the Polite Arts'.[11] In the first four Annual Exhibitions, Gwynn contributed architectural drawings: from 'An architectonick drawing designed for the alteration of an old room in Shropshire' in 1769, to his last in 1772 for his most well-known structure, the famous Magdalen Bridge in Oxford, then under construction. Gwynn was also considered an 'improver', adding architectural features to paintings and illustrations, especially for his fellow Foundation Member, the painter and printmaker Samuel Wale.

There was, however, a fifth Foundation Member, William Tyler (d. 1801), who slipped between architecture and sculpture. In the first years of the Annual Exhibition, Tyler regularly showed architectural drawings; but he later submitted sculpture, and it is upon this discipline that his artistic reputation rests. His selection as a Foundation Member undoubtedly had as much to do with his connections with other Foundation Members as with his abilities, for he was a proper busybody. The painter Benjamin West, second President of the Royal Academy, who succeeded Sir Joshua Reynolds, explained that Tyler was included because the institution's originators needed to make up a quota of founders, saying that 'there was not a choice of Artists as at present, and some indifferent artists were admitted'.[12] In the history of the Royal Academy, Tyler is remembered mainly for so stirring up Reynolds over the appointment of a new Professor of Perspective that he resigned as President, only to come back a few months later by popular demand.

But it was Chambers who stood head and shoulders above his new architect colleagues, setting a precedent for architects to take a leading role in the running of the Royal Academy that continues to be disproportionate to their low numbers in relation to other categories of membership. The painter Sir Joshua Reynolds may have been the first President, and indeed he played a very active role in the day-to-day running of the Academy, but it was Chambers who was the institution's first Treasurer, an equally if not more powerful position, as holder of the purse strings and representative of the King, to whom appeal could be made in hard financial times. In the history of the Royal Academy, three-quarters of its Treasurers have been architects.[13] Moreover, Chambers literally built the new Royal Academy, designing new Somerset House on the Strand where from 1780 to 1837 the fledgling institution occupied the north wing.

Naturally, the Foundation Members were keen to be represented by some works within the Royal Academy's collection. Although the painters presented exemplars to be hung on the walls of the Royal Academy – in 1780 Reynolds gave two magnificent pendant portraits, one of Sir William Chambers and one of himself – of the original architect-members only Chambers submitted a 'specimen of his Abilities':[14] a copy of a drawing by his friend Jean-Laurent Legeay, made in red chalk, of a perspective of the Marino Casino near Dublin, the neoclassical garden house that Chambers had designed for James Caulfeild, 1st Earl of Charlemont.

11 John Gwynn, *London and Westminster Improved, Illustrated by Plans. To which is prefixed, A Discourse on Publick Magnificence; with Observations on the State of Arts and Artists in this Kingdom, wherein the Study of Polite Arts is recommended as necessary to a liberal Education: Concluded by Some Proposals relative to Places not laid down in the Plans*, London, 1766.

12 Kenneth Garlick and Angus Macintyre (eds), *The Diary of Joseph Farington*, New Haven and London, 1978–98, 16 vols, vol. 6, p. 2214 (8 January 1804).
13 Between 1768 and 2010 there have been 28 Treasurers, 21 of them architects.
14 RAA/CM/1, p. 155, Council Minutes, 16 March 1773.

This drawing, which hung on display for too long, has sadly faded to near extinction. Fortunately, another fine example of Chambers's work entered the Royal Academy's collection in the mid-nineteenth century, an important drawing illustrating his theory on the origin of the Corinthian order (see pp. 42–43).

Perhaps it is no great loss to have no demonstration pieces by Tyler or Gwynn. However, it is a real disappointment that there is no architectural drawing by George Dance the Younger in the Academy's collection, for he was a superb designer and draughtsman. Instead, in yet another example of the overlapping nature of the roles of artist and architect at this period, Dance is represented by the numerous drawn portraits that he made of his fellow Academicians, his so-called 'Academical Heads'.[15]

Dance, like Chambers, was well-versed in foreign architectural academic traditions, having been admitted to the Accademia di San Luca in Rome and having also won the gold medal from the Accademia di Belle Arti in Parma in 1763 with his design for a public gallery. Dance was therefore instrumental in shaping the Royal Academy's programme of academic architectural study. In practice, Dance was a major London town-planner and builder of public buildings, many of which have disappeared, including his greatest work, Newgate Prison, which was demolished in 1904. A collection of his very fine architectural drawings was acquired by his principal pupil, Sir John Soane, and they survive in a wooden boxed 'shrine' in the Sir John Soane's Museum.[16]

In the case of Thomas Sandby, the Royal Academy was fortunate to receive, in 1904, a fine example of one of his architectural drawings from a descendant (see pp. 44–45).[17] Thomas was another practitioner who slid between artistic genres, and his drawings and those of his brother Paul Sandby, a fellow Foundation Member, are often indistinguishable. Thomas Sandby's drawings, lifelike and picturesque, were instrumental in the development of the art of the architectural perspective, establishing this representational technique as the major form of architectural presentation.

As the Royal Academy's first Professor of Architecture, Thomas Sandby dutifully delivered an annual series of six public lectures 'calculated to form the taste of the Students to instruct them in the laws and principles of composition; and to point out to them the beauties or faults of celebrated productions'.[18] From 1780 until two years before his death in 1798, Sandby repeated the same lectures each year, as was the tradition, illustrating them with 33 large and impressive architectural drawings.[19] His lectures were highly influential in forming the tastes of subsequent generations of architects as well as the growing architectural profession.

Exactly a year after being elected the first architect-Academician in February 1785, James Wyatt presented his Diploma Work, showing his design for the Darnley Mausoleum (see pp. 46–47). Wyatt was an architect who perfectly met the rigorous academic standards of the founding Academicians. He had spent a year in Venice learning draughtsmanship from Canaletto's colleague Antonio Visentini, and then a further two years in Rome making the requisite measured drawings of ancient edifices. Election as an Associate of the Royal Academy (ARA) followed quickly, when he was 24 years old. As was expected of those desiring election as a full Royal Academician, he exhibited architectural drawings of his designs fairly regularly at the Annual Exhibitions. Wyatt was a likeable man but of famously desultory habits. Although he holds the distinction of having been elected in 1805 the first architect-President of the Royal Academy, he lost the position within a year because he neglected business and fell asleep in meetings. He also seems to have bent two of the cardinal rules concerning Diploma Works. First, he submitted his drawing not as required, before he had been accepted as a full Academician by Council, but a year afterwards. And secondly, there is a strong

15 Garlick and Macintyre, op. cit., vol. 1, p. 146 (19 January 1794).
16 Jill Lever, *Catalogue of the Drawings of George Dance the Younger (1741–1825) and of George Dance the Elder (1695–1768) from the Collection of Sir John Soane's Museum*, London, 2003.
17 At his death Thomas Sandby left about 100 drawings, which included those produced for his lectures. His brother Paul Sandby offered them to the Royal Academy, but the gift was declined. RAA/PC/3 p. 28, Council Minutes, 1 June 1799.
18 RAA/IF, Instrument of Foundation, 10 December 1768, Chapter 11.
19 David Watkin, *Sir John Soane: Enlightenment Thought and the Royal Academy Lectures*, Cambridge, 1996, pp. 40–57.
20 Garlick and Macintyre, op. cit., vol. 1, p. 146 (21 January 1794). Having dined at William Tyler's, Farington recorded: 'The name of the Artist who is employed by Wyatt to draw for him is Dixon. He has been with Wyatt from the time of the building of the Pantheon.'

likelihood that he did not make his own drawing but that it is the work of his long-time assistant and draughtsman John Dixon.[20]

In fairness to Wyatt, tardiness and surrogacy were common. By the mid-1790s, overdue Diploma Works had become such a problem that a new law was passed within the Academy giving an Academician-elect an allowance of a year in which to submit.[21] Today, that period is six months, and the law continues to carry the late eighteenth-century wording that describes the firm penalty awaiting those who do not submit a Diploma Work: 'in failure of which, his Election shall become void, unless such an apology be made by him for the omission as may be deemed sufficient by the Council.'[22] Nevertheless, a blind eye is usually turned because Royal Academicians appreciate that it is rarely straightforward for any new candidate, not just an architect, to produce an example of work of such prestigious importance. There is usually pressure and a sense of responsibility; much decision-making goes into making a choice. Do I have a work at hand that is creditable? Should I make a new and specific piece as my Diploma Work? Will it measure up to those by my colleagues past and present? How will it stand for posterity? And the central question for architects: how well does it represent my achievements and my view of architecture?

The thorny question of whether architects should produce their own Diploma Works remains. Should the work be in the architect's own hand? Some believe so, even today when the *modus operandi* of architectural practice and representation are continually pushing back the boundaries. This issue reached a head in the mid-1930s at a time when architectural perspectivists, professional hired artists who were almost always architect-trained, were commonly employed to make presentation drawings. In the light of this type of perceived encroachment, architect-artists representing the work of other architects, the Academicians passed a law concerning architectural Diploma Works that still stands today: 'Only drawings made by architect-Academicians elect themselves are eligible as their Diploma Works.'[23] Whether such a principle is tenable is open to debate, especially as in the last several decades architectural drawings are no longer the staple.

One historical consistency, however, is that within architectural practice, the making of an architectural representation has not always been as straightforward as it is, say, for an artist painting a canvas, although of course artists and sculptors do often have assistants who take part in production. Wyatt, if he did have Dixon make his drawing, no doubt considered it a perfectly legitimate action because it came from *his* office. In an architect's practice, no matter who makes the drawing or image, model and even the design itself, logically and usually legally the maker is subsumed by the name of the owner, principal or practice, unless express permission is given for an individual's name to appear in connection with the work. Wyatt even forced Dixon to stop showing at Royal Academy exhibitions, claiming that Dixon's designs were borrowed from his drawings.[24] In a busy office – and Wyatt can probably boast more buildings to his name than any of his rivals from the late Georgian period – architects obviously cannot be expected to produce every major drawing.

And why therefore, it can be argued, should a Diploma Work be an exception? It is usually the case that a master architect maintains such intellectual control over the design that it bears the overwhelming characteristics of his personal drawing style, which have been absorbed by pupil, office and hired hand to become near synonymous with and indistinguishable from the archetype. But, when a master architect hands the making over to a perspectivist whose artistic style he admires, he allows that outsider to make a sympathetic artistic interpretation. However, even such drawings, which are often made for presentation, for instance Diploma Works, must be worked up from the master architect's drawings. Furthermore, such pieces often do not represent the end of the process, no matter

21 RAA/GA/1/1, p. 343, General Assembly Minutes, 4 April 1795.
22 *The Laws of the Royal Academy of Arts, 1768 to 2008*, September 2008, p. 24, Section 5, Clause 11.
23 Ibid.
24 Garlick and Macintyre, op. cit., vol. 2, p. 630 (4 August 1796).

Fig. 5
Stephen Burchell (1806–c. 1845), Drawing of a plaster cast of a marble fragment in the gardens of the Villa Medici, Rome, 1825. Pen with black ink and brown and black washes, 600 × 860 mm (RIBA Drawings Collection, London). Burchell made this drawing as his testimonial work for entrance to the School of Architecture at the Royal Academy Schools when he was about nineteen years old. He was apprenticed in the architectural office of Sir John Soane, where the cast he depicts was displayed on the north side of the dome, as it still is today at the Sir John Soane's Museum in Lincoln's Inn Fields. In the lower right of the drawing, Soane verifies that his pupil has made the drawing.

how polished they look, but are instead part of the process towards the finished design and the built work, both of which are guided by the creative and overarching mind of the master architect.

Concerns about authenticity, however, did not trouble John Yenn, the second architect Royal Academician to be elected, in 1791; his Diploma Work (see pp. 48–49) was of his own making.[25] Yenn was the first of a trio of architect-Academicians – followed by John Soane in 1802 and Robert Smirke in 1811 – to be nurtured in the Royal Academy Schools, and who thus achieved the high standards that the Foundation Members sought. Apprenticed as a youth of fourteen to Chambers, Yenn developed in his shadow, gradually taking on many of his mentor's smaller architectural jobs. Upon Chambers's death, Yenn was elected in his place as Treasurer of the Royal Academy. Although not a high-profile architect, Yenn nevertheless produced exceedingly skilled academic architectural drawings aimed specifically for the Annual Exhibition (many now in the possession of the Royal Academy). Almost all are theoretical, rendered in elevation, enlivened with light and shade, with cloudy blue skies and areas of green shrubbery. Yenn's drawings, based on Chambers's continental experience of drawing style and exercises set in the Royal Academy Schools, mark both the zenith and the rapid demise of the use of the elevation in presentation. The elevation was not to return to presentation drawing for more than a hundred years, when it was transformed by the more austere and compositionally complex style of the French Beaux-Arts (see pp. 120–21). The more painterly, natural style of the perspective advocated by Thomas Sandby had already begun to overtake Yenn's flat method of representing buildings.

Yenn had been admitted as a student in the architecture section of the Royal Academy Schools in 1769, the year of its formation.[26] He was the son of a barber and wig-maker, and private tuition with architectural perspectivists and draughtsmen of the

time would probably have been beyond the means of his family. But by joining the Royal Academy Schools he entered the first organised establishment to offer an architectural education in Britain at no cost to the student. Admittance, a great privilege, was granted through merit in draughtsmanship (fig. 5). Unsurprisingly architect-Academicians often sent their favoured pupils along to sharpen their skills. The programme was part-time and supplemented pupilage, the training received in an architect's office, which generally involved basic office routine, the keeping of accounts, measuring, sketching and making copy drawings. Attendance at the Schools was unregulated, and it was often a complaint that some students registered for the prestige and were then rarely seen again. Over the years, student numbers depended upon the quality of the Professors (a few of whom were themselves tardy in their attendance, failing to deliver their lectures or to visit the Schools) and were dependent upon the rise and interest in alternative architectural facilities and classes, a trend that increased around the mid-nineteenth century and eventually evolved into the establishment of full-time schools of architecture.

In the nearly two-hundred-year existence of the Royal Academy's Architecture School – its doors closed in 1964 – the curriculum inevitably underwent modifications. Change, however, was never radical, which speaks of the tenacity of the academic tradition that the Royal Academy strove to maintain and apply in the ever-changing world of architecture and architectural education. The basics of the programme remained unaltered: the Architecture School was not concerned with debate and social problem solving, which is the modern approach that finally overwhelmed the Academy, but was rooted in the timeless, essential elements of architecture as it had been sanctioned by the past. The Schools neither promoted lessons in construction nor in the making of working drawings, which is reflected in the fact that,

25   John Yenn's Diploma Work was honoured by appearing in the background of the painting The Royal Academicians assembled in the Council Chamber to adjudge the Medals to the successful students in Painting, Sculpture, Architecture and Drawing by Henry Singleton, completed in 1795 (Royal Academy of Arts, London). Chambers appears prominently in the centre of the Academicians, leaning on a table upon which can be seen an architectural student's large drawing of a domed building.

26   See Neil Bingham, 'Architecture at the Royal Academy Schools, 1768 to 1836', in Neil Bingham (ed)., The Education of the Architect, Proceedings of the 22nd Annual Symposium of the Society of Architectural Historians of Great Britain, London, 1993, pp. 5–14.

Fig. 6
This albumen print of a photograph by Henry Bedford Lemere (1839–1911), taken in c. 1876 and belonging to the Royal Academy of Arts, shows an example from the extensive collection of architectural plaster casts of parts of historic buildings that adorned the Architecture School in the Royal Academy. Students were obliged to 'draw from the cast' for at least the first year of the architecture course. Only when they had reached proficiency in this skill were they allowed to measure buildings and make designs of theoretical projects. Although the Architecture School closed its doors in 1964, many of the casts still hang in situ in the former Architecture Room in Burlington House, now used by today's postgraduate fine arts students at the Royal Academy Schools.

from the outset, Chambers kept all pattern books, copy guides and builders' manuals out of the Library.[27] This was an 'academic' education where the art of drawing was the handmaiden of history. Architecture students might rub shoulders with painters and sculptors in other parts of the Schools – in perspective classes, at the lectures given by the Professors, sometimes in the Antique School for drawing the casts of antique sculpture, even in the Life School, and certainly at the annual prize-giving – but on the whole, students in architecture kept to themselves, spending long hours drawing from the ever-growing collection of architectural casts of fragments of ancient buildings (fig. 6) before moving on to attempt mastering the intricate complexity of the classical orders, guided at first by textbooks such as Chambers's *Treatise on Civil Architecture*, first published in 1759. Having gained these accomplishments, students were required to make measured drawings of parts of existing London buildings that were considered worthy of study by the Professors. And then, bringing all this knowledge together, they worked on design drawings for original compositions. The ultimate achievement was to win one of the drawing competitions in a battle for medals: silver for measured drawings and gold for design drawings. Gold medallists were often afforded, wars aside, the opportunity to travel on a scholarship.

Both Robert Smirke and John Soane had won the silver and the gold medals. Smirke travelled to Italy and on to Greece, while Soane set off to Rome on the King's Travelling Studentship. Unlike Yenn, who stayed at home to gain the new style of classical architectural education, Smirke and Soane went to live among the ancient ruins. Smirke profited from the experience by submitting a 'restoration' of the Acropolis (see pp. 52–53), the Royal Academy's only architectural Diploma Work that is not based upon an architect's own building project. As a scholar of the antique, he interpreted what he had seen, studied,

sketched, measured and drawn, and then romanticised it as a reconstruction with an architect's accuracy.

This was a very different approach from that of Soane, whose Diploma Work, a design for a new House of Lords (see pp. 40–41, 50–51), was unabashedly a piece of self-promotion. But this is hardly unusual: many Diploma Works have a touch of self-publicity about them. And it would be unfair to characterise Soane as someone solely concerned with his own interests: he was one of the great supporters of the Royal Academy, sending his pupils to the Royal Academy Schools, giving memorable lectures as Professor of Architecture between 1806 and 1837, and even setting up his office like a mini-Academy with a cast collection and a régime in drawing that was to influence the teaching practices at the Royal Academy Schools.

Over the course of the first half of the nineteenth century, academic interest in the history of architecture deepened with the intensification of scholarship. The Royal Academy was at the top of its game, the Diploma Works reflecting the growing appreciation of past eras and styles: the design by William Wilkins for King's College, Cambridge, showed the early flirtation with gothic in the mid-1820s (see pp. 56–57), while a decade later, C. R. Cockerell worked up an Elizabethan medley with his competition entry for the Houses of Parliament (see pp. 58–61). Increasingly hardy examples of the Greek revival, the most prevalent and purely derived of the antique styles, appeared. Both the drawing by John Peter (Gandy) Deering (see pp. 62–63) and that by Philip Hardwick (see pp. 64–65) were for modern adaptations of propylaea, entrance portals to sacred Greek sites. With Hardwick's Euston Arch for the railway station, the ancient truly met the contemporary in a design for a new building type. Sir Charles Barry made the leap into the Italian Renaissance vocabulary with his design for a Pall

27 Nicholas Savage, 'The Academicians' Library: A Selection not a Collection', *Apollo*, 128, October 1988, pp. 258 63.

Mall clubhouse (see pp. 66–67), which his son Edward Middleton Barry inflated into a wonderful baroque scheme for London's Whitehall (see pp. 74–75) that would have vied with Vatican City had it been built. Also during this period, the Royal Academy publicly paraded its neoclassical architectural colours by moving in 1837 into the new temple-fronted building on Trafalgar Square designed by William Wilkins, where it shared premises with the recently created National Gallery.

The historical, classical ideals upon which the Royal Academy was founded reached a high point when from 1841 to 1856 Cockerell gave his annual lectures as Professor of Architecture. As both a brilliant scholar and a draughtsman, Cockerell was able to extend his range over the entire history of architecture, from the ancient world to the present, illustrating his lectures with charts, tables, drawings and a 'drop-scene', a back-cloth ten feet by fourteen feet that depicted a collection of historical buildings. In 1848 he polished this teaching aid into probably one of the most celebrated architectural watercolours of the period, *The Professor's Dream*, exhibited at the Annual Exhibition and now in the collection of the Royal Academy (fig. 7). On a single sheet of paper, nearly four feet by six feet, Cockerell created a visionary world vested in architectural fact, a technique that had been brought to perfection by Soane's great perspectivist Joseph Michael Gandy ARA. In Cockerell's comparative drawing, airy Renaissance domes and medieval spires stand before the apexes of the great Egyptian pyramids, the scene falling in layers through Greek and Roman temples to a darkened base of ancient Egyptian monuments and the minute figures of travellers crossing the desert sands to enter this heavenly city. 'Architecture belongs to history,' said the Professor. 'With her a hundred years are but as a day. Calculated for endurance to the future she *must* be founded on the principles of the past.'[28]

Victorian Virtuosity, 1840–1890

Although in the mid-nineteenth century the basis for new architecture remained a sound understanding of historical principles, the favoured style shifted from the antique-based neoclassicism that the founders of the Royal Academy and their followers had nurtured towards a revival of the gothic. Many classicists abhorred the return of the gothic, but within the Royal Academy little such rivalry existed: leading gothic-revival architects showed in the Annual Exhibitions, became Royal Academicians, taught in the Schools, delivered lectures, and helped to run an arts institution that had by now become a respected force in British culture. When, with his Diploma Work (see pp. 70–73), Sir George Gilbert Scott fired a significant volley in the 'Battle of the Styles', it was done respectfully but very publicly. Forced in the early 1860s by the Prime Minister, Lord Palmerston, to change his gothic design for the new Foreign Office in Whitehall to one of classical inspiration, Scott recalled in his autobiography: 'I had a splendid view made … I placed it with my other Gothic designs in the exhibition at the Royal Academy as a silent protest against what was going on.'[29]

Scott, by his own admission, had the drawing 'made'. The laying out of architectural perspectives for presentation in exhibitions and the ever-increasing number of architectural competitions had always been a complex and time-consuming affair, but now it became even more so as expectations grew in terms of their increased size and artistry. The art of the perspective had reached a standard that required a virtuoso watercolour technique. But there were dissenting voices. The architect William Burges (1827–1881) disapproved of the Academy's encouragement of perspectives; his outspokenness did him no favours, and delayed his election as an Associate until the year of his early death.[30]

In large architectural offices such as those of Scott, John Loughborough Pearson (see pp. 82–83) and Alfred

28 See the chapter 'The Royal Academy Lectures, 1841–1856' in David Watkin, *The Life and Work of C. R. Cockerell*, London, 1974, pp. 105–32.
29 George Gilbert Scott, *Personal and Professional Recollections*, London, 1879, p. 200.
30 J. Mordaunt Crook, *William Burges and the High Victorian Dream*, London, 1981, p. 75.

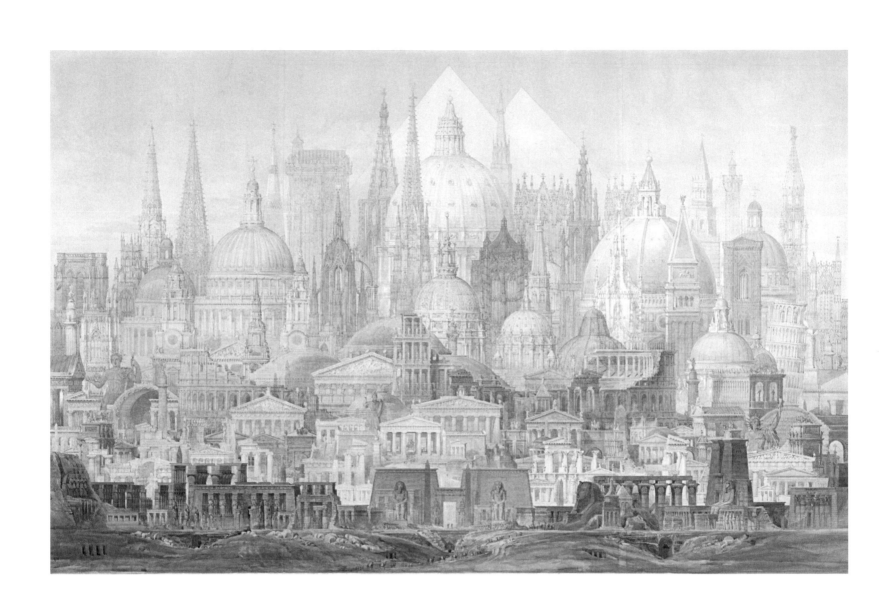

Waterhouse (see pp. 84–85), teams of assistants would have worked for many weeks to create a show-stopping perspective. The right size and strength of support had to be purchased, usually something like a good English-made Whatman cartridge paper from the mills in Kent, hot-pressed and smooth. This had to be stretched and mounted onto a drawing table or board; drawing pins left holes, which were acceptable for working drawings, but certainly not for presentation. The complicated drawing process usually began with projecting planes up from the plan so that the building looked life-like and, most importantly, was accurately represented. Out came the drawing instruments: dividers and scales for noting dimensions; T- and set-squares for straight lines and angles (pearwood or mahogany with ebony edges were considered the best materials for these); compasses and French curves for circles and arcs. Pencils were sharpened, and ink was loaded painfully slowly, just a few drops at a time, into fiddly ruling pens with screws that adjusted the line thickness. Mistakes were rectified by sponging out, never scratching with a wet knife or an ink-eraser. And then the master architect himself might intervene, as Waterhouse almost ways did, and breathe artistic life into the architecture and its surroundings by adding his own inking, layered over with delicate watercolour, shading and highlights. Finally, a skilled outsider, someone to depict objects, people, horses and carriages, might be required.

In smaller practices, or even larger offices that were busy or preferred a certain draughtsman's style of drawing, the demand for large perspectives made it perfectly acceptable to put the work out to specialists. However, there was always a nagging doubt among some architect-Academicians about this. Was not drawing the foundation of design, the cornerstone of the Royal Academy's School of Architecture? How could this fundamental architectural skill be so blatantly swept aside, especially in the Diploma Works, which were held up to students and fellow Academicians alike as an architect's masterwork? In 1874 the architect George Edmund Street petitioned the Council of the Royal Academy to accept the resolution that at the Summer Exhibition 'preference this year be given in the selection of Architectural Drawings as much as possible to those which were evidently the work of the Architects themselves, and elevations and details of buildings were admitted as well as Perspective Drawings'.[31] Leading by example, Street certainly finished off his own Diploma Work of the entrance to the Law Courts on the Strand (see pp. 78–79), and even more probably created it in its entirety.

Street's plea for drawings that showed detailed features of a building reflected the working practices and types of drawings common in architectural offices at the period. For architects of the Victorian gothic revival and emerging Arts and Crafts movement in the 1870s and 1880s, the aesthetic of the working drawing and the principles of construction were morally intertwined, and their integration was reinforced by the idealisation of the craftsman advocated by John Ruskin and William Morris. Many architects prided themselves on the simplicity and directness of their working drawings. The challenge was to fit onto a single sheet as much beautifully arranged information as possible: elevations, sections, a sketch perspective and a detail of a specific part of the building, perhaps a wooden door latch or an inglenook bench. But although such drawings were fine for students in the Architecture School at the Royal Academy to study, Academicians were not encouraged to submit workmanlike drawings as Diploma Works.

The Beaux-Arts and Academic Entrenchment, 1890–1960

By the 1870s and 1880s, a schism had arisen among architects over the question of whether architecture was a science or an art. The architects of the Royal Academy took a decided stand. There is no doubt that at the time of the foundation of the Academy, the institution was viewed as a means of raising the

31 RAA/PC/10, Annual Report, 1874, p. 16.

professional profile of the architect. Yet, by the late nineteenth century, this attitude had hardened in some circles into a form of protectionism, with a strong campaign being led for the title of 'architect' to be legally registered only to those who had completed an approved system of education regulated by the Royal Institute of British Architects. This went against the grain of the Royal Academy's culture, which held that although artists, sculptors and architects worked in distinct artistic fields, nevertheless they shared a commitment to unity through design. The architect-Academicians Norman Shaw (who had been Street's chief assistant) and Sir Thomas Graham Jackson Bt (who had been articled with Sir George Gilbert Scott) led the movement against registration. They edited an important book of essays that was published in 1892 and entitled *Architecture: A Profession or an Art?*. Contributions were included by, among others, their fellow architect-Academicians Sir Reginald Blomfield, G. F. Bodley and Ernest Newton. Shaw felt so strongly about the matter that he declined at least twice the Royal Gold Medal in Architecture, annually given by the Royal Institute of British Architects, declaring that the Royal Academy was the place for architectural development, not the Institute. For the time being, the artist-architects were successful; registration was held off until the 1930s.

Shaw and Jackson were as good as their word with their Diploma Works (see pp. 80–81, 86–87), working up their own drawings, abandoning the large, colourful flourishes of their predecessors in favour of the simple use of pen and ink. Shaw, Jackson, Street and Ernest George (see pp. 100–01) were the masters of the line drawing, usually executed without washes. Their technique translated well when the drawings were published in the building journals using the new technology of photolithography, which could reproduce line accurately but not tone.

The Royal Academy's move from its cramped quarters in the National Gallery's building in Trafalgar Square to Burlington House in 1868 enabled the institution to expand. Sydney Smirke built a suite of large exhibition galleries at the rear (fig. 8) in the Italianate style that he favoured and had used so forcefully in his Diploma Work, a design for the Carlton Club (see pp. 68–69); the exterior of his Academy galleries was, however, stripped down as the building could not be seen from the street. Not only did these new galleries give the Annual Exhibition greater space, but they also permitted the accommodation of winter loan exhibitions from 1870, which eventually developed into the international programme for which the Royal Academy is known today. Smirke also added a storey to Burlington House to create a set of special permanent galleries in which all the Academy's Diploma Works could be shown together for the first time. The three Diploma Galleries were linked with the Gibson Gallery, which was used to display the collection of work bequeathed by the neoclassical sculptor-Academician John Gibson. Highlights of the Academy's collection were placed throughout the galleries, such as Michelangelo's marble *Taddei Tondo* depicting the Virgin and Child with the infant St John.[32] Newly elected Royal Academicians now submitted Diploma Works in the knowledge that their drawings would hang on permanent display in the Diploma Galleries, open to comparison and public scrutiny.

The Royal Academy Schools were also given spacious new quarters. To Smirke's range of studios, Shaw added a large room for the Architecture School in 1886, set out with drawing tables, its high walls hung with the Academy's extensive collection of architectural plaster casts. Reform of the curriculum was also on the agenda as architectural education became an increasingly heated topic. The Visitors, three or sometimes four architect-Academicians, continued in rotation to assist in tutoring the students and setting the subjects for drawing competitions. With the appointment of Richard Phené Spiers as Master of the Architecture School in 1870, a position he was to hold until 1906,

32 The Diploma Galleries were finished in 1885 (RAA/PC/10, Annual Report, 1885, p. 5); in 1919 the architectural Diploma Works were placed on screens along the centre of the Gibson Gallery (RAA/PC/10, Annual Report, 1919, p. 14); in 1926 six architectural drawings 'whose condition had so deteriorated that they were no longer suitable for exhibition' were removed to the Library (RAA/PC/10, Annual Report, 1926, p. 8). By 1939 seven drawings – by Sir Charles Barry, Sir William Chambers, Philip Hardwick, Sir Robert Smirke, Sir John Soane, William Wilkins and James Wyatt – were listed as unfit to be shown (Royal Academy of Arts, *Catalogue of the Diploma and Gibson Galleries*, London, 1939).

the Academy gained its first full-time teacher in architectural drawing.[33] Spiers was a highly influential drawing master, who also wrote on the history of architecture in ancient Egypt, Greece and Rome, as well as the standard textbook on the classical orders. His *Architectural Drawing*, first published in 1887 and revised in 1902, is a lucid, instructive and beautiful examination of the various methods of architectural representation, and includes illustrated examples by many architect-Academicians.

Having been trained at the Ecole des Beaux-Arts in Paris, Phené Spiers was instrumental in introducing elements of the French Beaux-Arts system of architectural training into Britain, especially as they related to drawing process and technique, although he found that he had to moderate many of the highly disciplined aspects of the French methods to the more flexible British context of the Arts and Crafts

movement. With a wide interest in the arts as they related to building, architects of the Arts and Crafts movement moved steadily towards the revival of English and French Renaissance styles. By the first decade of the new century these had evolved into the Edwardian baroque, a style boldly classical, rich in sculpted elements, and suitably grand for those opulent years. These developments overlapped with the Beaux-Arts ideals in architecture and urban planning: designs that were symmetrical, formal and complex in their composition. The Beaux-Arts tradition rapidly established itself as orthodoxy, especially in the Royal Academy, where the French academic tradition reawakened an awareness of the institution's origins as formulated by Sir William Chambers while simultaneously consolidating the achievements of the 'architecture as an art' crusade of the previous generation.

Sir Reginald Blomfield, a Renaissance scholar and authority on historical drawing – his *Architectural Drawing and Draughtsmen* was published in 1912 – was the archetype of the new classicising architect-Academician. Under his guidance, and during the presidency of the architect Sir Aston Webb, the Academy attempted in the early 1920s to institute an advanced architectural training in the Schools based upon the Beaux-Arts system, complete with *ateliers* of supervised workshops for students to produce *esquisses*, rapid sketches to be worked up into elaborate competition designs *en loge*, in private cubicles.[34] The aim of this programme was to emulate the now more established schools of architecture, especially the Architectural Association and Liverpool University, which were by then offering full-time study. In the end the venture failed because the facilities at the Royal Academy were inadequate for such an ambitious programme, which made external educational governing bodies unwilling to offer support. Moreover, the aftermath of the First World War had left tragically fewer and less qualified men to undertake the course.

33 Richard Phené Spiers, 'The Architectural School of the Royal Academy,' in Arthur Cates (ed.), *Papers on Education*, London, 1887, pp. 47–52.
34 RAA/PC/10, Annual Report, 1920, p. 91.

Fig. 10
Booklet accompanying an exhibition of suggested designs for rebuilding London held at the Royal Academy in 1942, during the Second World War (Royal Academy of Arts, London). Organised by the Royal Academy Planning Committee, a group of architect-Academicians, all the schemes followed the academic principles of Beaux-Arts planning – neoclassical, symmetrical and axial in plan with a focus on monuments. The cover drawing shows a committee design, drawn by the architectural perspectivist J. M. D. Harvey (1895–1978), for opening a view of St Paul's Cathedral from the River Thames.

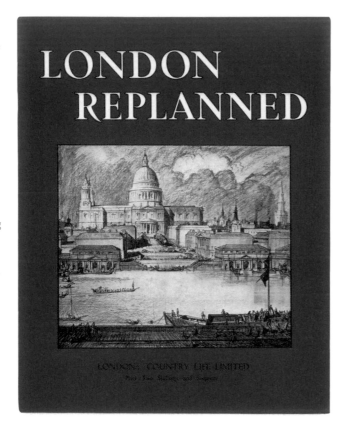

In his Diploma Work Blomfield showed the gentler side of Edwardian classicism, with his 'Wrenaissance' design for an Oxford college (see page 98–99). But many of his colleagues submitted drawings of schemes in full-blown neo-baroque overlaid with Beaux-Arts planning, creating potent manifestations of the wealth and power of the British Empire. Sir Aston Webb designed a processional way consecrated to Victoria, Queen and Empress (see pp. 92–95); John Belcher erected another memorial, this one to a king of industry (see pp. 96–97); Sir John J. Burnet fashioned a museum building dedicated to King and Emperor (see pp. 108–09); and Sir Herbert Baker and Sir Edwin Lutyens, the two greatest imperial architects, produced great governmental complexes in South Africa (see pp. 110–11) and India (see pp. 104–05) respectively. This was

the group of men who ruled the British Empire from an architectural standpoint, and their drawings, hanging in the Diploma Galleries, reinforced the authority and power of the Royal Academy's position during this period as the arbiter of national and imperial taste.

By the beginning of the twentieth century, professional architectural perspectivists had begun to sign the drawings they made for others. Sir Aston Webb had several favourites whom he allowed to do this, alongside his own signature. When it came to his Diploma Work, however, Webb did not seem to feel obliged to include the signature of T. Raffles Davison on the perspective of his design drawing of 1903 for replanning the area around Buckingham Palace in the Queen Victoria Memorial scheme, although Davison's style was very recognisable. Similarly, Lutyens's Diploma Work of 1920 of the Jaipur Column in India was obviously done by William Walcot with his distinctive watery brush stroke.[35]

The first Diploma Work to be co-signed by the architect and perspectivist was submitted by Ernest Newton for a country house to be built in France, a soft watercolour by Cyril Farey dated 1919 (see pp. 102–03) that the Council accepted without quibble.[36] Farey was then just hitting his stride as the most popular draughtsman for presentation drawings of the interwar years. He crowned this reputation with his bestselling book *Architectural Drawing: Perspective and Rendering*, which was first printed in 1931 and republished with colour plates in 1949.[37] Farey had trained as an architect and had won the Gold Medal in drawing at the Royal Academy Schools. In the history of architectural representation at the Royal Academy, probably no other perspectivist has exhibited more than Cyril Farey. Nevertheless, although the architect-artist was encouraged within the Academy, the artist-architect was not. Farey was never put forward for membership.

In fact, with the Council of the Royal Academy, the body responsible for judging the acceptability of Diploma Works, comprising mainly painter-

35 Walcot was put up for election as an Academician but never gathered enough votes. RRA/GA/11/2/2, Nominations for Associateships, p. 36.
36 RA Council Minutes, vol. 24, 27 May 1919, p. 115.
37 His co-author was the architect, historian and critic A. Trystan Edwards (1885–1973).

Academicians, it is perhaps not surprising that these members viewed the outside artist-perspectivists as interlopers. When in 1932 Sir Herbert Baker submitted a drawing for his Diploma Work signed jointly by himself and his perspectivist, the question of the architect presenting a work in his own hand again came out into the open. Council were displeased and requested that Baker submit 'if possible a design drawn by himself'. Baker resisted, saying that he was 'unable' and would they please reconsider. In the end, there was a supposed compromise, although in fact Baker really won by giving 'a revised drawing' of the same scheme, the Government Buildings in Pretoria, by the same perspectivist, H. L. G. Pilkington.[38] Three years later a similar thing happened when Guy Dawber submitted a watercolour by the perspectivist Philip Dalton Hepworth (see pp. 116–17); the Council asked him 'to add a plan or section of his own design by himself'. Having considered the matter, Dawber did nothing, undoubtedly considering that Hepworth's drawing *was* his design.[39]

The painter-Academicians now made their bid, led by the artist Philip Connard (1875–1958). In December 1935 Connard argued that in future architects exhibiting in the Summer Exhibitions and depositing Diploma Works should only be allowed to submit 'geometrical drawings' – in other words, plans, elevations and sections – and certainly no perspectives unless they had been done by the architect himself.[40] The extremity of this measure was not acted upon. Nevertheless, so strong was the opposition to architectural Diploma Works being executed by someone other than the elected Academician that the Royal Academy did pass a law in February 1936 that Diploma Works must be in the hand of the architect.[41] This law has never proved tenable.

Away from Burlington House, however, the mood was changing and a concerted campaign was underway to win perspective artists the right of acknowledgement. Reviewing the Royal Academy's Annual Exhibition of 1940 in the building press, Professor Charles Reilly gave credit to Lutyens, who had now come around to allow his draughtsmen to sign his drawings. But Reilly censored E. Vincent Harris for showing his design drawing for Nottinghamshire County Hall – which Harris was to submit two years later as his Diploma Work (see pp. 122–25) – saying 'I can hardly think, with his vast practice, Mr Vincent Harris has drawn his Stockholm-like tower twice over himself … This building is much more delicately detailed, if one can judge from these eighth-scale drawings, than is usual with this architect whose hand often lies rather heavily on his buildings.'[42]

In 1937 the Royal Academy held its first architectural exhibition, entitled simply 'Exhibition of British Architecture'.[43] On display were an exhaustive 1,570 drawings, models and photographs, supplemented by seventeen painted and sculpted portraits. The majority of pieces concentrated on newer work from the past ten years, although the timeline stretched back to 1900. All projects included had either been built or were in construction; there were no conjectural or fantasy schemes. Moreover, there was also a substantial retrospective section, with historic drawings by artists ranging from the Renaissance master John Thorpe to the fin-de-siècle designs of Charles Rennie Mackintosh. In this retrospective section were a selection of Diploma Works by Hardwick, Waterhouse, Bodley, Pearson and Belcher.

As bombs fell on London during the Second World War, skylights shattered and doorways were blown out at Burlington House, but exhibitions never ceased. A group of architect-Academicians, led by the Academy's President, the architect Sir Edwin Lutyens, formed the Royal Academy Planning Committee and mounted designs in October and November 1942 for a grand reconstruction of London after the war, envisioning a city based on Beaux-Arts planning with formal buildings laid out along symmetrical street patterns radiating off piazzas (fig. 10).[44] The exhibition,

38 RAA/PC/1/26, Council Minutes, 22 March 1932, p. 145; 18 April 1932, p. 150; 10 November 1932, p. 184.
39 RAA/PC/1/26, Council Minutes, 19 November 1935, p. 436.
40 RAA/PC/1/26, 10 December 1935, p. 443.

41 RAA/GA/13, *The Laws of the Royal Academy of Arts*, 1938, p. 38, Clause 8.
42 *Architects' Journal*, 91, 16 May 1940, p. 501.
43 Some small exhibitions of architectural drawings had taken place, including one held for a few weeks in October 1910 that presented drawings and models to coincide with a RIBA Town Planning Conference.

44 *London Replanned: The Royal Academy Planning Committee's Interim Report*, London, October 1942; this was followed by *Road, Rail and River in London: The Royal Academy Planning Committee's Second Report*, London, July 1944.

Fig. 11
Albert Richardson, Professor of
Architecture, giving a lecture to
art and architecture students in
the Architecture School of the
Royal Academy Schools, the
walls covered in plaster casts,
1953. Richardson was elected
President the following year.
The lantern slide projected
on the screen shows the
Edwardian baroque town hall
of Deptford, South London.
Photograph by Russell
Westwood.

in the midst of the darkest days of war, provided a positive and uplifting message of hope.

In 1939 the Diploma Works had been taken into safe storage, but with the advent of peace they were never rehung in their purpose-designed galleries. From then on, they were treated as an historic collection to be drawn upon for special occasions. The first instance of this was when four were hung alongside Cockerell's *Professor's Dream* in a small selection of architectural drawings that was arranged as part of the celebration 'The First Hundred Years of the Royal Academy 1769-1868' during the 1951-52 exhibition season.

After the Second World War, architecture at the Royal Academy underwent dramatic change. The Architecture School, which had been suspended during hostilities, reopened somewhat shakily, offering postgraduate study in 'advanced' civic design. Sir Albert Richardson, a die-hard classicist who attempted to keep the Beaux-Arts tradition alive in the face of advancing modernism, was responsible for the programme. He was joined by Arthur Davis, who had been a top student at the Ecole des Beaux-Arts in Paris during the 1890s, and by Curtis Green; both these architects submitted Diploma Works exemplifying the Beaux-Arts drawing tradition (see pp. 120-21, 112-113). Although Richardson's lively and popular lectures were the high point of the course, only a few students were attracted to *en loge* contests for a Grand Prize (fig. 11). And of those three or four students who registered each year, some even balked at the classical values being taught: Peter Smithson, who with his wife Alison was to go on to become the influential leader of the New Brutalist movement, insisted upon following 'current fashions', as a pained Richardson observed when Smithson submitted a competition design influenced by Mies van der Rohe (fig. 12).[45] Now that the national official system of architectural education was no longer based on pupilage in architect's offices but instead completely in universities, polytechnics and independent schools, such as the Architectural Association, the Architecture School within the Royal Academy Schools was suspended in 1957. It made a brief comeback under Sir Basil Spence in 1961 but, with only a few evening students attending, it closed for good in 1964.

The post-war years were difficult and controversial as the Royal Academy attempted to find an accommodation between the older, classical values of patrician Royal Academicians and the dramatic tidal wave of modernism. With the exception of Raymond Erith, a full-blown classical survivor (see pp. 146-47), all the newly elected architects of the 1950s and 1960s practised in what can either be described as a historical-modern synthesis or a form of stripped-back modernism, whose appearance to ardent followers of the avant-garde represented the dying embers of historicism.

The stylistic eclecticism of this period is evident in its Diploma Works. Edward Maufe's drawing of 1948 was for Guildford Cathedral (see pp. 130-31), in the gothic style. Howard Robertson's was for a prominent high-rise commercial building, the Shell Centre on London's South Bank (see pp. 138-39); but even this met with scathing reviews, both architecturally and in presentation – an *esquisse*, a sketch, it satisfied neither camp. Although the buildings were decidedly modern, William Holford's perspective of Kent University retreated into the picturesque, with a view largely of countryside (see pp. 148-49). Basil Spence submitted one of his beautiful chalk drawings of Coventry Cathedral (see pp. 140-41), but nevertheless this seemed to hard-line modernists to be a mediating exercise, popular but not avant-garde. It was a period during which blame was cast in all directions, and the architects of the Royal Academy, in attempting to uphold the values of an academic tradition that stretched back to the Renaissance, found themselves either in head-on opposition to the modernists or at least trying to appease their younger colleagues outside the Academy who had little time for history.

45 RAA/PC/10, Annual Report, 1949,
p. 41; Simon Houfe, John Wilton-Ely,
Alan Powers and W. A. Downe (eds),
Sir Albert Richardson 1880-1964,
exh. cat., Heinz Gallery, Royal Institute
of British Architects, London, 1999,
pp. 63-66.

Fig. 12
Peter Smithson (1923–2003), *Student Competition Entry for a New Fitzwilliam Museum, Cambridge*, 1949 (Smithson Family Collection). This drawing is from a set submitted by Smithson when he was a postgraduate student at the Royal Academy School of Architecture in 1948–49. Its forward-looking design was at odds with the academic classicism then being taught by Albert Richardson PRA. Smithson, in partnership with his wife Alison, went on to become an international leader of post-war avant-garde architecture associated with the New Brutalist movement.

The Modern Academy, 1960–2010

It took the diplomatic skills and engaging personality of the architect Hugh Casson, President from 1976 to 1984, to convince artists and the public that the Royal Academy could both embrace the new and respect the old (fig. 13). Casson represented the human face of modernism: an accomplished watercolourist, he had trained as an architect in the burgeoning modern movement of the 1930s, and was able to design buildings such as the Elephant and Rhinoceros Pavilion at London Zoo (see pp. 152–53), constructed in what many perceived as that most dreaded of materials, concrete, yet making it all seem so joyful.

The door was now open for a generation of architects who had not gained their initial training in an architect's office, but in schools of architecture in the 1930s: Maxwell Fry, Richard Sheppard, Jim Cadbury-Brown, Ernö Goldfinger, Leslie Martin, Denys Lasdun and Geoffrey Jellicoe. Although in the 1930s architectural schools were still run along the lines of the Beaux-Arts system, albeit tempered to accord with British taste, these architects when young had found themselves attracted to modernism emerging from Europe. After the war they became the new leaders and teachers, using principles modelled on those of the German Bauhaus in the 1920s. All these practitioners could draw the classical orders and make exquisite drawings, but they had moved on to create an architecture concerned with abstract form and geometry, using new technology and materials, especially glass, steel and concrete, which they often left exposed. In socially conscious post-war Britain, they also subscribed to a programme driven by state planning, social welfare and civic development.

Although the group of Diploma Works submitted by these Royal Academicians reflected the architects' rational and experimental aesthetic, at the same time their works were still grounded in traditional drawing skills. The drawing by Ernö Goldfinger (see pp. 160–61) is the purest, reflecting the fact that in the 1920s he

had studied at the Ecole des Beaux-Arts in Paris and rubbed shoulders with such titans of modernism as Le Corbusier and Auguste Perret. Goldfinger's drawing is about circulation, the sense of volume and the rationale of geometry, all refinements of Beaux-Arts principles. And yet the work also portrays the concrete world of Brutalist architecture, with a walking figure reminiscent of one of Le Corbusier's modulor men. Goldfinger added colouring to his drawing to give it a personal touch, but the base image is a print, the product of a mechanical process that reflects the modern obsession with the machine-made. Although such reproductive prints had been rejected as Diploma Works in the past, they came to be considered acceptable, doubtless because their character, as is exuberantly conveyed in the case of the futurist Peter Cook (see pp. 228–29), is integral to the modern idiom of design expression.

Architects such as Maxwell Fry abandoned all intention of finesse in draughtsmanship, letting the pen flow with the building line (see pp. 154–55). And 65 years after Sir John J. Burnet had tentatively inserted small photographs of a model and a plan into his 1925 Diploma Work drawing (see pp. 108–09), as did Philip Powell in 1977 (see pp. 162–63), in 1991 Denys Lasdun unabashedly presented a photograph of his models for the National Theatre, albeit with a drawing in his own hand added at the request of Council (see pp. 186–87). In the photograph, Lasdun's models, however, lie in a heap, the works of art having been discarded; this was a radical and pessimistic comment upon the traditions of the Royal Academy, and especially on the object as being a creation of enduring beauty. The tide had definitely turned.

Although occasionally models of buildings had been shown in Annual Exhibitions during the Regency period, in 1895 E. S. Prior started the modern trend for exhibiting models by including one of his designs for a country house, The Barn in Exmouth. But it was to be another century before the first architectural model was to be submitted as a Diploma Work – by Michael Manser, for an office building (see pp. 214–15), accepted in 1995.

SECTION THROUGH THE LIBRARY BLOCK   1:24

Fig. 13
Leonard Rosoman RA, *Sir Hugh Casson PRA*, 1992. Pencil and watercolour, 800 × 1120 mm (Royal Academy of Arts, London). Casson, a popular President of the Academy from 1976 to 1984, is pictured in the recently opened Print Room of the Royal Academy Library, designed by the architect-Academician Jim Cadbury-Brown.

Subsequent contributions by Michael Hopkins (see pp. 204-07), Chris Wilkinson (see pp. 232-33) and Spencer de Grey (see pp. 240-41) introduced the new sophistication of the modeller's art with the precision of laser-cutting to create three-dimensional representations of exacting form.

Philip Powell was the first Royal Academician to have been architecturally trained in the post-war years and since his election another two generations have followed. In the twenty-five years between 1985 and 2010, thirty-two architects were elected, exactly twice as many as in the entire nineteenth century, mainly as a result of the abolition in 1991 of the Associate (ARA) category, which had begun to look like a second-class membership rather than an entry level.

The election of Richard Rogers as an Associate in 1978, the year after the completion of his Centre Georges Pompidou in Paris, marked a shift towards architects working in high tech, the engineer-based movement that was to catapult many of its practitioners into international prominence. Rogers's Diploma Work, a 1980 drawing of the Inmos Microprocessor Factory in Newport, South Wales (see pp. 170-73), was a fine example of this movement, overshadowing the work of such older leaders as Sir Leslie Martin, one of the great reformers of post-war architectural education, whose Diploma Work drawing of his Gulbenkian Centre of Modern Art in Lisbon (see pp. 174-75) from about 1985 still upheld the geometric and concrete forms of the now passing Brutalist movement. The elements of a refined engineering aesthetic are noticeable in the Diploma Works of Norman Foster (see pp. 190-93), Nicholas Grimshaw (see pp. 210-213) and particularly the lightbox of photographs by Eva Jiricna (see pp. 216-17), the first woman architect-Academician. The election in 1986 of Sir Ove Arup, the first and so far the only civil engineer to be a Royal Academician, acknowledged the strong reliance upon engineering that is such a motivating force behind much modern architecture.

Arup's Diploma Work, a drawing of Kingsgate pedestrian bridge in Durham (see pp. 178-79), was, moreover, the first drawing to show a working detail, for an expansion joint.

Technology now not only entered architecture as a vocabulary of style but also radically changed architects' working practices. The use of computer programs to assist with many of the processes of building design quickly became the norm in the 1990s. The first Diploma Work drawing to incorporate a computer-crafted image was submitted by Paul Koralek, a large tableau overlaid with text, photocopies and drawings for his 1993 competition entry for the Royal Library in Copenhagen (see pp. 194-97). Nevertheless, although works by Nicholas Grimshaw and David Chipperfield (see pp. 236-39) are full computer renderings - in the case of Grimshaw with colour added by hand - there is no doubt that these architects maintain full control of the design submission.

Interestingly, although all architect-Academicians are now computer-literate, none were raised in the lap of a processor. They were all traditionally trained in drawing, and not a single one uses programming as their primary means of design. The design expressions of these architects are as broad and diverse as their individual approaches to the contemporary world. Zaha Hadid's deconstructivist paintings are her trademark (see pp. 230-31), and she began using the traditional medium of oil and acrylic to create designs that had the look of being computer-generated in the years just before architects made the big switch to digital imaging. Ian Ritchie finds his muse through printmaking (see pp. 218-19), while Will Alsop crosses the boundaries between the arts in response to the integrated approach subscribed to by the Academy (see pp. 220-21). Many architects, among them Edward Cullinan (see pp. 188-89), Piers Gough (see pp. 226-27), Eric Parry (see pp. 234-35) and Gordon Benson (see pp. 222-25), persist in freehand drawing, extending the vocabulary of architectural draughtsmanship in a way that only master-architects can.

Although today's Royal Academy has no Architecture School, and the position of Professor of Architecture no longer carries any responsibility for delivering lectures, the institution's promotion of architectural design may be said to be greater than ever before in its long history. In former days the Architecture Room at the Summer Exhibition sometimes attracted little attention from members of the public: as one wag sneered in 1890, it was 'only patronised by old ladies, who take refuge in it to devour the contents of their luncheon baskets; fat old gentlemen who wish to get cool; and thin young men who want to get married, and can spoon undisturbed'.[46] These days, visitors of all kinds linger as much there as in the other rooms, and the architectural models, now the predominant means of display, are often more comprehensible, beautiful and intriguing to the general public than the works of art in the other galleries.

Architecture has never received as high a profile in the Main Galleries during the winter exhibition season as the other arts or in thematic exhibitions. But 1986 marked a shift in public interest in architecture with an exhibition focusing on three Academicians of international reputation, Britain's first 'starchitects' Norman Foster, Richard Rogers and James Stirling (fig. 14). The exhibition's success contributed to the establishment of an architecture programme in 1991, beginning with the Royal Academy Annual Architecture Lecture, which is delivered by an architect of international standing. An Architecture Committee of architect-Academicians was formed as a sub-committee of Council, and a lively series of lectures, forums, touring exhibitions and on-going shows is created by a Curator of Architecture through an endowment given by Mrs Drue Heinz HON DBE. Major architectural exhibitions in the Main Galleries followed, with the popular *Living Bridges* in 1996. And finally, exhibitions on historic architects were inaugurated in 1995 by, appropriately, one about the Palladian revival forged by Lord Burlington and his circle. This was followed four years later by a major retrospective on Sir John Soane. In 2009 the finest and largest exhibition on Andrea Palladio ever mounted saw the temporary return of many of the Italian Renaissance master's drawings, once part of Lord Burlington's collection, to Burlington House, where they had resided nearly three centuries earlier.

These exhibitions have been only the tip of the iceberg. The Royal Academy Library is the oldest institutional fine-arts library in the United Kingdom, and its collections continue to grow and serve Academicians, staff, students and the public. The creation of a new double-height library in 1986, which Jim Cadbury-Brown RA transformed out of the Gibson Gallery, followed by his print room in 1992, as well as the restoration of the John Madejski Fine Rooms, have afforded the institution an opportunity to exhibit works from its collections of archival material, paintings, drawings, prints and photographs. Architecture has figured large in these displays that often focus upon past and present architect-Academicians. As the Diploma Works form the core of the Royal Academy's collections of painting, sculpture and drawing, selected pieces are usually to be found on display and loan.

Since 1768 the Royal Academy has played a prominent role in the encouragement of the 'Arts of Design' in Britain. Architecture has had a particularly strong presence at the Academy, and the assembly of architect-Academicians has always included leading British practitioners and teachers, whose collective presence has long raised the profile of architecture by means of exhibitions and programmes of study. The Royal Academy's historic and ever-growing collection of architectural Diploma Works is a body of exemplars that offers an exceptional and matchless retrospective of style and technique in architectural presentation within the academic tradition.

46 Harry Furniss, *Royal Academy Antics*, London, Paris and Melbourne, 1890, p. 65.

Sir William Chambers RA
1723–1796
Foundation Member 1768

Design for a capital illustrating the origins of the Corinthian order, c. 1757–70

Pen with black ink and grey, brown and red washes with a border of black and brown washes, 370 × 353 mm
Bequeathed by Mrs Augusta Thackeray, 1856

Sir William Chambers was the moving force behind the creation of the Royal Academy in 1768. As architectural tutor to the future King George III, he was in the king's confidence when George came to the throne. Together, architect and royal pupil established a much-needed and financially secure institution to foster British art and architecture. Although Sir Joshua Reynolds may have served as the first President, Chambers more importantly was the first Treasurer, holding the purse strings.

As a Foundation Member of the Royal Academy, Chambers was not required to deposit a Diploma Work, although he did present as a 'Specimen of his Abilities' a red chalk perspective of the Casino at Marino that has sadly faded beyond recognition. The present drawing, illustrating the mythic origins of the Corinthian order, came to the Academy through Chambers's protégé, John Yenn RA, whose collection of drawings and topographical watercolours was presented in his memory by his daughter, Mrs Augusta Thackeray, in 1856.

Chambers, like many of his contemporaries, was fascinated by the evolutionary history of architecture, a new subject of study at the time. The classical orders were of particular interest and many far-fetched theories about their development were unearthed. In his seminal *Treatise on Civil Architecture* (1759), Chambers recounted the ancient story of the origin of the Corinthian order as it was given in the first century BC by Vitruvius: 'A young Girl of Corinth being dead, her nurse placed on her tomb a basket, containing certain trinkets in which she delighted when alive, and covered it with a tyle to prevent the rain from spoiling them. The basket happened to be placed on a root of Acanthus, which in the spring, pushing forth its leaves and sprigs, covered the sides of it; and some of them, that were longer than the rest, being obstructed by the corners of the tyle, were forced downwards, and curled in the manner of Volutes. Callimachus, the Sculptor, passing near the tomb, saw the basket, and in what manner the leaves had encompassed it. This new form pleasing him infinitely, he imitated it on columns, which he afterwards made at Corinth, establishing and regulating, by this model, the manner and proportions of the Corinthian Order.'

Along with this charming account Chambers illustrated an acanthus growing in and through a basket, forced down under the tile. But in the pen and wash drawing in the Royal Academy collection, the acanthus plant is almost mature, in the final stage of growth: the tinted red seedpods ripening, the ornament formalised but the weave of the basket still visible, an architectural element recognisably derived from nature.

The inscription at the foot of this drawing in Chambers's hand must date from after 1770, since he signs himself 'K.P.S.' – Knight of the Polar Star – a title bestowed on him that year by King Gustav III of Sweden. However, the drawing itself may date from more than a decade earlier if it was made in connection with either the *Treatise* of 1759 or the illustrated manuscript that Chambers made for the young Prince George entitled 'The Origins of Buildings and Orders' (c. 1757; Collection of Her Majesty The Queen).

John Harris, *William Chambers: Knight of the Polar Star*, London, 1970

Robin Middleton, 'A Treatise on Civil Architecture, London, 1759', in John Harris and Michael Snodin (eds), *Sir William Chambers: Architect to George III*, New Haven and London, 1996, pp. 68–76; also pp. 26–27 for the Casino drawing

Michael Snodin (ed.), *Catalogues of Architectural Drawings in the Victoria and Albert Museum: Sir William Chambers*, London, 1996

Sir William Chambers. R.P.S. Invt. et. Delt.

Thomas Sandby RA
Baptised 1723; d. 1798
Foundation Member 1768

A Hall of Magnificence, c. 1775
Watercolour, 473 × 392 mm
Presented by William Arnold Sandby, 1904

The architect-artist Thomas Sandby and his younger brother Paul were Foundation Members of the Royal Academy in 1768. As such, neither had to deposit a Diploma Work. In 1904 Paul Sandby's great-grandson and first biographer William Sandby bequeathed a drawing by each of the brothers to the Royal Academy, which filled a historical gap on the walls of the Diploma Galleries where, from 1876 to 1939, Diploma Works by all the Royal Academicians were permanently displayed. Because it was painted in gouache, Paul Sandby's drawing of Windsor Castle has survived slightly better than his brother's delicate watercolour.

Thomas Sandby's drawing was misidentified from an inscription on the back as a depiction of his most famous and finest architectural work, the Freemasons' Hall in Great Queen Street, near Covent Garden in London. The hall was replaced in the 1860s, but hitherto, in 1828–29, additions were made to it by Sir John Soane RA, who so admired Sandby's work that he not only acquired his archive of drawings, but had his office create a drawing of Sandby's Masonic building for display during the lectures he gave for thirty years from 1806 as Professor of Architecture at the Royal Academy. Soane himself, when a pupil at the Royal Academy Schools, had sat in on the lectures that had been given annually by Sandby from 1780 to 1796 as the Academy's first Professor of Architecture. Anticipation would mount for the finale of Sandby's sixth and last lecture, when he unrolled his stunning design for a 'Bridge of Magnificence', the most celebrated British architectural drawing of the period, which stretched more than sixteen feet in length.

The subject of this much smaller drawing owned by the Royal Academy is unidentified. It appears to be another of Sandby's imaginative inventions. Sandby seems to have been partial to this scheme of a hall of magnificence because he made at least one other version (now in the collection of Tate, London, and also presented by his great-grandson). The design, with its cross-vaulted ceiling, giant Corinthian columns and Diocletian windows, emulates Michelangelo's church of Santa Maria degli Angeli e dei Martiri built within the Roman ruins of the Baths of Diocletian. The aspect and perspectival sensation of this drawing are similar to one that Sandby made for his bridge of magnificence. Looking down the length of the great hall, he emphasises the grandeur and elegance of the space to great effect by pulling the perspective of the embellished roof over nearly two-thirds of the sheet. Such an expression would have been considered to impart aesthetic and spiritual associations, a mixture of awe and pleasure in line with contemporary discussions surrounding the nature of the sublime and the beautiful.

One of Sandby's distinctive watercolour techniques was to eschew the usual application of black ink to outline forms, and instead to draw first a pencil underlay and then shade and colour over the top. 'This mode of delineation,' he told his architectural students, 'I recommend to those, who, from practice, are more experienced in the art, for the purpose of facilitating their operation as well as to give their drawings that soft and agreeable appearance this method is capable of producing, from it nearer approach to that of nature' (Sandby, manuscript of his sixth lecture, Sir John Soane's Museum, London). The present drawing is created by this method, using only washes.

Most importantly, this work illustrates the revolutionary shift that Thomas Sandby was making in the history of architectural drawing. This interior view, presented in full and lifelike perspective, shows people going about their business. Previously, architects had shown interiors in flat elevation, or in sketchy, lifeless perspectives. Similarly, when Sandby made exterior perspectives, he set buildings in seemingly natural settings, almost telling a story, in streets filled with passers-by, or an atmospheric countryside. This was a style that Thomas developed in tandem with his brother Paul, whose English landscape watercolours have come to overshadow Thomas's equally historic role in drawing and, more broadly, artistic representation.

The lower-right corner bears the collector's mark of Paul Sandby RA, an indication that Thomas's brother cherished this drawing.

William Arnold Sandby, *Thomas and Paul Sandby Royal Academicians. Some Account of Their Lives and Works*, London, 1892

[Adolph] Paul Oppé, *The Drawings of Paul and Thomas Sandby in the Collection of His Majesty The King at Windsor Castle*, Oxford and London, 1947

Johnson Ball, *Paul and Thomas Sandby, Royal Academicians*, Bath, 1985

John Bonehill and Stephen Daniels (eds), *Paul Sandby: Picturing Britain*, exh. cat., Nottingham City Museums and Art Gallery, National Gallery of Scotland, Edinburgh, and Royal Academy of Arts, London, 2009–10

James Wyatt PRA
1746–1813
ARA 27 August 1770
RA 15 February 1785

Mausoleum for the Darnley family,
Cobham Hall, Kent: perspective, 1786
Pen with black ink and coloured washes,
578 × 732 mm

James Wyatt began his career on a tide of success. When he was only in his mid-twenties, the opening in 1772 of his Pantheon in Oxford Street made him one of the most sought-after British architects. A few years earlier he had lain on his back, suspended hundreds of feet above the marble pavement of the Pantheon in Rome, taking measurements of its original second-century dome. He loosely translated these vertiginous labours into what quickly became the most fashionable assembly room in Georgian London, reaping him not only praise but monetary benefits as an investor. Soon he was enjoying royal and aristocratic favour, building large country houses and landing top jobs, among them Surveyor to Westminster Abbey and Surveyor-General and Comptroller to the Office of Works.

Yet when James Wyatt died in 1813 in a carriage accident, he was professionally in disarray and personally impoverished. Even the King had become disgruntled with Wyatt's disorganised and procrastinating habits. The architect had lost many of his positions, could not prise payments out of clients, and had been blackballed from the Society of Antiquaries of London for 'destroying' cathedrals. And at the Royal Academy, after campaigning against the long-standing presidency of Benjamin West, he was himself elected President in 1805, the first architect to occupy the post. But his disdain of his fellow artists and his tendency to fall asleep in meetings put West back in the president's chair after a year. Wyatt had upset almost everyone.

Wyatt's perspective drawing of his mausoleum design for the Darnley family was the first Diploma Work by an architect to be accepted by the Royal Academy. The work is signed and dated 1786, and Wyatt submitted it in February of that year, exactly twelve months after his election as a full Royal Academician, when the building was nearing completion. However, given Wyatt's dilatory methods, the drawing may well date from about four years earlier, when he created a whole set of design drawings for this project. And it is also probably not in his own hand.

The landscape designer Humphry Repton remarked favourably upon Wyatt's excellent draughtsmanship, stating that he had a 'wonderful command and facility of pencil' and could draw perfect circles and straight lines freehand (Colvin, p. 1108). Wyatt was a frequent contributor to the Royal Academy's Annual Exhibition, showing drawings from 1770, with three for the Pantheon, to 1799, with Fonthill Abbey for the eccentric and wealthy recluse William Beckford, a fantasy country house in Wiltshire, now demolished, in the picturesque gothic style whose tower grew so tall that absence of firm foundations caused it to collapse several times.

The mausoleum shown in Wyatt's Diploma Work was built in the isolated parkland setting of Cobham Hall, Kent, the home of the Darnley family. John Bligh, the 3rd Earl, had obliged his heirs to build a mausoleum in his will. Wyatt's design inspiration was the Pyramid of Cestius, the ancient tomb in Rome that the Earl would have seen on his travels. The architect knew it at first hand too, and also from Piranesi's etchings. The Darnley structure is impressive, square in plan but with chamfered corners carrying sarcophagi, the whole ringed in Roman Doric columns. A great staircase flows across a dry moat.

Wyatt, as usual much too busy, left supervision of the mausoleum's completion to the architect George Dance the Younger RA. By a quirk of fate, the building, with its chapel above and crypt below, was never used because of a disagreement with the Bishop of Rochester, who refused to consecrate it. After long years of standing in ruin, the mausoleum was restored and in 2009 ownership was transferred to the National Trust.

Today, sadly, despite careful modern conservation, Wyatt's drawing is badly burnt out and distressed by sunlight, having hung in former days for too long on permanent display in the Royal Academy's Diploma Galleries. Nevertheless, the nobility of his design and the drawing style are still apparent.

John Martin Robinson,
*The Wyatts: An
Architectural Dynasty*,
Oxford, 1979, p. 240

Howard Colvin,
*A Biographical
Dictionary of British
Architects 1600–1840*,
fourth edition, London,
2008

Roger Bowdler,
'A Mansion for the
Dead: The Story of the
Darnley Mausoleum',
*The National Trust:
Historic Houses and
Collections Annual
2009*, London, 2009,
pp. 4–11

James Wyatt 1786

John Yenn RA
1750–1821
ARA 17 October 1774
RA 10 February 1791

Design for a country house or public
building: front elevation, 1791
Pen with black ink and coloured washes,
615 × 765 mm

This is a purely theoretical design.
The architect had no client in mind.
Almost every year for more than a quarter
of a century, from 1771 to 1797, John Yenn
showed similar generic designs at the
Royal Academy's Annual Exhibition
with titles such as 'A gentleman's casine',
'A villa' and 'Design for a pavilion
supposed to be situated on a lake'. Even
Yenn's Diploma Work has not come down
to us with an official title, other than the
simple 'Architectural Elevation' recorded
in old catalogues, so its subject is
conjectural. Is it a country house?
Or perhaps a public building?

Yenn's drawings, of which a great
many survive in the Royal Academy's
collections, are as cool and chaste as their
titles. In their time they were greatly
admired. The architectural historian John
Harris, when curating the first exhibition
on Yenn in 1973 at the RIBA Heinz Gallery
in London, pronounced them 'supreme
examples' of British architectural
rendering in the late eighteenth century.
For today's vociferous tastes, the austerity
of the drawing style is perhaps somewhat
difficult to appreciate fully. Yenn rarely
broke from his formula, typified in his
Diploma Work drawing: a straightforward
elevation, never a perspective, the flat
surface set behind a dry foreground and
between a little foliage. Compared to the
presentation drawings of previous
generations, which had tended to be
simple elevations on white backgrounds,
Yenn's luxurious settings and
architectural detailing seemed more
naturalistic and immediate.

Yenn inherited this drawing style from
his architectural master Sir William
Chambers RA, a founder member of the
Royal Academy. In fact, Yenn's whole
career was lived in Chambers's shadow.
In 1764, at the age of fourteen, the usual
age to begin an apprenticeship, Yenn

entered Chambers's office. This was
perfect timing for the young man to
become one of the first pupils to enrol in
1769 in the newly formed Royal Academy
Schools, an evening course of study to
supplement his day job. Yenn's drawing
entitled 'A nobleman's villa' won him the
student Gold Medal. Graduating as
Chambers's most trusted disciple and
foremost advocate, he rose through the
ranks of his master's two principal
concerns: His Majesty's Office of
Works and the Royal Academy of Arts.
Yenn would have been a busy architect,
undertaking the innumerable small
jobs that go unnoticed but keep a royal
household safe and comfortable.
He gained small commissions too,
including a music room at Windsor
Castle and some additions to Greenwich
Hospital. At the Royal Academy, upon
Chambers's death, Yenn succeeded his
master in the crucial post of Treasurer,
a role that effectively made him chief
executive of the nation's most important
art gallery and art school.

In this drawing by Yenn, the glow of
Chambers's stylistic influence is strongly
evident. With its heavy rustication,
classical orders and balustrade with
sculpture, the projected building is like
a small, updated version of Chambers's
most famous work, Somerset House,
a structure that Yenn knew well, having
been given by Chambers the extremely
responsible position of clerk of works
there when he was only twenty-six.

John Harris, *John
Yenn, Draughtsman
Extraordinary*, exh.
cat., RIBA Heinz
Gallery, London,
3 September –
19 October 1973

Nicholas Savage, 'John
Yenn RA: Pioneer of the
Architectural Exhibition
Drawing', exhibition
handlist, Royal
Academy of Arts,
London, May–October
1997; revised handlist
with Neil Bingham,
Royal Academy of Arts,
London, March–July
2010

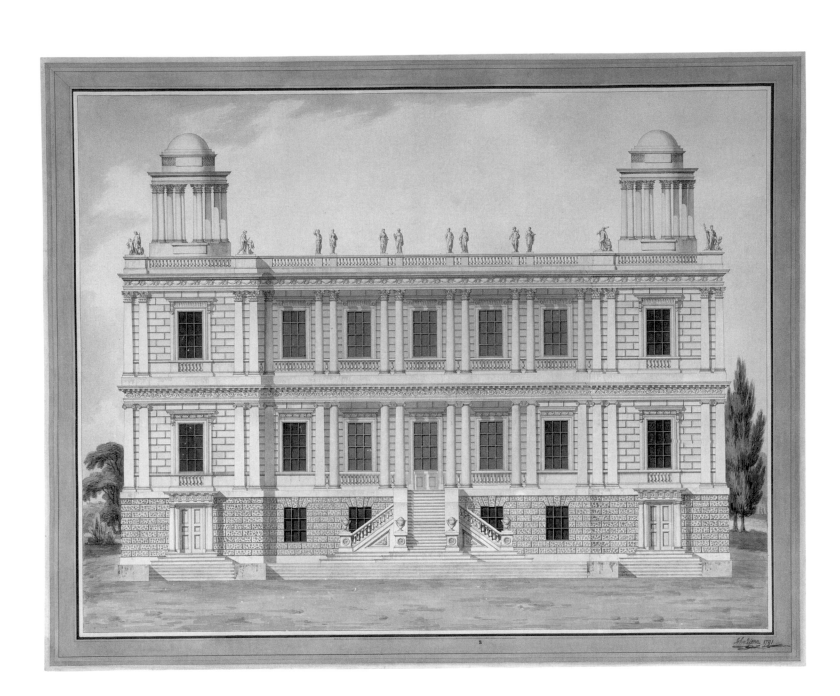

Sir John Soane RA
1753–1837
ARA 2 November 1795
RA 10 February 1802

New House of Lords:
perspective and plan (inset), 1794
Pen with black and brown ink and coloured
washes, 702 × 1254 mm

The Royal Academy played an important role in the long career of Sir John Soane. During the early 1770s, when he was an architectural pupil first of his 'revered master' George Dance the Younger RA and then with Henry Holland, Soane studied at the Royal Academy Schools. Winning the student silver and gold medals brought him to the attention of Sir William Chambers RA, the founding architect-father of the Royal Academy. Chambers was instrumental in persuading George III to approve Soane for the King's Travelling Studentship to study ancient architecture in Rome. It was while he was in Italy that Soane also began to cultivate the rich British patrons who were to help him gain his first commissions upon his return to London.

Soane became a popular architect, mainly undertaking country houses and government projects. As a Royal Academician, he did not hesitate to voice his own often controversial views at Council and General Assembly meetings. But at the Royal Academy he is most famously remembered for his annual lectures that he delivered as the institution's Professor of Architecture from 1809 until his death in 1837. These he illustrated with his great drawings, which influenced generations of architects. Moreover, for over sixty years, from his student days until his death, Soane showed his drawings at the Royal Academy's Annual Exhibitions, missing only five.

Soane's most prestigious and long-running job was as architect to the Bank of England in a building programme that lasted from 1788 to 1833 (his building was replaced in the early 1930s by Sir Herbert Baker RA's existing structure). Soane's other great project, a new House of Lords at the Palace of Westminster, was to come to nothing, although this was not for want of tactical manoeuvring on Soane's part. In giving a drawing of this project to the Royal Academy as his Diploma Work, Soane attempted to keep his design before the public eye. He even applied a label to the drawing mount, misleadingly stating that he had been invited by a Lords' committee to submit the scheme to replace the old and dilapidated House of Lords. In fact, Soane had been requested only to investigate the possibilities of new heating and ventilation. He had rather more than stretched the brief.

Soane personally lobbied his design drawings to King George III and the Prime Minister, William Pitt. But the country was in financial crisis and preoccupied with the revolutionary situation in France. Undeterred, he continued to polish his scheme, making fresh drawings. Today, these sets of drawings still remain in his home and office at 13 Lincoln's Inn Fields, a museum of Soane's architectural collecting mania.

This perspective view shows Soane's idea for a great, classical House of Lords building, *Imperium Britannicum* made manifest. In front of the principal south façade, groups of ladies and gentlemen mingle and gesticulate in admiration. Henry VII's chapel is seen on the far left. In the shaded foreground, water stairs to the River Thames are guarded by nationalistic sculptures of lion and unicorn. Soane's building is arranged with a central temple in the Corinthian order flanked with domed pavilions in the Ionic order. A quadriga crowns the entrance that leads within to the *scala regia*, a theatrical space for viewing the pageantry of the monarch's procession.

Ralph Hyde, John Hoole and Tomoko Sato (eds), *Getting London in Perspective*, exh. cat., Barbican Art Gallery, London, 1984, p. 25

Gillian Darley, *John Soane: An Accidental Romantic*, New Haven and London, 1999, pp. 118–23

Margaret Richardson and MaryAnne Stevens (eds), *John Soane, Architect: Master of Space and Light*, exh. cat., Royal Academy of Arts, London, 1999, p. 256

·DESIGN·FOR·THE·INTENDED·NEW·HOVSE·OF·LORDS·
THIS·VIEW·WAS·MADE·FROM·THE·DRAWINGS·DESIGNED·IN·OBEDIENCE·TO·AN·ORDER·OF·
·A·COMMITTEE·OF·THE·HOVSE·OF·LORDS·AND·OFFICIALLY·SVBMITTED·TO·AND·HONORED·WITH·THE·APPROBATION·OF· HIS·MAIESTY·

·DESIGNED·BY·IOHN·SOANE·
·ARCHITECT·TO·THE·BANK·OF·ENGLAND·
·AND·
·MEMBER·OF·THE·ACADEMIES·OF·ARTS·
·IN·PARMA·AND·FLORENCE·
·MDCCXCIV·

Sir Robert Smirke RA
1780–1867
ARA 7 November 1808
RA 11 February 1811

The Acropolis of Athens, as seen
from the Areopagus; restored from
remains still existing, c. 1808
Pencil, gouache and coloured washes,
978 × 1537 mm

Sir Robert Smirke was among the leaders of the Greek Revival at the beginning of the nineteenth century. And there is no greater exemplar of the movement's historical origins in ancient Greek architecture than the sacred Acropolis in Athens, the subject of Smirke's Diploma Work. This large watercolour, sadly faded from extended exposure to light when on permanent display in the Royal Academy's Diploma Galleries, was Smirke's masterly reconstructive interpretation of the ruined site that he worked up from drawings made on a visit to Athens in 1803. Smirke returned to England in 1805 after four years abroad and quickly established his Greek credentials with his design for Covent Garden Theatre. The British Museum (1823-46) was to become his most celebrated work in the Greek Revival style.

As early as the 1750s, James Stuart and Nicholas Revett had measured and drawn the buildings on the Acropolis; their published findings were a revelation both to archaeologists and architects. However, a more widespread rediscovery of Greek culture did not take hold until the end of the eighteenth century, and this proved sporadic because the Napoleonic Wars interrupted continental travel for long periods. Robert Smirke was one of the first British architects to make the long and difficult trip, venturing into the lands of the Ottoman Turks.

The artistry of Smirke's Diploma Work is masterful. This is perhaps to be expected, as he had been taught drawing and painting under the aegis of his father, the distinguished painter Robert Smirke RA. The younger Smirke's drawing, like many of his father's works, is akin to history painting. It captures a moment more than 2,000 years ago based on the facts of historical study. The faded watercolour and sun-bleached paper have now created an Aegean mist through which shimmers the citadel temple of the Acropolis (Greek: *acro*, 'topmost'; *polis*, 'city'). Below in shadow lies the Areopagus (Greek: *Areos*, 'of the God Ares'; *pagos*, 'hill'), the terraced outcrop where toga-wearing citizens gather. The silhouetted monument is of Smirke's imagination: a great plinth modelled on that of the Choragic Monument of Lysicrates and crowned by a figure of Athena.

Behind rise the sheer ashlar walls of the Acropolis. To the right, distant figures mount the broad ceremonial stairs guarded by pairs of Delian lions. High above, the annual Panathenaic procession enters the sacred precinct. The young girls, the Arrephores, who have spent the last year weaving the *peplos* (a sleeveless robe) that will cover Athena's statue, carry the sacred garment upon a litter. Musicians accompany the rite with stringed lyres and *bukanes* (curved trumpets).

The procession enters beneath the most visible of the buildings, the monumental gateway of the Propylaea. The Parthenon temple looms behind. Smirke has drawn the buildings and their columns, capitals, metopes and famous pediment sculptures in pencil, precisely and sparingly. And even though the drawing has been almost obliterated by long-term exposure to light and layers of varnish, Smirke probably included little colour to begin with, restricting himself to broad neutral washes.

J. Mordaunt Crook,
*The Greek Revival:
Neoclassical Attitudes
in British Architecture,
1760–1870*, London,
1972, pp. 47–56

Frank Salmon, *Building
on Ruins: The
Rediscovery of Rome
and English
Architecture*,
Aldershot, 2001

Sir Jeffry Wyatville RA
1766–1840
ARA 4 November 1822
RA 10 February 1824

Mansion for the 1st Earl of Yarborough,
Brocklesby Park, Lincolnshire:
aerial perspective, 1824
Pencil, pen with black ink and coloured
washes, 354 × 475 mm

Although the great country house represented in this design was never built, Jeffry Wyatville must have considered it of great personal and professional importance when he chose to present it to the Royal Academy as his Diploma Work in 1824. The magnificent scale of the house would have made Brocklesby Park the architect's largest commission, rivalling his great transformations of Windsor Castle for King George IV and Chatsworth for the 6th Duke of Devonshire.

Although the drawing is dated 1824 on the front, it was probably made in 1822, the date Wyatville inscribed on the back with the name of the client and the location. The client was Charles Anderson-Pelham, 1st Baron Yarborough, but he had died in 1823. His seat had been Brocklesby Park, an enormous estate in Lincolnshire with an old country house. A dating of this drawing to 1822 would also correspond with a set of sketch plans of the house made by Wyatville and dated 1820 and 1821 that are now in the Royal Institute of British Architects in London.

A long note made on the back of the drawing by the architect also boasts of how he was granted permission to change his name from Wyatt to Wyatville by George IV on 12 August 1824 at the ceremonial laying of the cornerstone to the George IV Gateway at Windsor Castle. The signature on the front is thus 'Jeffry Wyatville', in block letters, and not in the architect's usual written hand, as if he were experimenting with how to sign his new name.

The drawing is a small masterwork even if the power of the architectural design is not particularly strong. The house is seen from the heights of a wooded hill, looking northeast, with a lake or river beyond, and another range of hills in the distance. The viewer is placed in the shade of a stand of trees, in cool contrast to the valley scene, which is washed in the bright sunlight of midday. The raised elevation reveals the complexity of the house's plan. The most arresting part of the design is the circular entrance court with an open colonnade, reminiscent of the circular courtyard of Inigo Jones's unbuilt scheme for Whitehall Palace. In fact, the whole of Wyatville's design for Brocklesby owes a great debt to Jones's Whitehall precedent, both in its plan and its classic detailing. Beyond the entrance court is a square forecourt before the main porticoed entrance, crowned by a cupola that resembles a small temple. The long south range, part of which faces onto a grassed terrace, was to have housed an orangery, a picture gallery and a library. Beyond, around the domestic courtyard, were the principal rooms of the house.

Wyatville's drawing resembles a fine miniature, for the actual size of the image is relatively small and the detailing delicate and intricate. The long terraced façade, for example, is only some 19 cm in length. Over the basic underlay of the building, which is drawn in pencil, coloured washes have been applied meticulously. The extraordinary draughtsmanship is especially noticeable in the effects of light and shade: a delicate graduation in luminosity moves along the terraced south façade, while the white sunlight bounces off the roofs. The serried ranks of columns are not in fact painted at all, but are represented by leaving the paper untouched.

Derek Linstrum,
*Sir Jeffry Wyatville:
Architect to the King*,
Oxford, 1972,
pp. 122–26, 231–32

William Wilkins RA
1778–1839
ARA 3 November 1823
RA 10 February 1826

Gateway and Cloister, King's College,
Cambridge: perspective, c. 1824
Pencil, pen with black and brown ink and
black and brown washes, 510 × 985 mm

Of all the many important buildings that William Wilkins designed in his career, critics and even the architect himself considered the entrance screen to King's College, Cambridge, his finest work. Wilkins presented this perspective for the screen and gateway as his Diploma Work upon election as a full Royal Academician in 1826. The drawing probably dates from two years earlier when, as the inscription at the bottom reads, it was 'now building'.

With the regimented railings marching the whole length of the bottom of the drawing, Wilkins stretches the view down Trumpington Street. His gothic screen and gateway are seen in the centre of the sheet. To the left, with a pair of oriel windows, is a new range that Wilkins built at the same time as the screen. Looming over the whole scene is the great backdrop of the famous King's College Chapel. And, at the far right, in the faded distance (for this drawing has faded badly) is the classical frontage of James Gibbs's Senate House.

Wilkins's screen, like the chancel screen of a medieval church, consists of a series of pierced pointed-arch openings topped by crockets. The gateway, accommodating the porter's lodge, a splendid small building bristling with spires and an octagonal-domed confection, is placed centrally. Although he did not imitate it, Wilkins paid his stylistic respects to the college's great chapel, a building that he held in high esteem, having measured and drawn it while he was a student at Cambridge in the late 1790s. He applied a similar gothic adaptation to the buildings around Front Court, or as he refers to it, with medieval propriety, the 'cloister'. His gothic is quite fanciful, not enslaved to historic precedents nor seeking archaeological correctness, as with the gothicists of the next generation.

William Wilkins practised in both the gothic and classical styles. Very much a scholar of the antique, he spent as much time writing about the architecture of the ancient world as he did in designing his own neoclassical examples. In fact, Wilkins has come to be known principally for large cultural buildings that echo his knowledge of the Greco-Roman period. The National Gallery in Trafalgar Square – when it opened, also the third home of the Royal Academy – is his most famous work, although the design is often considered weak because Wilkins was forced to use the columns and capitals from the recently demolished Carlton House. Moreover, opinion differs over whether his classicism could be too doctrinaire at times, weakening the impact of his architectural designs. But with gothic there is no doubt about his prowess. As the architectural historian Sir Howard Colvin observed: 'The pierced screen at King's College … was a stroke of picturesque invention that shows what Wilkins could do when he was released from the shackles of classical scholarship.'

R. W. Liscombe,
*William Wilkins
1778–1839*, Cambridge,
1980, pp. 125–28

Howard Colvin,
*A Biographical
Dictionary of British
Architects 1600–1840*,
fourth edition, New
Haven and London,
2008, pp. 1122–25

WM·WILKINS·A·M   R·A·ARCH!

THE·GATEWAY·AND·CLOISTERS·OF·KINGS·COLLEGE
NOW·BVILDING·AT·CAMBRIDGE

**Charles Robert
Cockerell RA**
1788–1863
ARA 2 November 1829
RA 10 February 1836

Houses of Parliament: competition design,
plan and elevation of the riverfront, *c.* 1835
(detail opposite, full drawing overleaf)
Pencil, pen with black ink and grey wash,
363 × 1658 mm

C. R. Cockerell lived and breathed the cultural and stylistic civilisations of the Greco-Roman world. 'By the body of Bacchus,' he would curse, venting oaths straight from ancient times. As a young man, just in his twenties, Cockerell had shot to fame by discovering two separate but equally famous groups of ancient Greek sculptures: the Ægina Marbles now in the Glyptotek, Munich, and the Phigaleian Marbles, acquired by the British Museum. This was a dazzling start to a long and richly symbiotic career as an antiquarian and an architect that made Cockerell a leading European figure in neoclassicism during the early Victorian period.

As the learned and longstanding Professor of Architecture at the Royal Academy, Cockerell delivered first-hand accounts of his seven years of travel and research around the embattled shores of the Mediterranean at the end of the Napoleonic Wars. In his later professional practice, he created such mighty icons of Victorian neoclassicism as the Ashmolean Museum in Oxford and, after the early death of its original architect James Elmes, St George's Hall in Liverpool. Both buildings evoke the power of resurrected ancient ruins fit for a new urban environment.

In 1835, fairly early in his architectural career, Cockerell joined the mixed throng of entrants, acknowledged and unknown, in the greatest and most prestigious of all architectural competitions in British history: to rebuild the Houses of Parliament. The nation sought a replacement to the Thames-side building that had largely been burnt down the previous year. In the search for a national architectural identity, the competition rules stated that the entries had to be in a Gothic-Elizabethan style. The scholarly Cockerell immediately queried this period classification offered up by the Government. Elizabethan was a new term, much debated at the time, associated with Tudor – but separated from 'Henrician' – evoking such beloved English figures as Good Queen Bess and Shakespeare. Elizabethan architecture was interesting, claimed Cockerell with little enthusiasm, useful for its 'National Association'. But it was his belief that during the sixteenth century the best architects had not been English but Italian: Michelangelo, Palladio, Vignola. It comes as little surprise then that Cockerell's competition design drawing for the Houses of Parliament – which he soon afterwards presented to the Royal Academy as his Diploma Work – is for a stylistically cloned building of an array of classical periods hung on an Elizabethan carcass. This experimental exercise gave rise to such curious features as the outer Tudor ranges with bays inset with Palladian windows.

Cockerell's design failed to impress. Besides its curiously fabricated style, his plan ignored the committee's recommended clean sweep of the site to start afresh: a true antiquarian, a worthy preservationist, Cockerell retained and enhanced many of the architectural remains that had survived the fire, 'antiquities' that were, he said, 'sacred in English breasts'.

Catalogue of the designs offered for the new Houses of Parliament, now exhibiting in the National Gallery, 7th edition, London, 1836

David Watkin, *The Life and Work of C. R. Cockerell*, London, 1974, pp. 155–57

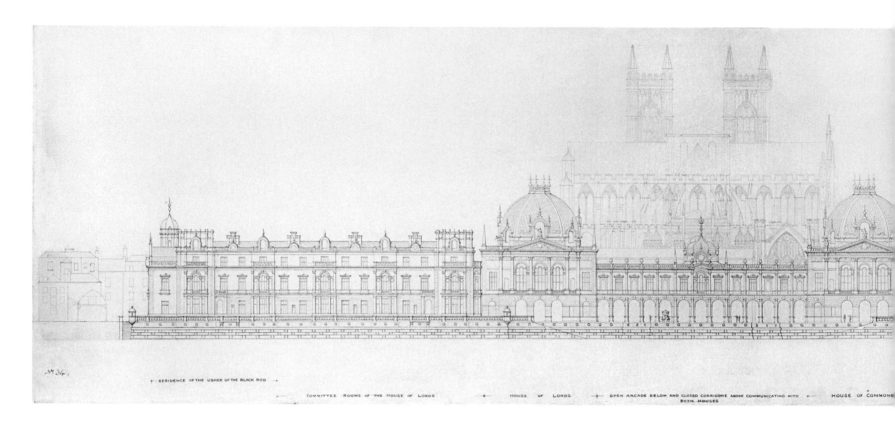

Nº 34.

·RESIDENCE OF THE USHER OF THE BLACK ROD·

COMMITTEE ROOMS OF THE HOUSE OF LORDS · · HOUSE OF LORDS · · OPEN ARCADE BELOW AND CLOSED CORRIDORE ABOVE COMMUNICATING WITH · · HOUSE OF COMMONS
BOTH HOUSES

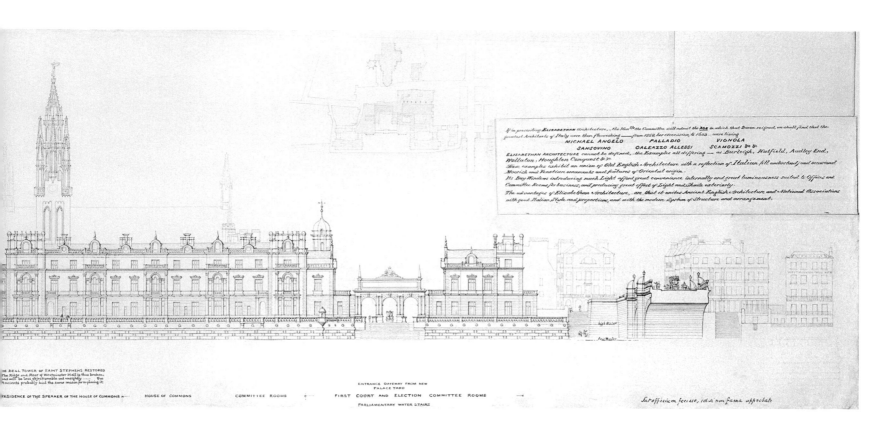

If in presenting ELIZABETHAN Architecture, the Hon.ble the Committee will admit the AGE in which that Queen reigned, we shall find that the greatest Architects of Italy were then flourishing — from 1558 her accession, to 1603 — were living

MICHAEL ANGELO   PALLADIO   VIGNOLA
SANSOVINO   GALEAZZO ALLESSI   SCAMOZZI &c &c

ELIZABETHAN ARCHITECTURE cannot be defined, the Examples all differing — as Burleigh, Hatfield, Audley End, Wollaton, Houghton Conquest &c &c. These examples exhibit an union of Old English Architecture with a reflection of Italian fell understood, and occasional Moorish and Venetian ornaments and features of Oriental origin.

Its Bay Windows introducing much Light afford great convenience internally and great luminousness suited to Offices and Committee Rooms for business; and producing great effect of Light and Shade externally.

The advantages of Elizabethan Architecture, are, that it unites Ancient English Architecture and National Associations with good Italian Style and proportions, and with the modern system of Structure and arrangement.

THE BELL TOWER OF SAINT STEPHENS RESTORED
The Ridge and Roof of Westminster Hall is thus broken, and will be less objectionable and unsightly ———— The Ancients probably had the same reason for so placing it.

RESIDENCE OF THE SPEAKER OF THE HOUSE OF COMMONS   HOUSE OF COMMONS   COMMITTEE ROOMS

ENTRANCE GATEWAY FROM NEW
PALACE YARD

FIRST COURT AND ELECTION COMMITTEE ROOMS

PARLIAMENTARY WATER STAIRS

Sat officium fecisse, id si non fama approbat

**John Peter Gandy
(afterwards
Deering) RA**
1787–1850
ARA 6 November 1826
RA 10 February 1838

Exeter Hall, Strand, London:
design perspective, *c.* 1830
Pencil, pen with black and brown ink
and coloured washes, 720 × 455 mm

Two years after being elected an Associate of the Royal Academy in 1826, the architect John Peter Gandy inherited a fortune from his friend Henry Deering, and with it the Lee estate, near Great Missenden, Buckinghamshire. Out of respect, Gandy assumed his friend's surname. Soon afterwards he received the commission for Exeter Hall. This proved to be not only his largest building, but also his last, other than a few alterations to a country house; the responsibilities of running his estate and being High Sheriff of Buckinghamshire and Member of Parliament for Aylesbury forced him to give up architecture. Deering's election to a full Academician in 1838 was criticised, therefore, as he was no longer practising. This is especially ironic since his brother, Joseph Gandy ARA, who was widely respected as the most imaginative architectural draughtsman of the age, was never to be admitted to full membership of the Royal Academy.

In fairness, Deering himself had been exhibiting accomplished drawings since his student days at the Royal Academy Schools. Many of these works had been topographical and reconstructive, based upon his travels and research in Greece and Asia Minor on behalf of the Society of Dilettanti. And there had also been the architectural designs submitted in conjunction with the architect William Wilkins RA, another scholar in the field with whom he sometimes collaborated.

When the time came for Deering to present a Diploma Work, he retrieved this drawing of the entrance to Exeter Hall, which he had exhibited at the Royal Academy Annual Exhibition in 1830 under the title 'Principal portal of entrance to the great hall now building in the Strand for religious and charitable purposes'. Naturally enough, the design's Greek Revival style shows the influence of his intimate knowledge of classical antiquity. The entrance is narrow and simple: a pair of columns within a pair of pilasters, crowned by a high attic, subservient within the façade to the more commercially viable ground-floor shops along the Strand, one of the most important shopping thoroughfares in London at the time. The capitals are very fine, based upon those of the Choragic Monument of Lysicrates in Athens. The cleverness of the drawing lies in the diminishing one-point perspective through the entrance, across the dark vestibule with its ocular glass skylight, to the light of the double staircase, and then into the bright hall with its sense of infinite space beyond.

In the drawing, the building's name, EXETER HALL, is carved into the entablature. When built, however, this was replaced by the Greek PHILADELPHEION, meaning brotherly love and imparting Masonic overtones, as the new hall was intended to supplement the nearby Masonic Temple for large public gatherings. The heart of the building was its great hall, with a capacity of 800 (it was later increased in size to hold 2,000), for meetings, concerts and services of various Protestant congregations. In 1842 *Punch* magazine carried a spoof on the evangelical pretensions of the assemblies, declaring: 'Reader, pause and humble yourself at the steps of the fabric, for Exeter Hall is an amulet about the neck of wicked London – a pillar of camphor in the city of the sick.'

Exeter Hall was demolished in 1907 and replaced by the Strand Palace Hotel.

Anon. [attributed to John Henry Newman], A Critique of 'Random Recollections of Exeter Hall in 1834–1837. By One of the Protestant Party', *British Critic*, 24, July 1838

Howard Colvin, *A Biographical Dictionary of British Architects, 1600–1840*, fourth edition, London and New Haven, 2008, pp. 404–05

Philip Hardwick RA
1792–1870
ARA 4 November 1839
RA 10 February 1841

Euston Arch, Euston Railway Station,
London: perspective, c. 1837
Pencil, pen with brown ink and brown
and blue washes, 745 × 1120 mm

The Euston Arch is Philip Hardwick's most famous work. The structure served as the entrance gateway to his Euston Railway Station, London's first intercity station building, the terminus of the London to Birmingham Railway.

Hardwick's Diploma Work, given upon his election as a full Royal Academician in 1841, appears to date from about four years earlier, and is probably the drawing shown in the 1837 Annual Exhibition as 'London and Birmingham Railway; the principal entrance of the London Station now erecting near Euston-square'. In the same year Hardwick also exhibited its companion piece, the principal entrance to his Birmingham station, at the other end of the line, also 'now erecting'.

The monumental character of the Euston Arch is powerfully captured in this perspective. The massive Doric structure presents Hardwick's reconstructed interpretation of the fifth-century BC Propylaea (*pro*, 'in front of' and *pylon*, 'gate'), the processional entrance gateway to the Acropolis in Athens. Hardwick's Propylaea is crowned by a pediment and flanked by a pair of lodges, as was its venerable Athenian predecessor. Although Hardwick never travelled as far as Athens in his four-year study tour in Europe, he was familiar with the Greek Doric temples at Paestum, south of Naples, which he had sketched and measured in 1819.

There is little indication from Hardwick's Diploma Work that this archway is the entrance to a railway station, a new building type. Hardwick has instead concentrated upon antiquarian precedent: behind the arch is a long row of Doric columns forming part of the station building but looking more like a temple within the sacred precinct. The figures' contemporary dress is the only concession to the Victorian era

(1837 was the first year of the new queen's long reign). A trio of working men idle about as a young man receives instruction from a gentleman, probably the architect himself, carrying what appear to be drawings tucked beneath his arm.

Amid great protest, the Euston Arch, along with the station as a whole, was demolished in 1962. In 2009 great chunks of the Yorkshire stone arch were dredged up from their watery grave in a tributary of the River Lea in East London where they had been dumped; there is an intention to reuse these pieces in a reinstatement of the Euston Arch on its original site.

Hardwick's little Curzon Street Station in Birmingham still survives.

Survey of London: Volume 21: Tottenham Court Road and Neighbourhood, Part 3, London, 1949, pp. 107–14

Alison and Peter Smithson, *The Euston Arch and the Growth of the London, Midland & Scottish Railway*, London, 1968

Hermione Hobhouse, 'Philip and Philip Charles Hardwick: An Architectural Dynasty', in Jane Fawcett (ed.), *Seven Victorian Architects*, University Park, Penn., 1977, pp. 32–49

Sir Charles Barry RA
1795–1860
ARA 2 November 1840
RA 10 February 1842

The Travellers Club, Pall Mall, London:
elevation of south front, c. 1842
Pencil, pen with black ink and coloured
washes, 525 × 695 mm

Charles Barry presented his elevation of the garden front of this gentlemen's club on Pall Mall as his Diploma Work in 1842. The drawing records the final form of one of Barry's smaller but nevertheless important works, incorporating his original proposal for a 'smoking tower', a penthouse haven for smokers on the roof, which had been omitted for reasons of economy at the time of the building's execution in 1830-32.

Barry's decision to give this seemingly modest design as his Diploma Work may seem curious. Why, for example, did he not give one of his drawings for his Houses of Parliament, one of the greatest of British buildings? Or a magnificent perspective, such as that for the grand country house Highclere Castle that he had exhibited to such acclaim at the Royal Academy in 1841? Part of the reason was that such flashy showpieces were usually carried out by hired hands or by staff in his large architectural office; this piece he almost undoubtedly drew himself. But even more important was Barry's great pride in the Travellers Club, a building that had broken down stylistic barriers by adapting the Italian Renaissance to local circumstances and thereby giving him his first taste of architectural fame.

Before Barry's club, Greek Revival had been the favoured style for prestigious buildings, among them a number of other gentlemen's clubs in Pall Mall. But the Grecian look, went the argument at the time, was peppered with porticoes and colonnades, and resulted in temples with no room for windows; it was therefore a style not practically suited to modern building. And when Italian architecture had been embraced in the previous century, it had followed the cool sixteenth-century precedent of Andrea Palladio, little embellished with ornament and with more porticoes and colonnades, a style which was 'the most vicious and extravagant … almost the poorest and most insipid', as one critic wrote in an essay eulogising Barry's Travellers Club (Leeds, p. 18). With the Italian Renaissance style, however, as revived here so successfully by Barry, the path was laid for a freedom of adaptation. Moreover, because more variation was possible, the different sides of a building need not be the same as long as they were harmonious; Barry proved the point with the Travellers Club, for the north front to Pall Mall and the south aspect shown in this Diploma Work are dissimilar although both designs are based upon Renaissance palazzi. As Sir Charles's son and biographer Alfred Barry pointed out, here was a club 'certainly like nothing which had preceded it in England; it was certainly recognised as a model for future imitation. These two facts alone stamp the design as having a real place in architectural progress' (A. Barry, pp. 86-87).

Unfortunately, this is one of the Royal Academy's architectural drawings that hung on display for more than half a century in the Diploma Work galleries at Burlington House, with the result that all delicate colour has been bleached out.

W. H. Leeds, *Studies and Examples of the Modern School of Architecture: The Travellers Club House, by Charles Barry, Architect*, London, 1839

Alfred Barry, *The Life and Works of Sir Charles Barry RA FRS*, London, 1867, pp. 81–88

Survey of London: Volumes 29 and 30: St James Westminster, Part 1, London, 1960, pp. 399–408

Sydney Smirke RA
1797–1877
ARA 1 November 1847
RA 16 November 1859

Carlton Club, Pall Mall, London:
perspective of the south front, c. 1855
Pencil, pen with black ink and coloured
washes, 560 × 815 mm

The early Victorian period was the golden age for building gentlemen's clubhouses. The prestigious addresses of Pall Mall and St James's Street are in the midst of the original clubland – and the architect Sydney Smirke built clubs in both streets. His first, with his fellow architect George Basevi, was the Conservative Club (today an HSBC headquarters) at 74 St James's Street. In 1845, at its completion, Smirke and Basevi received the commission for their second, the Carlton Club. However in October of that year Basevi fell to his death while inspecting Ely Cathedral, and Smirke had to continue alone.

The Carlton Club became another in the collection of recently completed clubhouses set side by side along the southern stretch of Pall Mall. Starting at Waterloo Place there is the United Services Club (today the Institute of Directors) by John Nash. This faces the Athenaeum by Decimus Burton; next door to this is the Travellers (see pp. 66-67), then the Reform, both by Sir Charles Barry RA. And then comes Sydney Smirke's club at the west end. The Carlton Club already had a building on the site by Smirke's older brother Sir Robert Smirke RA; completed in 1836, this had soon proved too small. To keep the Carlton Club running during building works, the 1836 clubhouse was initially retained. Construction therefore took place in two stages: the first at the western end was finished by 1848, and the whole was completed in 1856 after a further two years of building from 1854.

Smirke's Diploma Work drawing represents the last phase of the design. Stylistically, Smirke drew his inspiration from the mid-sixteenth-century Library of San Marco in Venice by Jacopo Sansovino. His Carlton Club is shown two storeys in height with a triple-arched attic room. The ground floor is composed of columns of polished pink granite and a series of arched windows edged in articulated voussoirs and topped by keystones with grotesque heads. The upper storey is richly decorated with stone sculpture, with angels in the spandrels and swags and cherubs in the opulent frieze. The interior too was resplendent, especially the staircase, with its painted decoration by Frederick J. Sang. The luxurious ornamentation of the Venetian baroque was seen as an advance on the austerity of the adjoining clubhouses, which were modelled on ancient Greek architecture and Roman and Florentine palazzi. Moreover, the Carlton was the bastion of the Tory party, and the stylistic gesture was intended as a comeuppance to the liberal Whigs' Reform Club opposite.

Unfortunately, the Carlton Club building suffered poor weathering of its Caen stone mouldings. In 1923-24 the architect Sir Reginald Blomfield RA recased the entire building in his own design of Portland stone. And then in 1940, the building was destroyed by enemy action. Today on its site there is a large office building designed by Donald McMorran RA in 1958-59, known simply as 100 Pall Mall. The Carlton Club's members moved to other premises in St James's Street.

Although Sydney Smirke's Carlton Club has now vanished, his architectural legacy endures through many of his public works. His famous circular Reading Room, occupying the centre of his brother's British Museum, may no longer echo to the thumps and thuds of closing books after its conversion to an exhibition space in the 1990s, but at the Royal Academy, Smirke's great Main Galleries (fig. 8) still see daily crowds of exhibition visitors. The Academy's perfectly lit axial galleries, etched in decorative gold-leaf mouldings, were the largest part of Smirke's transformation of old Burlington House in Piccadilly when the Royal Academy moved to its new home in 1867. He also heightened the façade by adding a third storey to house a permanent display of the Diploma Work of every Royal Academician.

J. Mordaunt Crook, 'Sydney Smirke: The Architecture of Compromise', in Jane Fawcett (ed.), *Seven Victorian Architects*, London, 1976, pp. 58-60

Margaret Richardson (ed.), *Catalogue of the Drawings Collection of the Royal Institute of British Architects. Volume S*, Farnborough, 1976, p. 77

'Pall Mall, South Side, Past Buildings: The Carlton Club', *Survey of London: Volumes 29 and 30: St James Westminster, Part 1*, London, 1960, pp. 354-59

**Sir George Gilbert
Scott RA**
1811–1878
ARA 5 November 1855
RA 28 November 1860

Government Offices, Whitehall, London:
perspective from St James's Park, c. 1864
(detail opposite, full drawing overleaf)
Pen with black ink, coloured washes and
gouache, 838 × 1727 mm

Sir George Gilbert Scott's Diploma Work
is an embodiment of vindication and
redemption. His great drawing was
shown in the Royal Academy's Annual
Exhibition in 1864 and then, as his
Diploma Work, it hung in the Academy's
permanent collection for all to see that he
was right. The subject is his design for a
massive government building spreading
from Whitehall to St James's Park. As he
himself made clear in the exhibition
catalogue, the design is 'as in the style
desired by the Architect'; in other words,
it is in the gothic style, not the classical
style that was forced upon him by the
government after lengthy controversy.

Scott did not win the much-publicised
1857 competition for the building, but by
a twist of fate, or perhaps a bit of string-
pulling, he was nevertheless appointed
as its architect. Asked to work up his spiky
gothic competition design and submit it
for approval, he found himself suddenly
up against the new Prime Minister, Lord
Palmerston, who as both former Secretary
at War and Foreign Secretary took
a personal interest in the design of the
building that was to house both his
previous departments.

Palmerston detested the gothic,
a revival style that had recently become all
the rage as a manifestation of the search
for an appropriate style for an imperially
British nation. The classical style stood
for the old, solid values of the ancients,
with which Palmerston identified, while
the gothic style had religious overtones
of morality and deified truth, which
the church-orientated Scott understood
in all their architectural complexity.
Having been told to alter his design to
classical, Scott submitted a compromise:
a Byzantine scheme. Palmerston would
have none of it – 'neither one thing nor
t'other; a regular mongrel affair,' he
snarled – and Scott, forced to capitulate,

remodelled his government building
again, in a style this time derived from the
architecture of the Italian Renaissance.

The whole affair was the pivotal
moment in the famous 'Battle of the
Styles' that came to dominate British
architecture in the mid-Victorian period.
As a result, Scott's Diploma Work became
one of the most important drawings in
Victorian architectural history. It is also
one of the finest, a masterful architectural
watercolour showing Scott's gothic goliath
sitting comfortably in its park setting,
enjoyed by all walks of British society:
working men repairing the park railings,
soldiers on parade, and gentlefolk
promenading.

The Government Offices were the only
substantial classical building that George
Gilbert Scott designed and he went on
without apology to create such
magnificent public structures in the
gothic style as London's St Pancras
Railway Station and the Albert Memorial,
content in the knowledge that his public
protestations had helped to turn the tide
of public taste.

John Physick and
Michael Darby, *Marble
Halls: Drawings and
Models for Victorian
Secular Buildings*, exh.
cat., Victoria and Albert
Museum, London, 1973,
p. 43

Ralph Hyde and John
Hoole, *Getting London
in Perspective*, exh.
cat., Barbican Art
Gallery, London, 1984,
pp. 53–54

M. H. Port, *Imperial
London: Civil
Government Building
in London 1851–1915*,
New Haven and
London, 1995,
pp.198–210

Edward Middleton Barry RA
1830–1880
ARA 29 January 1861
RA 30 June 1869

Government Offices, Whitehall, London: perspective with two block plans inset, c. 1858 (detail opposite, full drawing overleaf)

Pencil, pen with black ink and grey wash, 430 × 1339 mm

Not even the noble dream designs of Inigo Jones and John Webb for a new Whitehall Palace in the mid-seventeenth century could rival this Victorian mega-structure for the same area of London. By the mid-nineteenth century, Whitehall had become the centre of government officialdom serving the nation, the fast-expanding empire and those who governed from the nearby Palace of Westminster. Edward Middleton Barry's great drawing was a visionary scheme for concentrating all the government departments scattered about Whitehall and beyond into one magnificent building. Whereas the proposals of Jones and Webb had been for a palace for the monarch, Barry's design was for an even more splendiferous palace for the civil servant.

One of the first steps in replacing Whitehall's cramped and dilapidated accommodation finally came in 1857 with a major architectural competition for a new War Office and Foreign Office, each in separate buildings but on one site. The result was a fiasco, and although Sir George Gilbert Scott RA was eventually chosen to build a single large building on the chosen plot, he was to end up depositing as his Diploma Work (see pp. 70–73) a drawing showing what he had *really* wanted to build, not the compromise forced upon him by the government.

In deliberate contrast to the architectural small play of the competition, Sir Charles Barry RA, working in close partnership with two of his four sons, Charles Jnr and Edward Middleton, developed a vast and comprehensive scheme: a domed wonder 'in one mass of building', spreading over all Whitehall and housing all the public offices. To show his project, Barry made a large and beautiful presentation drawing,

his greatest work on paper (now in the RIBA Drawings Collection), and included it in the 1858 Royal Academy Exhibition.

In *The Life and Works of Sir Charles Barry RA FRS*, the Revd Alfred Barry (later Bishop of Sydney and another son) discussed how important this project had been to his father and included large foldout drawings of the scheme tucked into a pocket at the back of the book. In fact, as Alfred relates, his father's government-office palace was intended to be only part of a yet-greater scheme for 'metropolitan improvements' in an updated version of Wren's plan for rebuilding London after the Great Fire of 1666. 'That it would be but an ideal he knew well … It was, in fact, brought forward in the names of his sons Charles and Edward, in the hope that, if it secured public attention and approval, some of its leading features might be executed by their hands' (p. 293).

Edward Middleton Barry's Diploma Work drawing thus forms part of this great family project. In both top corners of the drawing are two small block plans taken directly from his father's design and simplified. The upper-left plan considers future expansion of the design, while the upper-right plan shows a more immediate scheme. Both variations are based upon retaining the Privy Council Offices (designed by Sir John Soane RA in 1826 but refaced by Sir Charles Barry twenty years later) and maintaining the layout of the 1857 competition scheme for the Foreign and War Offices. That the competition results, and the layout, were abandoned soon after the competition indicates that this Diploma Work dates from around 1857–58, and that it probably took many weeks or even months to make.

The perspective is stunning. The view is of the east frontage imagined along Whitehall and Parliament Street.

Although the drawing almost looks like an elevation, it is a perspective, with the added charm of pedestrians and traffic. Stylistically, Edward has amplified the repeating element of his father's Privy Council Offices and then added his own neo-baroque elements to the recipe, throwing in a seasoning of French detailing that can be especially savoured in the central pavilion.

Barry submitted this superb drawing as his Diploma Work out of a strong sense of family loyalty to his father's Whitehall scheme. According to Bishop Alfred, Sir Charles devoted much time in his final years to working on his great drawing; Edward's own Diploma Work, exquisitely executed and almost certainly in his own hand, was proof that the son could rival his more famous father and yet remain loyal to his inheritance.

Alfred Barry, *The Life and Works of Sir Charles Barry RA FRS*, London, 1867

Margaret Richardson (ed.), *Catalogue of the Drawings Collection of the Royal Institute of British Architects. Volume B*, Farnborough, 1972, p. 44, for Sir Charles Barry's scheme

SLOCK PLAN SHEWING PROPOSED CONCENTRATION OF PUBLIC OFFICES IN ONE BUILDING TO BE COMPLETED HEREAFTER. THE PRESENT GOVERNMENT BUILDINGS IN WHITEHALL AND S.T JAMES PARK BEING PRESERVED TO FORM PART OF THE SAME.

ULTIMATE EXTENSION OF PUBLIC OFFICES.

WAR OFFICE AND GENERA

BLOCK PLAN SHEWING WAR AND FOREIGN OFFICES AS THEY MIGHT BE ERECTED SO AS TO BE COMPLETE IN THEMSELVES BUT YET TO FORM PART OF A GENERAL SCHEME AS SHEWN IN OPPOSITE SPANDRIL IF THOUGHT DESIRABLE

ANCE TO PUBLIC OFFICES.

PRESENT BOARD OF TRADE &c. WITH ROOF RAISED AND ADDITIONAL STORY OBTAINED AT BACK.

**George Edmund
Street RA**
1824–1881
ARA 8 May 1866
RA 29 June 1871

Royal Courts of Justice, Strand, London:
perspective of south front entrance,
December 1871
Pen with brown ink, 561 × 985 mm

George Edmund Street was above all else a church architect, so it is little surprise to find that his most famous building, the Royal Courts of Justice, usually known more simply as the Law Courts, wears the ecclesiastical apparel of the gothic style as if it were a medieval cathedral.

Having won the competition for the building, Street was appointed architect in 1868. His built design, however, bore little resemblance to his winning entry. The Government, always inclined to meddle when it came to prestigious public commissions, forced Street continually to revise his design, especially in plan, and then make one alteration after another. Moreover, in the three years it took Street to work up his final design, he modified the building's architectural style, moving from a rather strict interpretation of French and English gothic to a gentler approach, with touches of the burgeoning Queen Anne revival.

It was Street's contention that all important perspective drawings – for competition, exhibition or to show the client – should be in the hand of the architect, not an assistant or hired draughtsman. This, he felt, gave a straightforward truth and honesty to the building process with no outside artistic trickery. But of course Street could afford to make this argument: he was a master of architectural drawing skills, especially in pen and ink. He records in his diary how a presentation drawing might take him sixteen hours to make, a relatively short time for such a complex task. Working four hours a night for four nights, from 9 pm to 1 am, Street devoted the first session to making the pencil underlay before inking.

In this perspective of the Law Courts (now discoloured by over-exposure to light), Street concentrates on the central section of the principal façade facing south on the Strand. David Brownlee points out in his book on Street and the Law Courts that, by not presenting a full elevation, the architect avoided showing the design for his clock tower at the far southeast corner, where he had been obliged to place it; Street had really wanted a much more elaborate freestanding tower in a prominent position. So in the Diploma Work the focus is shifted to the Great Hall with its flèche spire, Street's Victorian interpretation of the medieval flèche on Westminster Hall, former location of the high courts.

An elevation by Street published in the *Building News* in 1871 illustrates the same portion of the south front of the Law Courts. This was taken from a contemporary contract drawing, made at the same time as this Diploma Work. All the architectural features of the magazine illustration correspond to those of the Diploma drawing, except one. Here we see the addition of a screen of pointed arches at street level along the right-hand side of the frontage. It is as if Street had decided to pay his respects to the Diploma Work submitted by William Wilkins in 1826 for his great gothic screen in front of King's College, Cambridge (see pp. 56-57).

Building News, 21,
17 November 1871

Arthur E. Street,
*Memoir of George
Edmund Street*,
London, 1888

David Brownlee,
*The Law Courts:
The Architecture of
George Edmund Street*.
Cambridge, Mass.,
and London, 1984

NEW·COURTS·OF·JUSTICE·LONDON·VIEW·OF·PRINCIPAL·ENTRANCE·IN·SOUTH·FRONT·

R. Norman Shaw RA
1831–1912
ARA 29 January 1872
RA 13 December 1877

Adcote, Shropshire: perspective
from the southwest, 1878
Pencil and pen with black ink,
647 × 971 mm

Norman Shaw was a Royal Academy success story. He had been a student at the Royal Academy Schools from 1849, winning both the Silver and Gold Medals. Then with a Royal Academy Travelling Studentship he spent two years making drawings that he published as *Architectural Sketches from the Continent* (1858). Once established as a highly successful architect and Royal Academician, he became one of the most respected Visitors (part-time teachers) at the Schools. He also undertook much design work at Burlington House, adding extra galleries, the Refreshment Room (today the RA Restaurant) and the adjacent turn-of-the-century staircase with Art Nouveau flourishes in its ironwork, now named in his honour – the Norman Shaw Stairs.

Shaw's architecture was the watchword for the late Victorian and Edwardian well-to-do classes. His houses, in town and country, captured a gentle domesticity in their solid exteriors and aesthetic interiors. These were the houses inhabited by children dressed in smocks and petticoats in the pages of popular illustrated books by Kate Greenaway, who herself lived in a house designed by Shaw in Hampstead. In his commercial work, Shaw was eclectic in his use of styles: New Scotland Yard on the Embankment (appropriately renamed the Norman Shaw Buildings, now that it houses offices for MPs) savoured a romantic past in red-brick fortress walls and turreted corners. Later in his career, Shaw embraced a robust English neo-baroque style best characterised in his Piccadilly Hotel (now Le Méridien Piccadilly Hotel) in London's West End.

Adcote in Shropshire, now a girls' school, is a large country house that Shaw designed for Rebecca Darby, a descendant of Abraham Darby, a pioneer of iron production. Shaw had four large country houses on the go at the time, all of a similar nature. The rendering of his perspective drawing of Adcote, presented as his Diploma Work, is typical of his accomplished drawing style, which was much imitated by his office staff and pupils at the Royal Academy Schools. It is in his favoured pen with black ink alone, no brushwork, no wash. The intensity of the image lies in the dense and meticulous penmanship. The perspective shows the house looming up from across the garden, viewed from a low viewpoint, a favourite Shaw device that he often reversed by zooming in close from above; both perspectival tricks were a means of making the building appear more dramatic.

The composition of the stone structure is complex, a medley of parts of differing scales which the architect is keen to emphasise by showing the house from this corner aspect. Shaw's genius lies in making the whole sing in harmonious unity. At the corner of the building, with its large pitched roof, is the great hall, shored up by a trio of buttresses and lit by an enormous bay window. To its right is a block in three storeys of diminishing height with the drawing room on the ground floor. To the left is a long range, triple-gabled, with the principal entrance at its centre. Overhead, the roofline bristles with clusters of attenuated chimneystacks.

Mark Girouard,
The Victorian Country House, New Haven and London, 1985, pp. 359–65

Andrew Saint, *Richard Norman Shaw*, New Haven and London, 2010, pp. 130–33, 438

John Loughborough Pearson RA
1817–1897
ARA 29 January 1874
RA 16 June 1880

Cathedral Church of the Blessed Virgin Mary, Truro, Cornwall: perspective, view from northeast, *c.* 1887
Pen with brown and black ink,
790 × 562 mm

John Loughborough Pearson's cathedral in Truro was the first Church of England cathedral to be built in the British Isles since Wren's St Paul's in London two hundred years earlier. Pearson won the commission in a limited competition held in 1878. A prolific church builder, his gothic revivalism was based upon sound ancient examples so that his buildings, unlike those of some of his contemporaries who experimented more freely within the style, had an atmosphere of good manners about them. Many of Pearson's buildings, such as St Augustine, Kilburn, London (1870-97), are positive highlights of Victorian church architecture, with sublime vaulted spaces, rich decorations and dramatic planning for the revived rites of worship. Truro Cathedral was not as dazzling, preferring a monumental dignity derived from its historical detailing. Pearson took the cathedral's principal form from examples of Early English gothic and added great spires like those of the famous Early French gothic cathedral in Caen, just across the English Channel.

In 1880, the year of his election as a full Royal Academician, Pearson deposited a drawing of an unrecorded subject as his Diploma Work but withdrew it seven years later, replacing it with this perspective of Truro. By 1887, the cathedral had been consecrated upon the completion of the choir, transepts and two bays of the nave. Moreover, Pearson was then being approached to create another cathedral, to be closely modelled on Truro; the Cathedral of St John, Brisbane, Australia, was consecrated in 2009, more than one hundred years after Pearson made the initial designs.

Pearson's Diploma Work, in his own hand, is a masterpiece of High Victorian wash drawing. The view is picturesque, with the mighty cathedral throwing its heavenly presence over the intimate riverside scene, with potted plants on a windowsill, a young woman resting from her heavy load, and men casually leaning over the quayside railings of the River Truro.

The cathedral is seen from the northeast in a view showing proposed future stages of building. The completed west front and towers are hidden by the low viewpoint. Instead the design concentrates on the octagonal chapter house, which was never built, and the great crossing tower that was not begun until after Pearson's death.

Anthony Quiney,
John Loughborough Pearson, New Haven and London, 1979, pp. 133–48, 277

Alfred Waterhouse RA
1830–1905
ARA 16 January 1878
RA 4 June 1885

Manchester Town Hall: perspective, 1887
Pencil, pen with black ink and coloured
washes, 762 × 1092 mm

A big man with a bushy beard,
Alfred Waterhouse designed colossal
Victorian buildings. Born in Liverpool,
he undertook his architectural
apprenticeship in Manchester, where
he started up his own practice. In 1859 he
landed the job of building the local Assize
Courts, a landmark now demolished,
whose appearance marked the emergence
of the gothic revival as an acceptable style
for public buildings in Britain. By opening
another office in London, Waterhouse
built up one of the country's largest
architectural practices. His portfolio
ranged from the terracotta-clad Natural
History Museum in London's South
Kensington to numerous college buildings
in Oxford and Cambridge. As principal
architect for the Prudential Assurance
company, Waterhouse built their fiery
red-brick headquarters in London's
Holborn (now renamed Waterhouse
Chambers and the headquarters of
English Heritage) and, like a brood of
little chicks, the company's branch offices
up and down the country.

Alfred Waterhouse secured the job
of designing Manchester Town Hall by
winning a competition that had been
held in stages between 1867 and 1868.
The building campaign lasted for a
decade. Thus this large watercolour, dated
1887, is not a design but a record of the
building after completion. A romantically
charged view, it shows the architectural
centrepiece of the booming industrial city
in all its gothic magnificence. The town
hall's principal front rises over Albert
Square, a scene teeming with street life
in the smoggy purple haze of sunset.
On the left, in shadow, is the memorial to
Prince Albert, designed in a sympathetic
gothic style in friendly rivalry by the
Manchester architect Thomas
Worthington. The clock tower of
Waterhouse's town hall soars above the
entrance; the large windows on the raised
principal storey light four great rooms:
the banqueting hall, the reception room,
the mayor's parlour and the council
chamber. The right-hand side of the
building is only partially glimpsed as it
takes the inward angle of Lloyd Street,
a configuration that gives the structure its
triangular plan and allowed Waterhouse
the opportunity of placing an enormous
public hall at its centre.

One of the most brilliant architectural
watercolourists of his generation,
Waterhouse often worked up drawings
for presentation. Before adding the
watercolour, Waterhouse usually assigned
to members of his office the tricky
business of setting up the building's
perspective lightly in pencil. For example,
in 1868, at an early stage in the design for
Manchester Town Hall, Waterhouse and
his staff made a watercolour to be shown
at the Royal Academy's Annual
Exhibition. The office register records
that the assistant George Steane devoted
seven days on the drawing before
T. Cooper took over and spent a further
five, while Waterhouse himself spent
three and half days on it (Cunningham
and Waterhouse, p. 181). The total
expenditure in man-hours on the
exhibition drawing, which was less
elaborate than this one Waterhouse
created for his Diploma Work, was thus
in excess of fifteen full days.

John Archer, 'A Classic
of Its Age', in John
Archer (ed.), Art and
Architecture in
Victorian Manchester:
Ten Illustrations of
Patronage and
Practice, Manchester,
1985, pp. 127–61

Colin Cunningham and
Prudence Waterhouse,
Alfred Waterhouse
1830–1905: Biography
of a Practice, Oxford,
1992, pp. 51–62

Examination Schools, Oxford: perspective
from Merton Street, 24 March 1897
Pencil and pen with black ink,
610 × 980 mm

'The Examination Schools were finished and inaugurated on 1st May 1883 by a concert at which the Prince of Wales was present. My wife and I were there,' dryly recalled the architect in his memoirs, 'and I was presented to His Royal Highness, who was very complimentary.' Although created as a place for students to take their exams, Jackson's Oxford building was reminiscent of a great Elizabethan-Jacobean prodigy house, expensively enriched and costing out at double its estimate.

An independent architect, with a small office and few imitators, Jackson nevertheless carried enough prestige to fill the vacancy of Royal Academician left in 1896 by the death of the institution's highly regarded President, the painter Sir John Everett Millais PRA. The Academy's choice of Jackson was perhaps not an obvious one, as he thrived almost exclusively on designing university buildings in Oxford and Cambridge in gently revived styles from Tudor through to Queen Anne. But these buildings were much admired, and Jackson's knowledge of these historic styles made him a valued scholar in the Academy's membership at a time when scholasticism was considered a necessary part of an architect's profession.

He was also a master draughtsman. Acknowledging that his Examination Schools had been the turning point in his career and his most prestigious commission to date (as indeed they have remained), Jackson created a fresh drawing of the building for his Diploma Work, nearly a decade and a half after its opening. Instead of a fully coloured-up rendition, as he had shown at the Royal Academy's Annual Exhibitions several times in previous years, this drawing is reflective, worked up in pen with black ink alone, like one of his highly finished

sketches from his annual continental jaunts. The view is not of the principal front, which faces onto Oxford's High Street, but of the open-sided quadrangle on Merton Street. A pioneer of photography, Jackson delighted in recording a precise moment in time: the clock over the entrance tells us that it is morning, 9.30 am, as a pair of scholars stand conversing before the great ornamental iron gates, while an excited child tries to escape his mother's care. Jackson even gives us the exact date in the lower left: 24 March 1897.

In the top right-hand corner, the architect labelled the project's name beneath the coat-of-arms of Oxford University bearing the inscription *Dominus Illuminatio Mea* (from Psalm 27, 'The Lord is my light'). This is surrounded by twelve maces with the inscription *Ego Sum Via Vita Et Veri* ('I am the way, life and truth'), inspirational words for undergraduates who continue today to sit their exams in the Examination Schools wearing the traditional subfusc attire of black and white with carnations in their buttonholes.

James Bettley,
'T. G. Jackson and the
Examination Schools',
Oxford Art Journal, 6,
1983, pp. 57–66

Sir Nicholas Jackson Bt
(ed.), *Sir Thomas
Graham Jackson Bt RA,
Recollections: The Life
and Travels of a
Victorian Architect*,
London, 2003

James Bettley,
*In Search of
Architecture: The
Watercolour Albums
of Thomas Graham
Jackson RA*, handlist,
Royal Academy Library
Print Room exhibition,
2003–04

William Whyte, *Oxford
Jackson: Architecture,
Education, Status,
and Style, 1835–1924*,
Oxford, 2006

The new Schools of the University of Oxford

George Aitchison RA
1825–1910
ARA 2 June 1881
RA 19 January 1898

Royal Exchange Assurance, 29 Pall Mall,
London: elevation with ground- and
first-floor plans inset, 13 May 1898
Pencil, pen with black, brown and blue ink,
coloured washes, gouache and gold paint,
763 × 440 mm

On Friday 13 May 1898, less than four months after having been made a full Royal Academician, George Aitchison finished this architectural drawing for his Diploma Work. The slim little office building he portrayed had been built a decade earlier. In the 1885 Royal Academy Summer Exhibition Aitchison had shown a pair of drawings for his Royal Exchange Assurance building when it was in its design stage; these are probably the two fine perspectives, an exterior and an interior, now held by the Royal Institute of British Architects. For his Diploma Work, Aitchison chose to show the building in a more architectural manner, in elevation only, stretching the narrow façade down a long sheet, and then inserting two small plans of the ground and first floors on either side, near the lower corners.

The impeccably rich style of both the drawing and the architecture is typical of Aitchison. Many of his commissions were Aesthetic Movement interiors, usually domestic, for wealthy clients who revelled in lavish spaces interwoven with colour, decoration and pattern. Most of these are now lost, but the London house and studio that he designed at 12 Holland Park Road for his friend the artist Lord Leighton PRA is a well-known and striking survival. Its exotic interiors play upon a Moorish taste, the centrepiece of the house being the tiled 'Arab Hall', a miniature mosque-like space for smoking and drinking.

Whereas all previous Diploma Works had been designs for country houses or magnificent public architecture, such was the richness of Aitchison's touch that it could even elevate a small commercial building. On a façade with generously sized windows, Aitchinson has nevertheless managed to introduce much sculpture and ornamental stonework.

With its mix of French and Italian Renaissance features, touches of English Jacobean, and then slipping into Dutch up in the gable, the building becomes a fine example of the Queen Anne Revival. The sculptor and Aitchison's fellow Academician Joseph Edgar Boehm carved the four herms between the windows on the ground floor, repeating them in smaller versions on the attic level. The roofline is richly patterned and crowned by a pediment; it sports a splendid chimney. Across the façade on the drawing, ROYAL EXCHANGE ASSURANCE is lettered in gold, indicating the crafted gold mosaic used when the building was realised. Aitchison used gold extensively in his schemes, his interiors often hand-patterned or stencilled with gold leaf.

The two small plans show the insurance offices occupying the ground floor, with a counter separating the public space from the working office. The manager had his own private office at the rear. Aitchison said that his decorative inspiration for the interior had come from the Collegio del Cambio in Perugia, a mid-fifteenth-century banker's exchange of densely furnished rooms with panelling and walls saturated with frescoes. The rooms in the Pall Mall office building, if not quite rivals to these Renaissance spaces, certainly imitated their richness, with walnut panelling, carved green marble fireplaces, friezes and embossed ceilings applied above bronze cornices enriched, of course, with gold and silver. One of the plans also shows how a private residence accessed from St James's Square occupied the upper storeys, with the first floor taken up by dining and drawing rooms. Interesting is Aitchison's small labelling for 'Hyatts lights', a novel invention by a New Yorker, Thaddeus Hyatt, for setting glass into metal frames.

Aitchison's building no longer exists. The Royal Exchange Assurance, which had been granted legal status by Royal Charter in 1720, merged and was then finally absorbed out of existence in the late twentieth century. The company used 29 Pall Mall until 1907 when the building was let. In 1925 the Junior Carlton Club next door to the west acquired the freehold and a few years later demolished the building to make way for a ladies' annex. Aitchison's drawing has thus become a rare record of what was once one of the most enchanting buildings on Pall Mall.

Builder, 49, 15 August 1885, p. 220

Survey of London: Volumes 29 and 30: St James Westminster, Part 1, London, 1960, pp. 325–38, 339–45

Barry Supple, *The Royal Exchange Assurance: A History of British Insurance, 1720–1970*, Cambridge, 1970

ROYAL·EXCHANGE·ASSVRANCE

ROYAL·EXCHANGE·ASSVRANCE

GROUND FLOOR

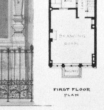

N° 23 ST JAMES'S
SQUARE, W.

FIRST FLOOR
PLAN

SCALE OF FEET

G. AITCHISON R.A.
150 HARLEY ST W
May 13. 1895

Church of St Mary the Virgin, Clumber,
Nottinghamshire: perspective, c. 1890
Pencil and coloured washes, 825 × 575 mm

George Frederick Bodley had been in pupilage during the early Victorian period under Sir George Gilbert Scott RA. Bodley inherited his master's gothic mantle and developed his own muscular but graceful response to this enduring, pointed style. In a career rich in church-building and extensive restorations, Bodley encouraged his own small group of pupils to continue exploring the gothic: C. R. Ashbee brought a medievalising tendency to the Arts and Crafts Movement, and Ninian Comper nurtured his gothic modernism into the middle of the twentieth century. Another of Bodley's young protégés, Giles Gilbert Scott RA, was to build the Anglican Cathedral in Liverpool (see pp. 106–07). Bodley himself designed several cathedrals that took many lifetimes to complete (which is fast, it has been joked, by medieval standards). His cathedral in Hobart, Tasmania, rose over fifty years, with dedication in 1936. And with his pupil James Vaughan, Bodley made initial drawings in 1902 for Washington National Cathedral, claimed to be the sixth largest in the world, which was not topped off until 1990 with its grand finial.

Bodley's designs for churches and their interior furnishings influenced the Anglican community worldwide. As co-founders of the ecclesiastical furnishers Watts & Co., London, Bodley and his architectural partner Thomas Garner created medieval-inspired patterns for clerical tastes in textiles and wallpapers that were exported around the globe. As a connoisseur and collector, and a collaborator with his Pre-Raphaelite friends William Morris and Edward Burne-Jones, Bodley often decorated his churches lavishly with stained glass, sculpture and pattern.

Bodley first exhibited his Diploma Work for St Mary, Clumber, in the Royal Academy's 1890 Summer Exhibition as part of a trio of drawings; hanging with this perspective were views of the interior and of the side chapel. Although the sheet is unsigned, it is likely that Bodley's favourite architectural perspectivist Henry William Brewer (1836–1903) made this full set. Watercolours by Brewer are rare in comparison to his prolific output of pen and ink drawings. Over forty years, Brewer produced perspective drawings for architects of their buildings in the pages of the weekly journal the *Builder*. However, he sometimes stepped out of his anonymity and contributed painstakingly detailed views of medieval cities, expansive fantasies based upon archaeological reconstructions.

St Mary, Clumber (1886–89), is one of Bodley's finest churches. The commission came from the twenty-two-year-old 7th Duke of Newcastle, who had inherited his dukedom in 1879, the same year as his ancestral home, Clumber House, burnt down. The duke rebuilt the house, using Charles Barry Jnr as his architect. However, as a high churchman, the duke chose the like-spirited Bodley as architect for St Mary. Unfortunately, in the course of the work, Bodley's relationship with his patron deteriorated and they fell out over the builder's estimates before fitting out was completed.

This exterior perspective looking from the southwest captures the visual power of Bodley's gothic style. Heavy buttresses grip the nave walls and a solid central crossing tower is topped by a delicate octagon and spire. The drawing is executed with minimal pencil underlay, lightly ruled in some places, and is then worked up in loosely applied watercolour. The order given by the ruling, overlaid with the freedom of the brushwork, reinforces the dual architectural character of the church: the muscularity of mass with the refinement of grace.

Today the church stands alone in the landscaped park, which was acquired by the National Trust in 1946, Clumber House having been demolished in 1938.

Richard Alcock, *The Chapel of St Mary the Virgin, Clumber Park: A Property of the National Trust*, London, 1967

David Verey, 'George Frederic Bodley: Climax of the Gothic Revival', in Jane Fawcett (ed.), *Seven Victorian Architects*, London, 1976, pp. 75–101

Sir Aston Webb PRA
1849–1930
ARA 23 March 1899
RA 17 June 1903

Queen Victoria Memorial, The Mall, London: plan and aerial perspective looking towards Buckingham Palace, November 1903 (detail opposite, full drawings overleaf)

Pencil, pen with black ink and dark grey washes, plan 330 × 1210 mm; perspective 472 × 1010 mm; label 490 × 140 mm
Perspective attributed to T. Raffles Davison

Within months of Queen Victoria's death in January 1901, her son King Edward VII had launched London's grandest urban-planning scheme as her memorial. Five eminent British architects were invited to compete for the prize of remodelling The Mall into a royal processional route, linking Buckingham Palace and Trafalgar Square. The scheme was to be an imperial rival to Paris's Champs-Elysées.

By July, Aston Webb had been selected. He was a good choice: a genial man who knew how to please, and how to use his budget to advantage. He was running the largest architectural office in the country at the time. His great gallery building for the Victoria and Albert Museum fronting Cromwell Road, practical and suitably imposing, was under construction.

The Queen Victoria Memorial was projected in three sections: first, a magnificent piazza in front of Buckingham Palace centred on a large statue of Queen Victoria by the sculptor Thomas Brock RA and enclosed by a sweeping colonnade with fountains; next, the widened and replanted long avenue of The Mall; and, finally, the opening of The Mall into Trafalgar Square, replacing old office buildings with the thoroughly practical Admiralty Arch, a ceremonial archway serving also as offices and accommodation for the adjoining Admiralty. An additional stage, not undertaken until 1913, was Webb's refacing of Buckingham Palace.

Aston Webb's Diploma Work drawing of the memorial scheme consists of three mounted sheets. It dates from November 1903, around the time when Webb was putting the finishing touches to the final design. Across the top stretches a sheet showing the plan of the whole scheme; the innovation by this time was that Webb had redesigned the area in front of the palace, bringing forward the sculpture – the big black dot – to a freestanding position at the heart of the *rond point*. Staccato points representing rows of trees line the processional route that culminates in the two alternative halves of Admiralty Arch.

The large aerial perspective looks towards Buckingham Palace, Brock's monument rising in the centre of the scheme. The pair of colonnades wrapping around the eastern side were later reduced to balustrades in the final design, making a financial saving which helped allow the rebuilding of the palace façade.

Although it is unsigned, the perspective is undoubtedly the work of the architectural draughtsman T. Raffles Davison (1853–1937). Aston Webb almost always turned his presentation work over to others, and Davison was his favourite. 'His peculiar power', when working with architects, wrote Webb's architect-son Maurice about Davison, lay 'in transferring their elevations and sections into perspective form, not only understandable by the layman, but truthfully portraying the design of the architect' (Davison, p, xiii). This is a typical Davison perspective, executed in black ink with a controlled and rapid hand.

T. Raffles Davison, *Raffles Davison: A Record of His Life and Work from 1870 to 1926 with a Selection of His Drawings and Sketches*, London, 1927

Ian Dungavell, 'The Architectural Career of Sir Aston Webb (1849–1930)', PhD thesis, Royal Holloway and Bedford New College, University of London, 1999, pp. 258–84

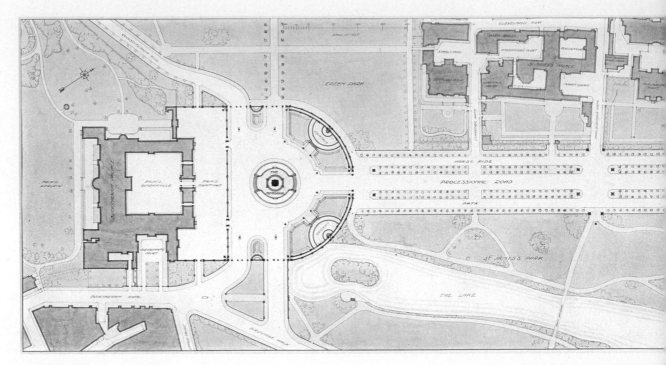

PLAN SHEWING THE SITE OF THE MEMO

GENERAL VIEW LOOKING TOWARDS BVCKIN

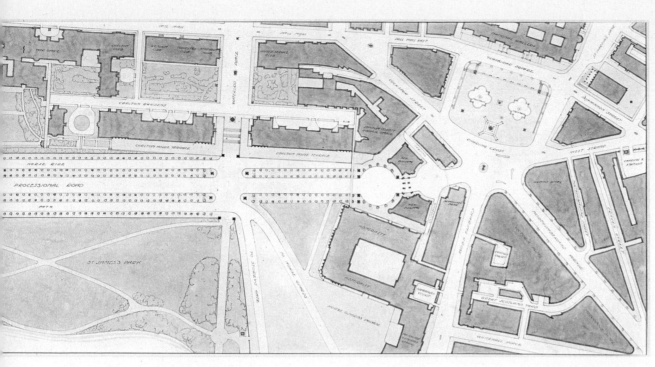

ND THE RECONSTRVCTION OFTHE MALL.

PALACE.

DIEV ET MON DROIT

DESIGN FOR THE
ARCHITECTVRAL
SVRROVNDINGS
TO THE
QVEEN VICTORIA
MEMORIAL
IN FRONT OF
BVCKINGHAM
PALACE
& THE TREATMENT OF
THE MALL

ASTON WEBB R·A·
ARCHITECT

THE MEMORIAL ITSELF
IS THE WORK OF
MR· THOS· BROCK R·A·

John Belcher RA
1841–1913
ARA 30 January 1900
RA 27 January 1909

Ashton Memorial, Lancaster:
front elevation, 1909
Pencil, black pen and coloured washes,
1300 × 710 mm

Upon a hill in Williamson Park, Lancaster, is the Ashton Memorial, a large, perhaps even the country's largest, memorial building. James Williamson, Lord Ashton, commissioned the structure in memory of his family. During the Edwardian period, Lord Ashton's one-hundred-year-old family business manufacturing oilcloth and linoleum was prospering, resulting in his many civic gifts to Lancaster, from the town hall to the Queen Victoria memorial.

John Belcher, architect of the Ashton Memorial, ran a large and successful London practice specialising in big, blustery public and commercial works. The first decade of the twentieth century was Belcher's finest. He had just completed Colchester Town Hall and, in the City of London, the sculpture-encrusted Institute of Chartered Accountants (with his young protégé Beresford Pite). Honours were coming his way, including presidency of the Royal Institute of British Architects followed by the Royal Gold Medal. And, finally, in 1909, as he was elected a full Royal Academician, the Ashton Memorial, the crowning achievement of these heady Edwardian years, was nearing completion.

The Ashton Memorial is Belcher's most spectacular work in the Edwardian neo-baroque style. He had always been attracted to designing in the renaissance and baroque revival styles, although he had not been averse to using gothic in his earlier work. But his reputation now lay in the English baroque, and this was reinforced by his collaboration with Mervyn Macartney in 1901 on an important historical survey of the period entitled *Later Renaissance Architecture in England*.

Belcher's Diploma Work shows the approach to the Memorial up the Cornish granite double-sweep staircase, which merges into a long flight of steps leading to the terrace. The Memorial itself, from the terrace to the top of the cross over the copper dome, is as tall as a twelve-storey building. From its vantage point it affords spectacular views over Morecambe Bay and in turn, the building creates a landmark silhouette on the hill. Stylistically, the building alludes to Sir Christopher Wren with touches of the Italian baroque thrown in. In his drawing, Belcher gives a distinct coloured highlight to the stained-glass window that illuminates the vast, domed interior. The building was originally used as a lounge, museum and reading-room; today it is a popular wedding venue.

Architectural Review, 25, 1909, pp. 248–52

A. Stuart Gray, *Edwardian Architecture: A Biographical Dictionary*, London, 1985, pp. 103–06

The Ashton Memorial
Lancaster

Scale of Feet

**Sir Reginald
Blomfield RA**
1856–1942
ARA 25 January 1905
RA 11 February 1914

Talbot Hall, Lady Margaret Hall, Oxford:
perspective looking northwest, east
and west elevations with ground
plan inset, 1914
Pencil, 848 × 850 mm

Dame Elizabeth Wordsworth, Founder and Principal of the first Oxford college for women, requested that the design of Lady Margaret Hall have 'somewhat of a homelike quality' about it. Sir Reginald Blomfield's response was a quartet of buildings, designed and built over a thirty-year span beginning in 1896, all constructed of red brick with stone dressings and clothed in the Wrenaissance style. Blomfield's design influenced the planning and style of women's colleges in Britain well into the twentieth century.

Blomfield presented this drawing showing the design for Talbot Hall, his newest addition to Lady Margaret Hall, as his Diploma Work in 1914. In the top perspective, the new building is shown sited alongside his earlier Wordsworth Building on the right, which was completed in 1909. Talbot Hall, however, was the *grande dame* of the college's buildings, serving as library, dining room and kitchens. The structure was restrained in scale and detail, domestic yet scholarly, a genteel country-house setting for its Edwardian lady students. Blomfield had designed and altered many country houses in his career, and gave Chequers its Tudor guise just before it became the country residence of the British Prime Minister.

Blomfield's Diploma Work is finely drawn in pencil alone. He uses the lead to full advantage, sharpening it for minute pointing in of such delicate work as the bead-and-reel borders and slashing with the side to create streaks of brooding sky. Blomfield has playfully hung the plan on a decoratively fringed curtain in the upper-right corner, and along the bottom he has placed the two principal elevations.

After the First World War, Blomfield achieved wide public recognition with such major works as the completion of London's Regent Street Quadrant and his most poignant design, the Menin Gate in Ypres, Belgium, a memorial inscribed with the names of the fallen of the Ypres Salient at the Western Front. He also published extensively on building and garden design. Many of his books were influential in their time. Wearing his scholar's hat as an historian of architectural drawings, he wrote the classic *Architectural Drawing and Draughtsmen* (1912) with a knowledgeable eye for representation and a sharp tongue for censuring buildings he disliked. Similarly, as a learned classicist, he found it difficult to accept the new modern movement as he grew older: approaching his seventieth year, he published his criticisms in *Modernismus* (1934), whose title made modernism sound like a disease.

Richard A. Fellows,
*Sir Reginald Blomfield:
An Edwardian
Architect*, London,
1985, pp. 85–89

Margaret Birney
Vickery, *Buildings for
Bluestockings: The
Architecture and Social
History of Women's
Colleges in Late
Victorian England*,
Newark, 1999,
pp. 79–91

LADY·MARGARET·HALL
OXFORD
Plan of Building &c &c
The S. Wing built in 1896
The Centre Block in 1904
The N. Wing now being
built 1914

West Elevation.

East Elevation.

LADY·
MARGARET·HALL
·OXFORD·
View of New Buildings
as completed.
Reginald Blomfield R.A.
Architect.
1914

Sir Ernest George RA
1839–1922
ARA 13 January 1910
RA 26 April 1917

Eynsham Hall, Witney, Oxfordshire:
perspective with ground plan inset, 1907
Pencil, pen with brown ink and coloured
washes, 608 × 982 mm

Sir Ernest George is known today for the highly collectable watercolours and etchings of continental views that he made and sold a hundred years ago. He enjoyed travelling, and was constantly sketching, measuring and painting. He was especially taken with historic Flemish and North German townscapes, often making drawings of picturesque views looking down stepped-gabled streets lined with prosperous merchant houses.

In his own architectural designs, George transferred the associations of old Low Countries canal-side houses to new London residences for the affluent classes of the late Victorian and Edwardian years. George's large gabled houses of red brick and terracotta, designed in collaboration with his then partner Harold Peto, cover extensive tracts of the Cadogan Estate in South Kensington. One of George's most famous clients was W. S. Gilbert, the librettist who worked so famously with Sir Arthur Sullivan. With the success of their operetta *Patience*, Gilbert was able to commission a flamboyant town house in Harrington Gardens. When he later decided to move to the country, he had George extensively remodel Grim's Dyke House (now a hotel) in the Harrow Weald for him.

George came to specialise in designing large country houses. His models were the older English great houses of the Jacobean and Elizabethan period that in turn had been stylistically much influenced by the Dutch Renaissance that George so admired. His Diploma Work is a presentation drawing of Eynsham Hall, one of his finest country houses in a revived Jacobethan style, combining elements of Burton Constable Hall, near Beverley in Yorkshire, with the more well-known Hardwick Hall in Derbyshire. His client was the industrial giant James

Francis Mason, whose father, a mining engineer, had established the family's fortune by mining copper in Portugal, thus enabling his son to acquire the splendid Portuguese title Visconde de Mason de San Domingoes e de Pomarão.

As might be expected from an architect who was also an accomplished artist, George's architectural drawings are magnificent. This drawing for Eynsham Hall, first exhibited in 1904, is characteristic. Although he uses his customary sepia ink, George's addition of coloured washes is a little atypical; he usually just touched in a wash for highlights. Interestingly, before presenting the work to the Royal Academy, George altered the inscription in the title in the upper-left corner, scraping off the name of his then partner A. B. Yates and adding the date of 1917, the year he submitted this drawing as his Diploma Work.

Eynsham Hall still belongs to the Mason family, who use it as a wedding and conference venue.

Academy Architecture, 25, 1904, 1, p. 45

Clive Aslet, *The Last Country Houses*, New Haven and London, 1982, pp. 130–32, 317

Margaret Richardson, *Architects of the Arts and Crafts Movement*, London, 1983, pp. 59–70

Ernest Newton RA
1856–1922
ARA 26 January 1911
RA 24 April 1919

House, Jouy-en-Josas, France:
perspective of principal north front
looking southeast, 1919
Pencil, coloured washes and gouache,
542 × 922 mm
Drawn by Cyril Farey

The house depicted in this pencil perspective is in Jouy-en-Josas, on the southwestern outskirts of Paris. The client was Ernest Mallet (1863-1956), a member of the distinguished French banking family, who for over thirty years sat as a Regent to the Bank of France. Mallet's wife, whom he married in London in 1905, was British, the Hon. Mabel St Aubyn, daughter of Lord St Levan. Members of the Mallet family seem to have had an Anglo-architectural streak in them: in 1898, Guillaume Mallet, Ernest Mallet's cousin, had commissioned Edwin Lutyens to design Bois des Moutiers, a beautiful Arts and Crafts house in Normandy with a garden by Gertrude Jekyll.

Construction of the house in Jouy-en-Josas began in 1913. The following year Newton exhibited a model of his building in the Royal Academy's Summer Exhibition. However, with work completed only to the roofline, construction was abandoned because of the outbreak of the First World War. Newton died in 1922. His son William Godfrey Newton continued his father's practice, publishing the finely illustrated *The Work of Ernest Newton RA* (1925), in which he showed two aspects of the model and noted that the house was still incomplete.

Although there is no record of anything comparable in French building registers, it seems likely that the house was eventually finished, as Ernest Mallet is buried in the local cemetery.

Newton's Diploma Work shows the main front of the house on its wooded hillside site. With picturesque historical references, such as the succession of diapered gables and clustered chimneys, the Mallet house, as the younger Newton noted, 'was to be definitely English in character though built near Versailles'

(p. 190). Very much an architect in the English historical tradition, Ernest Newton had been an articled pupil of R. Norman Shaw RA, rising to chief clerk, and had inherited Shaw's masterly technique of domestic arrangements. But Newton pared down plan and decoration, giving precedence to comfort over elaborate detailing, a realignment that the modern client preferred.

The perspective is by Cyril Farey (1888-1954), one of the most gifted perspective artists in British architectural drawing. In the first half of the twentieth century, so popular was Farey with architects in the Royal Academy's Summer Exhibition, that Sir Edwin Lutyens PRA quipped of the Architecture Room: 'What ho, the Farey Glen!' (*Builder*, 182, 17 February 1954, p. 976). Farey's usual technique was to have a draughtsman set out the perspective in pencil to his chosen aspect, before rubbing it all out to leave indentations as guidelines for adding his soft washes.

Another view by Farey of the front of the house, looking in the opposite direction, exists in the Drawings Collection of the Royal Institute of British Architects. Many of Newton's drawings in the RIBA collection illustrate his willingness to have others, among them T. Frank Green, W. R. Lethaby and T. Raffles Davison, create his presentation drawings.

Building News, 116,
7 May 1919, pp. 269–70

Builder, 116, 9 May 1919,
p. 454

W. G. Newton, *The
Work of Ernest Newton
RA*, London, 1925,
pp. 190–93

HOUSE AT JOUY EN JOSAS . FRANCE

ERNEST NEWTON A.R.A.
ARCHITECT

Sir Edwin Lutyens PRA
1869–1944
ARA 27 February 1913
RA 18 March 1920

Jaipur Column, New Delhi, India:
perspective, c. 1920
Pencil, coloured washes and gouache,
1075 × 565 mm
Drawn by William Walcot

'He is all for my star and not the one that makes a long nose at you seen sideways,' wrote the architect Sir Edwin Lutyens to his wife Lady Emily back in England. Lutyens was in New Delhi, creating the new capital of India, and had just shown the Viceroy, Lord Chelmsford, his design for the Jaipur Column (letter dated 15 January 1917, quoted in Percy and Ridley, p. 341). Crowning the column, surmounting an orb, which Lutyens felt represented power, he had set the Star of India, not a flat, cut-out star like a Christmas tree ornament, but a full sparkler, fashioned in glass, its six points facing in the cardinal directions north, south, east and west, and up and down. The star, Lutyens maintained, showed that as an architect he was doing his job, designing in three dimensions.

The Jaipur Column was erected on the cross-axis of Viceroy's Court before the east front of Lutyens's monumental Viceroy's House, today the Presidential Palace. It was a gift from the Maharaja of Jaipur. Rising more than 145 feet in height and standing on a broad red sandstone plinth, the column shaft is decorated with a pattern of British oak leaves. The orb, seen here in the perspective that Lutyens presented as his Diploma Work, was replaced in the final design by a bronze lotus flower. In the built column, the lotus was given a fuller profile, and the eagles at the foot of the shaft were executed as if they were in flight, instead of perching like pigeons. Lutyens and the later Viceroy, Lord Irwin, composed the inscribed motto:

'In thought faith
In word wisdom
In deed courage
In life service
So may India be great.'

Although Lutyens was brilliant at dashing off design sketches and scattering playful doodles and caricatures over any piece of paper that came close to hand, he always passed on his design drafts, usually drawn on lined paper, for his assistants to work up to scale. This Diploma Work perspective is by William Walcot, Lutyens's favourite architectural perspectivist and one of the most brilliant artists working in this specialised field. Born in Odessa into a Scottish-Russian family, Walcot was co-architect of the luxurious Art Nouveau Metropol Hotel in Moscow. But when he moved to London in about 1907, he worked mainly as a draughtsman and printmaker. Walcot's scenic reconstructions of ancient buildings have always been highly collectable. Lutyens was one of the first architects to employ him as a perspectivist, and he was particularly delighted with the way Walcot's unique shimmering style of drawing suggested the heat of India.

In 1921, the year after Sir Edwin Lutyens presented this drawing to the Royal Academy, he received the Royal Gold Medal of the Royal Institute of British Architects. He was at the zenith of his architectural powers, and celebrated for his large and imaginative country houses in the neoclassical or Arts and Crafts styles, often with gardens designed by his friend Gertrude Jekyll. Although his design for the great Roman Catholic Cathedral for Liverpool rose no further than the crypt for lack of funds (see also pp. 150–51), a fine pair of Lutyens churches forms the centrepiece of Hampstead Garden Suburb in London. Yet for all these grand projects, it is Lutyens's Cenotaph in Whitehall, a tapering block of stone undecorated but for a pair of wreaths, architecture in its purest form, that continues to resonate, more than the Jaipur Column, beyond boundaries of class, politics and religion.

Robert Grant Irving, *Indian Summer: Lutyens, Baker and Imperial Delhi*, New Haven and London, 1981, pp. 243–47

Arts Council of Great Britain, *Lutyens: The Work of the English Architect Sir Edwin Lutyens (1869–1944)*, London, 1982, p. 169

Clayre Percy and Jane Ridley, *The Letters of Edwin Lutyens to His Wife Emily*, London, 1985

Margaret Richardson, *Sketches by Edwin Lutyens*, London, 1994

**Sir Giles Gilbert
Scott RA**
1880–1960
ARA 26 April 1918
RA 27 March 1922

Cathedral Church of Christ, Liverpool:
interior perspective of east end from
the south aisle, 1922
Pencil, pen with brown ink, coloured
washes and gouache, with scoring,
842 × 490 mm

Sir Giles Gilbert Scott spent nearly sixty years of his life designing Liverpool's Anglican Cathedral. When he died in 1960, his work was still under construction; another eighteen years were to pass before the building's full consecration in 1978. And although his Liverpool Cathedral is a most magnificent achievement in British architecture, Scott might be bemused to discover that today his red telephone boxes attract armies of camera-clicking tourists and that his industrial Bankside Power Station no longer houses pumping engines but works of valuable art in its new guise as Tate Modern, a building with an annual number of visitors ten times greater than his cathedral.

Scott was only twenty-three when he won the invited open competition for Liverpool Cathedral that resulted in the final design of 1903. The assessors G. F. Bodley RA and R. Norman Shaw RA, a little taken aback at Scott's youth and probably by his being a Roman Catholic, insisted that the elderly Bodley act as his co-architect. But Bodley died in 1907 and so Scott became sole architect.

Design and work on the cathedral was carried out in stages, with the ebb and flow of economic and political forces shaping the building programme. In essence, Scott created three developing plans – in 1904, 1910 and 1924 – to suit major changes. His Diploma Work was drawn and submitted in 1922, the year that he was elected a full Royal Academician. The perspective is a design drawing showing a view from the south choir aisle looking into the sanctuary, with the high altar surmounted by a dramatic reredos, the east end window above. The scene is framed with a massive aisle arch. Adding contemplative charm to the moment are a seated gentleman reading and a smartly dressed woman

gliding along the aisle. The image is masterfully drawn and then rendered in brown ink and wash, with subtle coloured washes highlighting the stained glass and the woman's attire. Bright touches of white gouache illuminate the central cross, flanking candlesticks and frontal at the high altar. Scott scored the paper to form stone blocks, giving the surface a texture.

Fascinatingly, the drawing shows Scott changing his mind. When Scott made this drawing in 1922, the southeastern section of the cathedral was already under construction. High stone walls were being erected around the sanctuary, which would have hidden it from the aisles except through two bronze gates. To improve this situation, Scott made this watercolour of a scheme that opens up the view by removing the wall. Having then submitted the drawing as his Diploma Work, he had second thoughts about the design and worked it up with another, more satisfying solution, 'a pierced screen, which was approved just in time for the wall to be pulled down and the screen substituted before the Consecration' of 1924 (Cotton, p. 33).

Vere E. Cotton,
*The Book of Liverpool
Cathedral*, Liverpool,
1964

Joe Riley, *Today's
Cathedral: The
Cathedral Church of
Christ, Liverpool*,
London, 1978

Sir John J. Burnet RA
1857–1938
ARA 21 April 1921
RA 19 February 1925

King Edward VII Galleries, British Museum,
London: cut-away perspective of staircase,
north elevation of architectural model and
sub-ground-floor plan, *c.* 1925

Print with coloured washes added,
photograph of model and photograph
of plan, 860 x 560 mm

Although John James Burnet had intended to study at the Royal Academy Schools, Richard Phené Spiers, Master of the RA School of Architecture, persuaded him to attend the Ecole des Beaux-Arts in Paris under his old tutor Jean Louis Pascal. In the early 1870s, following the onslaught of the Franco-German War and torch-bearing Communards, Pascal was overseeing new work on the burnt-out Louvre. Burnet's parents were concerned for their son's safety, and for his morals, as a Scottish Congregationalist living in a Catholic country. Luckily, they relented, especially his father, himself a noted architect, who accompanied the young Burnet to introduce him personally to the great Pascal.

Under Pascal's tutelage, Burnet said that he and his fellow pupils found their 'eyes opened to artistic possibilities … of which we had not dreamed, giving us courage to go through the days and nights required to make the finished drawings' (*Dictionary of Scottish Architects*). At the Ecole des Beaux-Arts, everything revolved around making these finished drawings: competition pieces, large, complex and impressive, for schemes of grand urban planning and gigantic neoclassical buildings.

Returning to his native Glasgow, Burnet joined a flourishing school of Scottish art and architecture, made internationally famous by Charles Rennie Mackintosh. Burnet's Beaux-Arts style suited the booming industrial city. He revelled in the language of ancient Greece and Imperial Rome as much as he did in the baroque tradition. Standing in front of his staff, he would exhort them to read the classics so that they could build with the knowledge of the great imperial ages of the past.

In 1905 Burnet set up a second architectural office in London on the strength of winning the competition to create a new gallery building for the British Museum to be sited along the northern boundary of Sir Robert Smirke RA's original building. Burnet's Diploma Work is a finished drawing of the great north staircase for this project.

Reaching up through Burnet's Edward VII Galleries building, the staircase has become the daily scene of tourists lingering over the museum objects at the north entrance. Originally Burnet's building housed the intimate North Reading Room – a richly styled retreat for readers in the British Library when it occupied part of the museum – but this was remodelled in the 1990s when the British Library departed and Norman Foster RA created the Great Court.

Burnet's staircase, with its powerful, dark columns rising through the open well, is viewed in a cut-away perspective that strips away some of the walls in order for the viewer to appreciate the decorative panelling of the under-stairs and the hidden 'I'-beam supports. As part of his presentation, the architect added a small photograph of the plaster architectural model, mounted over the drawing and showing the external elevation as it was to be built, only lacking the installed sculptures of Art and Science by Sir George Frampton RA. Beneath the staircase drawing, Burnet attached another photograph, a much-reduced drawing of the sub-ground floor plan, which is in fact the entrance level. The plan reinforces the axial planning that underpins Burnet's Beaux-Arts sensibilities.

David Walker, 'Sir John James Burnet', in Alastair Service (ed.), *Edwardian Architecture and Its Origins*, London, 1975, pp. 192–215

Gavin Stamp, *The Great Perspectivists*, London, 1982, p. 116, preliminary drawing illustrated (in RIBA Drawings Collection)

'Sir John James Burnet', in *Dictionary of Scottish Architects*, www.scottisharchitects.org.uk

Sir Herbert Baker RA
1862–1946
ARA 23 November 1922
RA 16 February 1932

Union Buildings, Pretoria, South Africa:
perspective with ground plan inset, *c.* 1932
Pencil and coloured washes, 664 × 870 mm
Drawn by H. L. Gordon Pilkington

This soft-edged watercolour of the South African government offices in Pretoria, designed and built by Baker between 1909 and 1913, was made by H. L. Gordon Pilkington (1886-1968), an experienced architectural perspectivist who had worked on the building as an articled pupil in Baker's Pretoria office. Baker commissioned Pilkington to create this drawing especially for his Diploma Work in 1932 just before he had Pilkington make a set of illustrations of his South Africa House in Trafalgar Square, the building opening in the following year.

In his lifetime Sir Herbert Baker shared equal billing with Sir Edwin Lutyens PRA as the leading architect working in the British imperial tradition. Born in Kent and trained in London, and for a time at the Royal Academy Schools, Baker worked at first in the office of Sir Ernest George RA before moving to South Africa in 1892. His friendships with the diamond king and empire-builder Sir Cecil Rhodes and with Lord Milner, Governor of the Cape Colony, opened up a busy twenty-year career in South Africa.

With the Act of Union of 1909, South Africa required offices for its Prime Minister (today the President) and its government administration. And the buildings needed to be architecturally symbolic of the country's new self-governing power within the dominions of the British Empire. Choosing a site on Meintjeskop, a hill overlooking Pretoria, Baker created a modern Acropolis, a vision he said he took from his youthful travels in Sicily, visiting the temple and theatre at Segesta and the Valley of the Temples at Agrigento. The Union Buildings were to be Baker's last and largest commission in South Africa and, to judge by his selection of a design from so early in his career for his Diploma Work, they remained his most

memorable. Upon their completion Baker moved back to London and became co-architect with Lutyens in creating India's new capital of New Delhi, a great undertaking but one beset with squabbling. Having been his own man in South Africa, Baker was not used to compromise.

Pilkington's watercolour shows the Union Buildings from an extremely low angle, looking up the great terrace of steps to a semicircular central plaza enveloped by a colonnade that joins the two outer blocks of offices. The building shimmers in its neo-baroque splendour, which is appropriately based on the style of that most British architect, Sir Christopher Wren. The plaza, stepped to form a vast amphitheatre, is flanked by a pair of domes like those of Wren's Royal Hospital at Greenwich. A tempietto, the small domed structure visible on the plaza, houses a figure of Mercury. In front stands Baker's equestrian monument, designed in the 1920s, to those who fell in the First World War, a duplicate of his memorial to the South African dead on the Delville Wood battlefield in the Somme. The Temple of Peace, although cut in the design stage, much to Baker's regret, is just visible on the left, sitting high on the hill and on axis with the centre line of the building, although artistic license places it to one side to make it visible. In the upper-right corner of the drawing a general plan of the building shows its complex internal and external arrangements.

Pilkington's perspective is a fine example of his skill as a draughtsman, justifying his high reputation on the architectural scene as 'perhaps the one man in our profession today who can rival William Walcot in the romantic representation of architecture by brush and pen' (*Architect, Builder & Engineer,*

17, September 1933, p. 8). Like Walcot, one of the most popular British architectural perspectivists of the period, Pilkington favoured a broad, watery brush, floating spectral figures, and highlights of impressionistic colour.

In the post-colonial era, Baker's Union Buildings increasingly came to be seen as representative of South Africa's apartheid government. But this negative impression was cast off when the complex served as the backdrop for Nelson Mandela's presidential inauguration in 1994. Dignitaries from around the world filled the outdoor amphitheatre, while crowds collected on the terraces and audiences from around the world watched on television. Baker's architecture had been miraculously reformed along with the nation that it symbolised.

Herbert Baker, *Architecture and Personalities*, London, 1944, pp. 57–62

Doreen Greig, *Herbert Baker in South Africa*, Cape Town, 1970, pp. 173–96

Michael Keath, *Herbert Baker: Architecture and Idealism 1892–1913. The South African Years*, Gibraltar, 1992, pp. 165–80

'Henry Lionel Gordon Pilkington', in *Practitioners*, www.artefacts.co.za

War Memorial
Plan

Herbert Baker.

W. Curtis Green RA
1875–1960
ARA 27 April 1923
RA 14 February 1933

London Life Association, King William
Street, London: front elevation, c. 1933
Pen with black and red ink, 640 × 1072 mm

The Pevsner Architectural Guide for the
City of London observes that the London
Life Association building by Curtis Green
is '…nothing in the least original, but
distinguished in the serene handling of
the material'. The same may be said of
Green's Diploma Work. Plain and austere
in its presentation, the drawing is a
straightforward elevation, not a hint of
pencil, no shading, just the black inking of
lines interrupted by sculptural decoration.
Yet the ascetic serenity of this drawing
carries an extreme confidence, if perhaps
not originality, in architectural
representation.

Green was a very successful architect,
with works ranging from houses and
cottages in many of the new garden
suburbs to such London landmarks as the
Wolseley Building on Piccadilly and the
Dorchester Hotel on Park Lane. But to his
architectural colleagues, Green was just as
well known as a specialist in pen and ink
drawing. For nearly a quarter of a century,
beginning early in his career in 1890 and
continuing until the outbreak of the First
World War in 1914, Green wrote a column
about drawing in the popular weekly
magazine the *Builder*, illustrating it with
his own work, mainly sketches in pencil
or ink. So obsessed was he by drawing in
pencil and pen that it was not until after
1936, with the encouragement of his new
wife, the Dowager Lady Northbourne,
that he 'ventured into the watercolour
which up to then had been for Curtis
Green a secondary art' (RIBA Heinz
Gallery, p. 23).

Among the architect members of the
Royal Academy, Green was one of the
most prolific exhibitors at the Summer
Exhibition. Even as he grew older and let
others run his firm, he showed almost
annually, drifting away from architectural
design into topographical views,
particularly of Italian scenes. In 1949

he published his drawing autobiography,
The Drawings of W. Curtis Green RA, in
which he recalled that he 'mastered the art
of mechanical drawing' in his first years
before moving on to the Royal Academy
Schools to learn this fine art from the best
architect-artists of the late nineteenth
century, all of them Royal Academicians:
R. Norman Shaw, G. F. Bodley and Alfred
Waterhouse. 'Shaw', he reminiscenced,
'confined himself to such comments
as "beau-ti-ful drawing", and about
a particularly unsuccessful design,
"I dreamt about your design last night",
passing immediately on to the next
student.'

At the time of Green's election as a full
Royal Academician, his London Life
building had been one of his most recent
jobs, completed in 1927. He had shown an
exterior perspective of the scheme at the
Royal Academy's Summer Exhibition of
1925: an eye-catching watercolour
enlivened by motorcars and a double-
decker bus, with dozens of dark-suited
and behatted city gentleman milling
about the building. But this, of course,
was not in Green's own hand. His
Diploma Work was thus an extreme
contrast, a skilful snub to the popular
demand for the seductive perspective of
coloured washes. The year before, for
example, Sir Herbert Baker had presented
his large and lavish Diploma Work
(see pp. 110-11), not in is own hand,
but by a well-known perspectivist.
Green would have been fully conscious
of the comparison his more sober
Diploma Work was making.

Interestingly, on accepting Green's
Diploma Work, the Council of the Royal
Academy requested that he 'include in his
drawing a plan of the part of the front of
building' (Royal Academy of Arts Council
Minutes, 26, 6 April 1936, p. 228). Green
complied, but only just, and with wit:

he drew a very faint red-ink line running
across the central horizon, following the
recession and protruding elements of the
façade to create a plan that is extremely
discreet and nearly invisible. No one,
and certainly not his fellow Royal
Academicians, was to get the better of this
master draughtsman.

W. Curtis Green,
*The Drawings of
W. Curtis Green RA*,
London, 1949

W. Curtis Green RA:
*Architect and
Draughtsman
1875–1960*, exh. cat.,
RIBA Heinz Gallery,
London, 1978

Simon Bradley and
Nikolaus Pevsner,
*London. 1: The City of
London*, London, 1997,
p. 526

LONDON LIFE ASSOCIATION. LTD.   KING WILLIAM STREET. E.C.

Sir Walter Tapper RA
1861–1935
ARA 22 April 1926
RA 12 February 1935

Church of the Annunciation, Bryanston
Street and Old Quebec Street, London:
perspective from southeast, c. 1912
Pencil with coloured washes and gouache,
775 × 532 mm
Drawn by Charles Gascoyne

Walter Tapper was elected a full Royal
Academician on 12 February 1935,
was knighted on 23 July and died on
21 September. But, within a month of his
election, he had submitted his Diploma
Work, this drawing for the Church of the
Annunciation, a building squeezed into
the back streets near Marble Arch.

Tapper was a quiet and reflective
architect. He was chief assistant and then
manager in the office of George Bodley RA
and Thomas Garner before setting up full
time in his own practice at the relatively
ripe age of forty. Preferring to keep a close
check on his designs, he never employed
more than four draughtsmen at a time.
Tapper is said to have gained honours
for his 'positive goodness' and 'honesty',
qualities which the architect Charles
Reilly said commanded 'affection and
respect' (Reilly, p. 157).

Deeply religious and of a high-church
persuasion, Sir Walter Tapper was
principally an ecclesiastical designer, the
architect of many churches. He held the
position of Architect to the Fabric of
Westminster Abbey, where he now lies
buried in the cloisters. But he could also
turn his hand to more prosaic matters,
as he had a good sideline in creating
showrooms and gas fires for the Gas Light
and Coke Company.

His son and later architectural partner
Michael John Tapper recalled that the
Church of the Annunciation, a fine lofty
building, with something of the scale
of a cathedral or a major medieval
church, was his father's favourite work.
The street elevations are windowless
at ground level, but high windows and
vaulting throughout give the interior
spaciousness. The church's rich
furnishings are in keeping with the
Anglo-Catholic tradition.

In 1912, the year construction began,
Tapper showed this drawing and another
of the interior at the Royal Academy's
Summer Exhibition. Both were by
Charles Gascoyne, the popular
perspective artist who died as a prisoner
of war in Germany in 1917. This moody
and introspective scene is played out
beneath the great east window and flying
buttresses on the north side of the church.
The winter day is rainy and blustery.
A woman fights the wind with her
umbrella. Another, wrapped up against
the weather, skirts a puddle in the road.
But her umbrella is folded, the rain has
passed, and the church is bathed in the
emerging sun, catching on its spire -
created by a touch of gouache - hinting
at the heavenly light of hope.

'Memoir of Sir Walter
Tapper by Michael
Tapper', RIBA Mss
Collection, TaM/1/2

Builder, 103, 13
December 1912,
following p. 714

C. H. Reilly, 'Walter
Tapper',
Representative British
Architects of the
Present Day, London,
1931, pp. 157–67

Charles Grosvenor del.

Ashley Chase, Dorset: perspective
of south garden front, c. 1925
Pencil, coloured washes and gouache,
with scoring, 622 × 957 mm
Drawn by Philip Dalton Hepworth

Guy Dawber wished to be closely identified with his architectural drawings. In his RIBA presidential portrait, he is shown resting his hand upon a drawing sheet pinned to his work table, and a large array hang on the wall behind him. In a scurrilous review of the Royal Academy's 1930 Summer Exhibition, *Time* magazine ignored the iconography when writing about this painting and instead commented upon Dawber's fashion sense: 'Tailor & Cutter, London's sartorial trade sheet, reviewed the clothes painted by artists upon their subjects. "The collar seam is incorrect, the sleeve is a catastrophe!" railed Tailor & Cutter at Sir William Orpen's portrait of architect Guy Dawber. "Alas, all of Sir William's sleeves are wrong this year."'

Guy Dawber may not have been up on the latest in tailoring, but he understood its importance. In 1939 he wrote in his *The Book of the Modern House*: 'It is said that the best dressed man is the least noticeable in any assembly, so is the house most pleasing which fits in with its surroundings, and yet has a character and distinction of its own.' And Dawber's Ashley Chase, of which he submitted a drawing as his Diploma Work, is just such a best dressed house.

Dawber designed robust country houses, many of them in the Cotswolds and built of local materials. The stone for the walls of Ashley Chase was quarried practically on site, and the doorway and window dressings are in the indigenous Ham Hill stone, honey warm in colour. It was this sympathetic knowledge of rural architecture that led Dawber to write books on old cottages and farmhouses and to become a founding member and the first president of the Council for the Preservation of Rural England.

Dawber commissioned and exhibited the Ashley Chase drawing in 1925. It is not in his own hand; rather, he chose to put it out to the architect-perspectivist Philip Dalton Hepworth (1888–1963). When it came to drawings in the office, a young architect working for Dawber recalled that 'nothing but the best was good enough for E.G.D., and that is why all his important drawings were done on linen - paper would not stand the strain!' (*RIBA Journal*, 45, 9 May 1938, p. 633). The durability of linen was also an advantage when it came to rough handling on site. Of course, this more delicate watercolour made for presentation is on wove paper. Coloured mainly in grey and green washes, the tone is misty. Hepworth scored the sheet with a rule and a pointed drawing tool, adding texture and depth to the built features of the house, its garden and the terrace retaining wall. The view is across a plain landscape. This illustration of the L-shaped planned house shows the turreted staircase at the junction of the curve. To the left is the parlour wing, and on the right the hall and dining room with the service wing receding beyond. Typical of Dawber is the attention given to the massing of chimneys and interesting changes in rooflines.

Although Hepworth moonlighted as a perspectivist, he ran his own sizable architectural practice. He had trained at the Architectural Association in London, then at the Ecole des Beaux-Arts in Paris before being sent to the trenches in the First World War, where he suffered the effects of being gassed in 1917. His designs as a principal architect to the Imperial War Graves Commission after the Second World War therefore seem especially poignant. His two largest building successes were the Wiltshire County Council building in Trowbridge in the early 1930s and, on winning a competition in 1937, his fine, Swedish-influenced Art Deco-styled Town and Assembly Halls in Walthamstow in northeast London. Hepworth lived in and refurbished the historic London house of the painter Johann Zoffany RA in Chiswick.

Patrick Abercrombie (ed.), *The Book of the Modern House: A Panoramic Survey of Contemporary Domestic Designs*, London, 1939

Architect and Building News, 121, 24 May 1929, pp. 709–11, 715

Builder, 136, 11 June 1929, p. 106

Philip Dalton Hepworth, Obituaries, *RIBA Journal*, 70, April 1963, pp. 170–71, and *Builder*, 204, 1 March 1963, p. 447

Sir Edwin Cooper RA
1874–1942
ARA 24 April 1930
RA 22 April 1937

Port of London Authority, Trinity Square,
Tower Hill, London: aerial perspective
and ground-floor plan inset, 1930
Pencil, pen with black ink and colour
washes, 720 × 685 mm

Elected a Royal Academician in 1937, Sir Edwin Cooper presented as his Diploma Work this very fine drawing for one of his most important buildings. The Port of London Authority is a great Beaux-Arts-style office block whose tower rises above the north moat of its famous medieval neighbour, the Tower of London. Cooper made the drawing in 1930, although the building had been designed nearly two decades earlier, following a competition in 1912. The architect reinforces the interval between construction and drawing in his initialled Latin inscription near the bottom right – 'Invt 1911 / Delt 1930' (*invenit*, 'he conceived it' / *delineavit*, 'he drew it') – although he forgetfully dates his original design to 1911. Cooper's original reason for making this drawing was to exhibit it in the galleries of the Royal Institute of British Architects on the occasion of a substantial exhibition of his work when he was awarded the Royal Gold Medal in 1931.

Cooper views the building from a great height, enabling the onlooker to appreciate its size and study its clever layout. He even includes a plan, decoratively placed in the upper right, within a wreath, balancing the wreath and coat-of-arms of the Port of London Authority in the top left-hand corner. The building's plan is an irregular pentagon, a square cut at one angle by a diagonal. The shortest of the building's five sides is the principal entrance, and the four lengthy arms contain a medley of offices straddling long corridors. Glimpsed within the centre courtyard is the domed rotunda of the Port Rates Office, which was destroyed in the Second World War and replaced in the 1970s by an incompatible addition.

The London County Council established the Port of London in 1908 to bring together the scattered and conflicting interests of the many private dock companies. This new building for the centralised administration of the River Thames was a magnificent display of pride in the river and docks that played such an important role in the life and economy of London. Cooper designed many buildings for the Port of London Authority, including the baggage hall, the dock master's office, warehouses and offices at Tilbury.

The architectural historian Alan Powers has commented that Cooper's building 'was a *ne plus ultra* of Edwardian pomp in London, and, like the Albert Memorial, so irrational as to be outside the normal canons of taste'. Of particular magnificence is the great pile over the entrance, traditional enough at ground level with its giant Corinthian-columned portico, but developing above into an architectural fantasy. This was Cooper's interpretation of one of the seven ancient wonders of the world, the Mausoleum of Mausolus at Halicarnassus, a tomb that served as a model for architects around the globe, most notably John Russell Pope, who designed the Masonic House of the Temple in Washington DC at around the same time. In Cooper's lofty composition, the focus is upon a large sculpture by Alfred Hodge of Father Thames.

Builder, 123, 20
October 1922,
pp. 570–78

Alan Powers,
'Corinthian Epics:
The Architecture of
Sir Edwin Cooper',
in *The Thirties Society
Journal*, 2, 1982,
pp. 13–18

Arthur J. Davis RA
1878–1951
ARA 21 April 1933
RA 23 April 1942

Westminster Bank, Threadneedle Street,
London: front elevation, 1921
Pen with black ink and black and grey
washes, 720 × 1250 mm

At the age of only 22, Arthur Davis burst into the architectural aristocracy when the prominent French architect Charles Mewès took him into partnership. Having recently walked away with the top student prizes at the Ecole des Beaux-Arts in Paris, Davis returned to his native London to run the Mewès and Davis office there. He was perfectly attuned to the congenial upper-class world of Edward VII's England that loved nothing more than a lavish bit of French belle époque. He created the sumptuous grand salons of London's Ritz Hotel and the Royal Automobile Club in Pall Mall, and then richly appointed banks and boulevard architecture, stately country houses and interiors for such transatlantic ocean liners as the *Aquitania* and the *Queen Mary*; he redesigned no less than forty townhouses for wealthy clients.

But by 1942, during the dark days of the war, when Davis offered the Royal Academy this presentation drawing of his Westminster Bank building in Threadneedle Street, the heady years of prosperity and affluence were over. Nevertheless, he had just been elected a Royal Academician and was involved with the Royal Academy's plans for the reconstruction of London after the war; these were stimulating years for him.

This sombre pen and wash rendering is a fine example of Davis's drawing and planning skills, which had been nurtured at the Ecole des Beaux-Arts. His shading is extremely deft. Like a musician who plays from the quietest pianissimo to the loudest forte, Davis's range extends from the whiteness of the sheet through to the intensity of the black inking. In between are imperceptible gradations as he creates raking light in such areas as around the front entrance. Blackened window openings were a feature of Beaux-Arts draughtsmanship.

Davis based the style of the Westminster Bank façade upon Roman Renaissance precedents. The ground-floor level is sourced from Michelangelo's Palazzo Farnese; the upper sections pay tribute to the Palazzo Massimo alle Colonne in Rome by Baldassare Peruzzi. Even the long and gentle curve of the frontage along Threadneedle Street is similar to the curvature of Peruzzi's palace in Corso Vittorio Emanuele. These exemplary buildings were well known to every British architect and student from the full-page illustrations in Sir Banister Fletcher's textbook *A History of Architecture on the Comparative Method*, which, when Davis made this drawing, was in its twelfth printing since its first publication in 1896.

For his Threadneedle Street bank, Arthur Davis received the London Architecture Medal and Diploma from the Royal Institute of British Architects for 1930. At the award ceremony, in the company of his chief partner Charles Gage, Davis spoke of the necessity that architects 'designing buildings under the shadow of Wren's great dome [of St Paul's Cathedral] should remember their manners and conform in some measure to the standards which had been set by their famous predecessors. Here', he warned, 'was no field for excessive originality nor for wandering through the untrodden paths of architectural experiment.'

Charles Herbert Reilly, 'Arthur J. Davis', *Representative British Architects of the Present Day*, London, 1931, pp. 67–79

Architecture Illustrated, 23, April 1944, p. 47

LONDON COUNTY WESTMINSTER AND PARRS BANK

LONDON COUNTY WESTMINSTER AND PARRS BANK

THREADNEEDLE STREET ELEVATION

SCALE 3/16 EQUALS 1 FOOT

E. Vincent Harris RA
1876–1971
ARA 23 April 1936
RA 11 August 1942

Nottinghamshire County Hall, Nottingham:
four drawings – elevation to River Trent
and to Playing Field; elevation towards
Trent Bridge; site with ground plan;
and section and north wing, 1940
(detail opposite, full drawings overleaf)

Pencil and pen with black ink, light
and dark grey wash, 480 × 1640 mm
(all four drawings)

In 1942, during the Second World War, E. Vincent Harris presented this set of four drawings framed in one mount to the Royal Academy upon his election as a full Royal Academician. A new county hall for Nottinghamshire was his latest major project but it was on hold because of the war. The local county council, formed in 1888, had been using a small mid-eighteenth-century building that by the mid-1930s was proving inadequate. The chosen site for the new building was on the outskirts of Nottingham, in Bridgford, a pastoral location on the River Trent. Harris's design shows the strong influence that Stockholm City Hall, which had been completed in 1923, was having on English architects at the time. Harris's tower, especially, is reminiscent of its Swedish predecessor, which in turn had been based upon the famous campanile of St Mark's in Venice; both exemplars, like Nottingham, were set romantically on the water's edge.

When the construction of Nottinghamshire County Hall resumed, post-war restrictions and financial constraints meant that the dramatic tower was never built. In fact, the whole complex was not completed until 1965 and then in a very different way from Harris's conception: the county architect W. D. Lacey used the CLASP system of prefabricated parts in his alterations to Harris's original design.

The drawings of Harris's Diploma Work set are of delicate beauty and exceptional draughtsmanship. They appear to be the work of an unknown architectural artist. Throughout his career, when creating his presentation drawings, Harris was inclined to use architects in his large practice, sometimes supplemented by outside perspectivists. This quartet of sheets is by a hand that can blend soft, undulating pencil lines representing leafless trees, ephemeral human figures and a sailing boat marking the River Trent. This delicacy is contrasted with the intensity of the pen lines for the brickwork of the building, which are densely drawn at about three lines per millimetre before being given an overall wash. The large, top drawing is a particularly interesting orthographic projection, which positions opposing elevations separated by a piazza in one plane. This mirror-effect creates double impact, as if there were two buildings, each with a dramatic tower.

Nottinghamshire County Hall was one of many major British public buildings that Harris built and designed in the first half of the twentieth century. His first success had been winning the 1914 competition to design the Ministry of Defence building in Whitehall, although the structure itself was not erected until after the Second World War. His public library in Manchester (1927), with its circular reading room, was followed by a succession of civic buildings, including Sheffield City Hall, Leeds Civic Hall, and county halls for Glamorgan, Surrey and Somerset alongside his Diploma Work design for Nottinghamshire. His restrained use of the classical vocabulary within a 'modern' framework gave his buildings authority without pomposity.

Elain Harwood, *Pevsner
Architectural Guides:
Nottingham*, New
Haven and London,
2008, pp. 160–61

NEW CO...

SAPIE...

NOTTIN...

ELEVATION TO RIVER TRENT

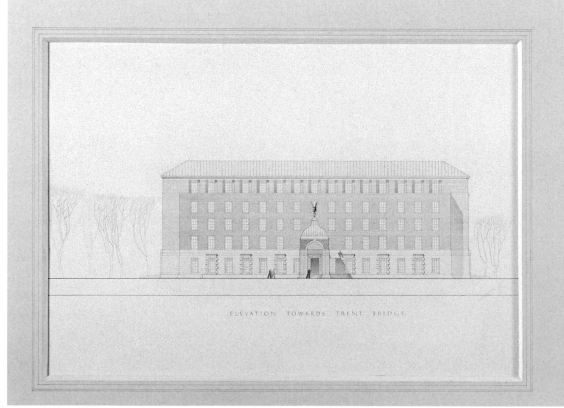

ELEVATION TOWARDS TRENT BRIDGE

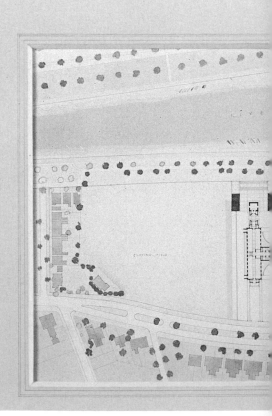

NTY HALL

HAMSHIRE

OFICIENS

ELEVATION TO PLAYING FIELD

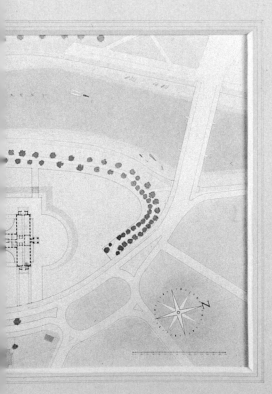

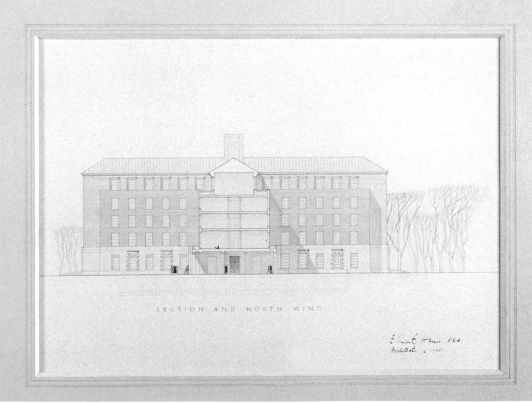

SECTION AND NORTH WING

E Vincent Harris RA
Architect . 1940.

**Sir Albert
Richardson PRA**
1880–1964
ARA 17 March 1936
RA 15 February 1944

Physics Building, University College,
University of London, Gordon Street,
London: south elevation and plan
to Gordon Place, 1944
Pencil, pen with black ink and grey
and brown washes, 502 × 1025 mm

Sir Albert Richardson's *Monumental Classic Architecture in Great Britain and Ireland* (1914) was a groundbreaking study in the reassessment of Georgian architecture. Richardson himself lived somewhat the lifestyle of an eighteenth-century gentleman, inhabiting his Georgian townhouse in Ampthill, Bedfordshire, initially without electricity, sometimes playfully wearing a powdered wig and getting about in a sedan chair. Keeping in character, he was never more comfortable than when designing contemporary buildings with a neo-Georgian spirit. The drawing that he submitted as his Diploma Work is illustrative of how he adapted his beloved classicism to modern circumstances.

Richardson cultivated a long association with University College London (UCL), adding new buildings for growing departments. He held the highest respect for the Wilkins Building, the palatial heart of the campus, a model example of the Greek Revival style from the 1820s that had been named in honour of its architect William Wilkins RA. Richardson's first work at UCL was a new Anatomy Building in 1922; his last was to be the Biological Sciences Building from 1959–64. In the meantime, he became Professor of Architecture at the UCL Bartlett School of Architecture. When he retired in 1946, he took up the same position at the Royal Academy when he briefly revived the School of Architecture with postgraduate courses meant to make up for the growing lack of historical design being taught to post-war architecture students. Richardson felt he could not stand by quietly as the academic ideals of the Royal Academy were overwhelmed by modernism. His students adored him and in his lectures (see p. 33) were always awed by his ability to make impromptu drawings of famous buildings from memory and to sketch his own classical designs while speaking.

This drawing, dating from 1944, shows a plan and elevation for an additional wing to UCL's original Physics Building, a victim of bomb damage; construction did not take place until after the post-war building restrictions had been lifted, with completion in 1954. Mis-titled 'Elevation to Gordon Street', the drawing actually shows the long south elevation that faces onto the inner court behind the Wilkins Building; the elevation to Gordon Street is only the short east end.

As is to be expected in a period of austerity, Richardson's design for the façade is plain. But this was his style anyway. Admiring as he was of the old, classical world, the lessons of the past for him were about proportion and scale, and how to fit a building comfortably onto its site alongside its neighbours. Ornament, unless he was working on a grander building, was of less concern to him. If the outside of his Physics Wing did not seem to keep up with the new lightweight and transparent character of the buildings of the growing modern movement, Richardson certainly embraced modern methods of construction, using a steel frame with solid reinforced concrete floors, aluminium windows and a heating system consisting of panels embedded into the ceilings. Kentish bricks and Portland stone dressings, however, place this plain and simple building firmly in the architect's beloved British tradition of practical beauty.

Builder, 186, 25 June 1954, pp. 1106–09

Simon Houfe, *Sir Albert Richardson: The Professor*, Luton, 1980

Simon Houfe, John Wilton-Ely and Alan Powers (eds), *Sir Albert Richardson 1880–1964*, London, 1999

UNIVERSITY COLLEGE LONDON
ELEVATION TO GORDON STREET

C. H. James RA
1893–1953
ARA 16 November 1937
RA 25 April 1946

Norwich Town Hall, Norfolk:
axonometric, 1933
Pencil, pen with black ink, gouache
and brown, grey and green washes,
766 × 746 mm

Rising up behind the colourful stalls of Norwich's large open market is the city's town hall, a splendid backdrop of civic pride. Today the building is deemed as Art Deco, but when it was designed and built by the architects C. H. James and S. Rowland Pierce, such stylistic terminology would have been anathema. For James and Pierce the direct inspiration was Swedish Modernism, a movement very fashionable for public buildings in Britain at that time, a blossoming in Swedish architecture having been made popular by the 1930 Stockholm Exhibition. The slender central columns of the building, lending the design its greatest elegance, were directly inspired by those of Stockholm Concert Hall (1923-26) by Ivar Tengbom HON RA. The tower with its cupola and the hooded windows at either end of the principal façade are features borrowed from Stockholm City Hall (1911-23) by Ragnar Östberg HON RA.

James and Pierce had won the Norwich competition in 1932, although financial difficulties resulted in the building not being completed and opened until 1938. The architect-assessor Robert Atkinson dictated the general layout with a ground plan set around an inner courtyard. The interior is restrained in its detailing, although the architects designed the principal furniture. The architect-artist James Beattie Michie and students of the Royal Academy Schools painted the staircase ceiling.

That James was elected to the Academy but not Pierce, when both architects were of comparable abilities and equals – together they also created Hertford County Buildings and Slough Municipal Building – was because the institution then upheld a tradition that architectural partners could not both be Academicians. In reputation, James perhaps had the edge over Pierce, having trained under Sir Edwin Lutyens PRA and then worked in the offices of Parker and Unwin, leaders of the Garden City Movement. Also, from 1919 to 1925, James, with his first partner C. M. Hennell, had established a reputation as an architect of good housing schemes in Welwyn Garden City and Swanpool Garden Suburb in Lincoln.

James submitted this drawing as his Diploma Work upon his election to full Royal Academician in 1946. The sheet, in his own hand, dates from 1933, during the design stage. The power of the drawing lies in its bird's-eye view, done in axonometric projection to permit an angled vantage to emphasise the plan.

Architectural Review,
84, November 1938,
pp. 203–06

Builder, 155, 11
November 1938,
pp. 911–15 and 920–28

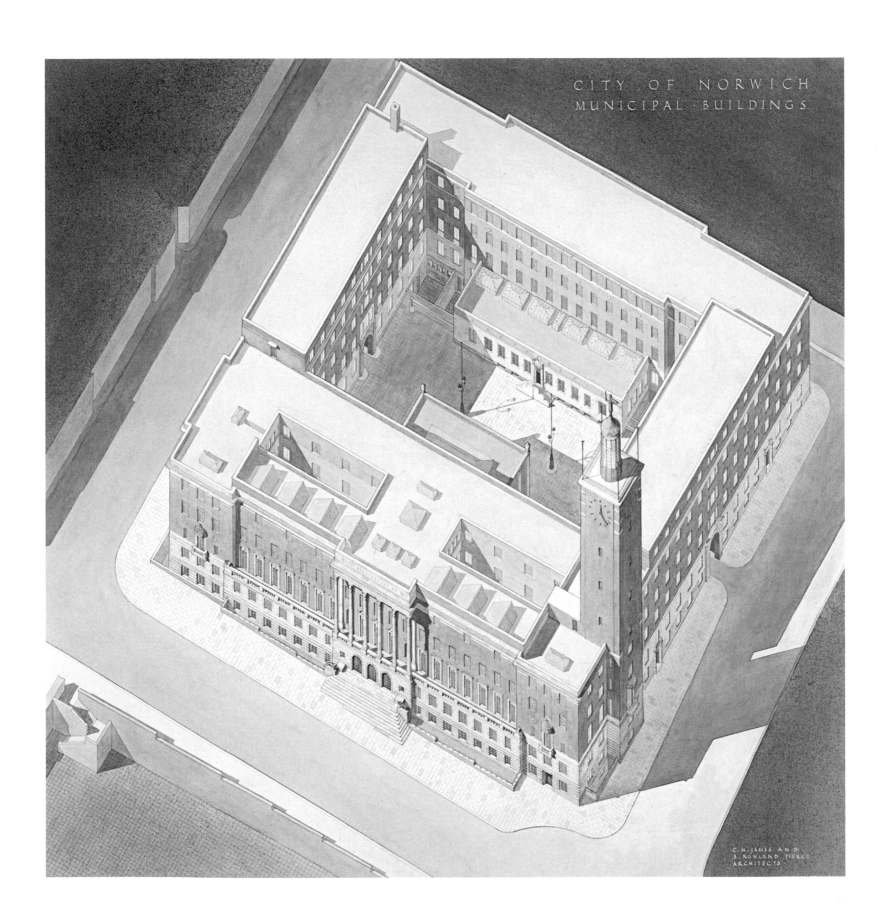

CITY OF NORWICH
MUNICIPAL BUILDINGS

C.H. JAMES AND
S. ROWLAND PIERCE
ARCHITECTS

Sir Edward Maufe RA
1883–1974
ARA 22 April 1938
RA 10 December 1947

Cathedral Church of the Holy Spirit,
Guildford, Surrey: south elevation, 1948
Pencil, pen with black ink and brown
and green washes, 749 × 1326 mm

Maufe's Diploma Work is a drawing of hope and faith. It is inscribed: 'Designed 1931 / Drawn 1948'. When Maufe made and presented this drawing of Guildford Cathedral, the building's construction had been halted by war and conditions for restarting were precarious. The foundation stone had been laid in 1936, but work ceased in 1939, and post-war Britain was placing all its energies into housing the displaced. Liverpool's Catholic Cathedral by Sir Edwin Lutyens PRA was in the same predicament, and was to be abandoned and its design handed over to another architect, Sir Frederick Gibberd RA (see pp. 150–51). But the economic situation eventually eased and funding was found for Guildford, and in 1952 work began again. Maufe's Cathedral of the Holy Spirit, built of brick in the gothic style, was consecrated on 17 May 1961.

This drawing is a straightforward elevation of the south side. Maufe took care to label each of the many works of sculpture. Collaboration between architects and artists was important to Maufe, who saw the process as being in the long tradition of cathedral building. In his little Pitkin guidebook to Guildford Cathedral, he wrote: 'The ideal has been to produce a design, definitely of our own time, yet in the line of the great English cathedrals.' And how did he make it of his time? In the caption to a photograph of his Diploma Work drawing in the Pitkin guidebook, he explains that he favoured space over decoration in his aim 'to build anew on tradition, to rely on proportion, mass, volume and line rather than on elaboration and ornament'.

Maufe had travelled throughout the 1920s and 1930s, seeking out new buildings in Scandinavia, Western and Central Europe; these were usually monumental churches by 'masters'.

Maufe's own church buildings from this period, as well as his better-known Playhouse Theatre in Oxford, shared a middle ground between tradition and simplicity that was similarly expressed in the buildings he visited and studied. Maufe's relentless use of the pointed arch in his design for Guildford Cathedral may show his reluctance to take up the new angular forms of modernism, but he was apprehensive about the rapidly emerging use of mass production. In his book on new 'modern' churches of the early twentieth century, he commented: 'I realise the way is narrow; that it is easy to slip over to the other side', the dark side where experiments in new materials and methods overpower traditional knowledge.

Edward Maufe, *Modern Church Architecture with Fifty Illustrations of Modern Foreign Churches*, London, 1948

Builder, 174, 14 May 1948, p. 575

Architect & Building News, 219, 17 May 1961, pp. 645–48

Edward Maufe, *The Cathedral of the Holy Spirit, Guildford*, London, 1972

GUILDFORD CATHEDRAL

SOUTH

Louis de Soissons RA
1890–1962
ARA 24 April 1942
RA 15 April 1953

Regent's Park Barracks, Albany Street, London: elevation, three plans and two sections of front to Albany Street, c. 1939
Pencil, pen with black ink and blue crayon, 582 × 792 mm

Louis de Soissons was born in Montreal. His full name was Louis Emanuel Jean Guy de Savoie Carignan de Soissons, Viscount d'Ostel, Baron Longroy. His family moved to England when he was young, and he was admitted as an architectural student at the Royal Academy Schools in 1906. He polished his design skills at the Ecole des Beaux-Arts in Paris and then studied ancient buildings at first hand as a scholar at the British School at Rome. In 1920, when he was thirty years old, Soissons was chosen as chief architect to create Welwyn Garden City. He spent the rest of his life shaping this satellite town just outside London's northern greenbelt into one of the finest models of the garden-city movement. By designing most of its principal civic buildings, housing and early factories, he balanced the benefits of a countryside town with clean industry. Soissons was entirely committed to the project and he and his family resided in Welwyn.

Although he never took a strong stand on any one style, including modernism, Soissons was a revivalist who tended to lean towards a traditional vernacular use of local materials and techniques. His neo-Georgian buildings were greatly admired and this design drawing for the entrance to the Regent's Park Barracks is a fine example. The criss-cross diapered brick façade, with stone dressings, is a restrained but imposing classical frontage, suitable with its wide entrance arch for troops on horseback and large military vehicles.

Louis de Soissons presented the drawing as his Diploma Work upon his election as a full Royal Academician in 1953. Drawn in his own hand, the sheet is undated. It is likely that it was made in the late 1930s when the architect was invited to design new quarters for the Royal Horse Guards who then occupied the Regent's

Park Barracks in Albany Street, London. However, the war intervened and the project was never realised. The drawing is a virtuosic performance in draughtsmanship. The layout is especially complex – a jigsaw puzzle of three plans and two sections layered over the elevation.

Builder, 186, 28 May 1954, p. 938

Maurice de Soissons, *Welwyn Garden City: A Town Designed for Healthy Living*, Cambridge, 1988

William Allen (revised by Andrew Saint), 'Louis de Soissons', *Dictionary of National Biography*, Oxford, 2004, vol. 51, pp. 528–30

ENTRANCE TO REGENT'S PARK BARRACKS N·W·I

DRAWN BY L. DE S.

LOUIS DE SOISSONS F.R.I.B.A.

**Sir Hubert
Worthington RA**
1886–1963
ARA 26 April 1945
RA 22 February 1955

Memorial for the Missing, British War
Graves Cemetery, El Alamein, Egypt:
plan, south, north and side elevations
and cross section, 1955
Pencil and brown wash, 645 × 1000 mm

Hubert Worthington visited El Alamein, Egypt, in July 1943, less than a year after the last of the two great battles had taken place in the western desert. The German forces under Rommel had been driven back, turning the tide of war in the Allies' favour, but at a terrible cost of life. Worthington, as principal architect for North Africa to the Commonwealth War Graves Commission, was required to design cemeteries and their memorial buildings from Alexandria to Tunisia, most prominently at Medjes el Bab in Tunisia, Valetta in Malta and this, the largest, at El Alamein.

Worthington served in battle himself during the First World War and was wounded on the Somme in 1916. He had been articled as an architect before the war with his brother, Sir Percy Scott Worthington – their father was Thomas Worthington, a well-known Manchester architect – and had then worked for two years in the office of Sir Edwin Lutyens PRA. After the war Worthington was Professor of Architecture at the Royal College of Art, London, from 1923 to 1928, while embarking on a successful architectural career, with much work in Oxford, including a new wing to the Radcliffe Science Library, New College Library and the remodelling of the interiors of the Radcliffe Camera and later the Old Bodleian Library. His rebuilding of the Inner Temple, London, and the restoration of Manchester Cathedral, where he is commemorated, were also important post-Second World War commissions.

Worthington married Joan Banham, who with her architectural training often prepared his presentation drawings. However, his Diploma Work is in his own hand, a record drawing of his El Alamein Memorial to the Missing made within a year of the structure's commemoration

in October 1954 by Field Marshal Montgomery, 1st Viscount Montgomery of Alamein. The drawing is a very fine example of pencil draughtsmanship, with only a touch of brown wash indicating the strength of the desert sun falling across the surface of the memorial building. The sheet is symmetrically arranged, with the long plan across the centre, the principal elevations above and below, and the short side elevation and a cross-section balancing the lower corners. The lettering – and there is much of it – is beautifully drawn. The whole scene is enlivened by small figures of soldiers and local gardeners tending the site.

Worthington was mindful of the special design requirements for desert sites of war graves memorials: high walls to keep out the drifting sands, and pergolas and terraces for shade. The El Alamein memorial structure, long and low, was made of locally quarried limestone with paving and copings of travertine marble brought from Italy. The round-headed arches are reminders of the ancient Roman architecture to be found in North Africa. The structure is a single 'cloister', a room pierced by a series of arches bearing Portland stone panels inscribed with the names of the missing soldiers who, unlike their comrades buried in the surrounding cemetery, do not possess marked graves.

Sir Hubert
Worthington,
Obituary, *RIBA Journal*,
70, October 1963,
pp. 422–23

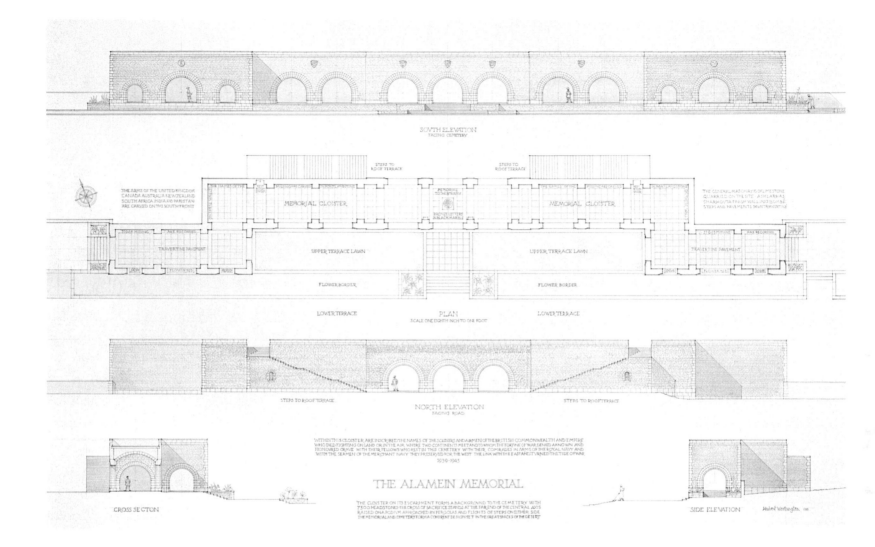

SOUTH ELEVATION
FACING CEMETERY

THE ARMS OF THE UNITED KINGDOM
CANADA AUSTRALIA NEW ZEALAND
SOUTH AFRICA INDIA AND PAKISTAN
ARE CARVED ON THIS SOUTH FRONT

STEPS TO
ROOF TERRACE

STEPS TO
ROOF TERRACE

THE GENERAL MASONRY IS OF LIMESTONE
QUARRIED ON THE SITE · ASHLAR HAS
SHARM QUTA FINISH WALL INSIDE OF THE
STEPS AND PAVEMENTS SAWN TRAVERTINE

MEMORIAL CLOISTER

MEMORIAL TO THE MISSING

BRONZE LETTERS
IN BLACK MARBLE

MEMORIAL CLOISTER

TRAVERTINE PAVEMENT

UPPER TERRACE LAWN

UPPER TERRACE LAWN

TRAVERTINE PAVEMENT

FLOWER BORDER

FLOWER BORDER

LOWER TERRACE

PLAN
SCALE ONE EIGHTH INCH TO ONE FOOT

LOWER TERRACE

STEPS TO ROOF TERRACE

NORTH ELEVATION
FACING ROAD

STEPS TO ROOF TERRACE

WITHIN THIS CLOISTER ARE INSCRIBED THE NAMES OF THE SOLDIERS AND AIRMEN OF THE BRITISH COMMONWEALTH AND EMPIRE
WHO DIED FIGHTING ON LAND OR IN THE AIR · WHERE TWO CONTINENTS MEET AND TO WHOM THE FORTUNE OF WAR DENIED ARNOWN AND
HONOURED GRAVE · WITH THEIR FELLOWS WHO REST IN THIS CEMETERY WITH THEIR · COMRADES IN ARMS OF THE ROYAL NAVY AND
WITH THE SEAMEN OF THE MERCHANT NAVY THEY PRESERVED FOR THE WEST · THE LINK WITH THE EAST AND SO TURNED THE TIDE OF WAR
1939-1945

THE ALAMEIN MEMORIAL

THE CLOISTER ON ITS ESCARPMENT FORMS A BACKGROUND TO THE CEMETERY WITH
7300 HEADSTONES · THE CROSS OF SACRIFICE STANDS AT THE FAR END OF THE CENTRAL AXIS
RAISED ON A PODIUM APPROACHED BY PERGOLAS AND FLIGHTS OF STEPS ON EITHER SIDE ·
THE MEMORIAL AND CEMETERY FORM A COHERENT DESIGN SET IN THE GREAT SPACES OF THE DESERT

CROSS SECTION

SIDE ELEVATION

Hubert Worthington 1953

Brian O'Rorke RA
1901–1974
ARA 25 April 1947
RA 21 February 1956

Ashcombe Tower, Ashcombe, Devon:
ground-floor plan and perspective
looking northeast, 1935
Pencil, pen with blue ink, coloured
washes and gouache, 508 × 737 mm

Brian O'Rorke's reputation as a designer rests mainly upon a vanished world of privilege – his Art Deco interiors for luxury liners, especially for the Orient Line, and most particularly the *moderne* chromium and bakelite interiors of RMS *Orion* that was launched in 1935. Later in his career, during the 1950s, O'Rorke became preoccupied with his designs for the National Theatre, which were never to come to fruition (but appeared in the Diploma Work sketch of the South Bank by Sir Howard Robertson RA; see pp. 138–39). O'Rorke did, however, build the quirky Royal Observatory Buildings at Hurstmonceux, Sussex, and the still very stylish Berkeley Hotel near London's Hyde Park Corner.

Perhaps O'Rorke hoped to present a drawing of one of these later schemes as his Diploma Work, as both were on the drawing board at the time of his election as a full Royal Academician in 1956. As it was, he deposited as only 'temporary' this drawing for Ashcombe Tower, made more than two decades earlier. He never replaced it.

Ashcombe Tower, a house designed for Major (later Brigadier Sir) Ralph Rayner and his wife Elizabeth, was one of O'Rorke's early works, and certainly one of his finest domestic buildings. Rayner, the local MP, had purchased a 2,500-acre estate that included an old ruin with remains of its tower. O'Rorke integrated these ancient features into his design, converting the tower into a staircase; in his Diploma Work drawing, a perspective view that concentrates instead on the sunny south front, its square squat stump is glimpsed over the roofline. Along the terrace of the south front are arranged the large open French windows of the dining room and a staccato effect of windows opening into the great room in the centre.

The cement-rendered exterior and lack of any reference to historical style made the house very modern, although it was nevertheless touched by the vernacular: the limestone for the dressings was local and the roof was covered in green Westmorland slate. The interior was the height of chic, furnished with carpets and curtains by Marian Dorn, with built-in electric clocks and light-coloured woods, including oak floors taken from the British Museum during a refurbishment. The son of the original clients still owns the house, and maintains it in all its Art Deco glory.

Builder, 148, 24 May 1935, p. 967

Country Life, 81, 13 February 1937, pp. 172–77

Country Life, 190, 12 December 1996, pp. 40–43

HOUSE AT ASHCOMBE DEVON:

GROUND
FLOOR
PLAN

BRIAN O'RORKE R.A. A.R.I.B.A.
ARCHITECT.

Sir Howard Robertson RA
1888–1963
ARA 22 April 1949
RA 24 April 1958

Shell Centre, South Bank, London: sketch perspective looking southwest, July 1953
Black crayon, 542 × 428 mm

This Diploma Work was part of Sir Howard Robertson's attempt at a rebuttal of the enormous criticism he was weathering at the time over the design of the building represented in the drawing. In 1959, when Robertson submitted this sketch, construction was just beginning on his Shell Centre, prominently sited along the River Thames on London's South Bank over land that had been cleared of the 1951 Festival of Britain pleasure gardens. The massive complex consisted of a 26-storey office block with a cluster of surrounding low-rise buildings, the whole providing office accommodation for 5,000 Shell employees as well as, when completed, restaurants, shops, a swimming pool, squash courts, a rifle range and a cinema.

Controversy and criticism dogged Robertson throughout the project, and these grew in intensity until the centre opened in 1962, when it was greeted as 'an inhuman monster of a building' (*Architects' Journal*, 135, 4 April 1962, p. 704). Robertson was taken aback by the vitriol from the press and his colleagues, saying he was 'very scarred but not bitter' about the episode that had come to dominate the last decade of his career (*Builder*, 202, 22 June 1962, pp. 1278-80). Part of the problem for his critics was that Robertson's architectural style seemed to sit on the fence. From early in his career during the 1920s he had been a proponent of the emerging modern movement while still adhering to the values of the Beaux-Arts training he had received in Paris before the First World War. It was this balancing act, almost ambivalence, that irritated progressive modernists who saw in the Shell Building a 'failure to create a building representing twentieth-century architecture' (*Architects' Journal*, op. cit.). Progressive eyes were now focused on

American high-rise buildings sheathed in curtain walls of glass, and not, as with the Shell Centre, in stone with small windows.

Robertson had been forced into a comprising situation. The architect Sir Leslie Martin RA had laid out the site and the guiding principles for new buildings on the South Bank, and Robertson followed restrictions on dimensions and height as well as the use of Portland stone cladding. Furthermore, the influential Royal Fine Art Commission insisted on tinkering with his design with typically muddled committee opinions. Perhaps if the Shell Centre had not been in such a prominent location on the river, its apparent shortfalls would not have been so noticeable.

This 'impression', as Robertson entitles this drawing in a rough hand, must have been his seminal sketch for the project. But it was to do him no favours. On seeing it at the Royal Academy's Summer Exhibition the critic Robert Paine wrote, 'perhaps one of the most interesting exhibits is a sketch by Sir Howard Robertson for the Shell Building, very slight but all too clearly revealing the fundamental dumpiness of the conception' (*Builder*, 196, 8 May 1959, p. 844). In the drawing, the tower is seen pressed close to the water's edge, its exterior a simple texture of vertical strips breaking the surface with rigid fenestration. Nestled at its base, to the right, is the circular form of the proposed but unrealised National Theatre by Brian O'Rorke RA, one of Robertson's younger protégés who had been elected a full Royal Academician two years before him.

Builder, 202, 22 June 1962, pp. 1278-80, and 29 June 1962, pp. 1326-27

Architect & Building News, 222, 1 August 1962, p. 844

South Bank Impression · Early Study for Shell Headquarters Buildings

· Howard Robertson ·

Sir Basil Spence RA
1907–1976
ARA 23 April 1953
RA 21 April 1960

Design for the Cathedral Church of
St Michael, Coventry: perspective through
nave towards altar, 15 February 1953
Coloured chalks, 910 × 830 mm

The commission to design a new
cathedral for Coventry proved to be the
most sought-after architectural prize
in Britain in the post-war era. The old
medieval church had been left in ruins
by the Coventry blitz on the night of
14 September 1940. In the aftermath, at a
time when post-war building restrictions
limited new construction to much-needed
public housing, the rebuilding of
Coventry Cathedral represented, for the
whole nation, a spiritual reawakening.
The architect who won the competition,
Basil Spence, dubbed his building a
'phoenix' rising from the ashes.

The competition took place in 1950
and after a relatively short building period
commencing in 1955, the cathedral was
consecrated in the presence of Her
Majesty The Queen on 25 May 1962.
This drawing, presented to the Royal
Academy by Spence in 1960 as his
Diploma Work upon his election as a
full Royal Academician in the same year,
dates from the early and intensive stage
of the cathedral's design. It is a key
drawing in the building's development,
marking a point when Spence made
a number of important changes as his
initial ideas were transformed into the
finished design. Spence considered the
drawing as pivotal and used it as one of
the illustrations in his book about
Coventry Cathedral (1962).

A perspectival view, the drawing looks
down the wide nave towards the east end.
More than half the sheet is taken up by the
roof, with its design of shallow concrete
mushrooms on tall tapering columns,
a modern twist on medieval stone piers
and cross-vaulting. The roof, 'faceted like
a fly's eye', said the architect, was a new
development upon Spence's earlier
smooth and rounded version. The
drawing also marked Spence's final
suggestion for extending the sightline

through the cathedral by fifty feet. He
replaced the wall that had been behind
the high altar in his previous designs with
a reredos, which permitted him to place
the great tapestry designed by Graham
Sutherland at the extreme east end of the
building, in the Lady Chapel.

Basil Spence was a consummate
draughtsman, recognised for his
perspectives in coloured chalks, which
he had started to make while a student at
Edinburgh College of Art. Chalk gives a
soft hue with vivid colouring. One of his
favourite drawing techniques was to set
buildings against black backgrounds
streaked with white gouache. Even when
his architectural practice became very
busy, Spence often reserved weekends for
working at the drawing board to create his
chalky perspectives.

Basil Spence, *Phoenix
at Coventry: The
Building of a Cathedral*,
London, 1962

Louise Campbell (ed.),
*To Build a Cathedral:
Coventry Cathedral
1945–1962*, Coventry,
1987

Louise Campbell,
*Coventry Cathedral:
Art and Architecture
in Post-war Britain*,
Oxford, 1996

Philip Long and Jane
Thomas (eds), *Basil
Spence, Architect*,
Edinburgh, 2008

Donald McMorran RA
1904–1965
ARA 22 April 1955
RA 31 October 1962

Estate cottages, West Wycombe,
Buckinghamshire: part-ground-
and part-first-floor plans, north, south
and east elevations, and sections, 1950
Pencil, pen with black and brown ink and
brown and red washes, 610 × 762 mm

Donald McMorran extended the language of classical architecture in a Britain increasingly obsessed by mid-century modern. As a disciple of the 'ancient art of architecture', he was outspoken about the modern movement's rejection of traditional styles and the accompanying loss of craftsmanship. 'The real danger of this situation', he warned, 'is that architects are putting themselves in an ivory tower and I am afraid they may be losing their position of master builders' (quoted in Denison, p. 123).

During his formative years in the 1930s, McMorran had practised in the established neo-Georgian style, slightly twisting the accepted classical principles to create innovative buildings. In the 1950s, however, his use of classicism became pared down and abstracted – mannerist modern – while growing more powerful. The brick halls of his design for the residence buildings at Nottingham University incorporated columns and stable-block planning; and his Wood Street Police Station in the City of London is a fortress of white Portland stone, a worthy neighbour to the stately architecture of Wren and Hawksmoor.

In 1962, as his Diploma Work, McMorran deposited this rather humble drawing dating from 1950. The subject-matter alone – a group of estate cottages – reflects his quiet, traditional values. The four cottages are in a single building with a triple-vaulted arched carriageway leading to an inner courtyard. The dwellings are rustic, with rainwater collected in barrels and windows tucked up under the eaves. Both the architecture and the drawing style are late examples of the Arts and Crafts Movement that always seems to flow quietly below the surface of much of British architecture.

The cottages, which were never built, would have made a highly appropriate addition to the principal and picturesque thoroughfare through the village of West Wycombe. The street is lined with properties built between the sixteenth and eighteenth centuries on the estate of the Dashwood family of West Wycombe Park. In the 1930s, the village was taken into the care of the National Trust. In place of McMorran's proposed cottages, the little Village Hall now stands.

Edward Denison,
McMorran and Whitby,
London, 2009

COTTAGES AT WEST WYCOMBE FOR THE NATIONAL TRUST

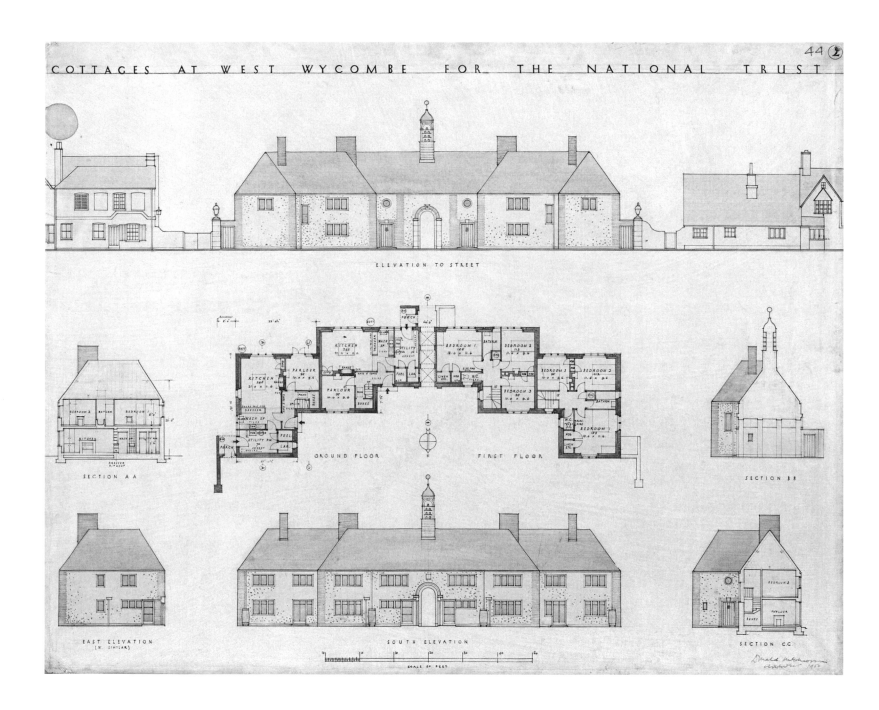

ELEVATION TO STREET

SECTION A A

GROUND FLOOR

FIRST FLOOR

SECTION B B

EAST ELEVATION
(W. SIMILAR)

SOUTH ELEVATION

SCALE OF FEET

SECTION C C

Marshall Sisson RA
1897–1978
ARA 26 April 1956
RA 26 April 1963

Alterations and additions to St Andrew-by-the-Wardrobe, Queen Victoria Street, London: ground- and gallery-floor plans, east and south elevations, and sections, *c.* 1958
Pen with black ink, 679 × 1103 mm

Marshall Sisson has suffered a mixed reputation, both personal and architectural. Like many of his fellow architect-Academicians who practised in the rapidly changing world of the mid-twentieth century, Sisson held entrenched academic views on maintaining the tradition of historical styles. Yet, ironically, when he was first setting out in practice in the early 1930s, he had made his name as a pioneer of the British modern movement, creating a series of progressive, flat-roofed houses, shorn of ornament and based on a standard unit of measurement. But Sisson soon returned to the historicist fold. He had been a pupil of the arch-classicist Sir Albert Richardson PRA (see pp. 126-27) at the Bartlett School of Architecture at London University, and after the Second World War he joined Richardson's attempt to steer young architects away from the new architecture by becoming Master of the revived Royal Academy School of Architecture. He moved to Dedham, Essex, where his close neighbour Raymond Erith RA (see pp. 146-47) also practised in the classical tradition. Sisson's later works, from the 1950s and 1960s, were especially criticised by the socialist-minded moderns, who also could not forgive him for having joined Oswald Mosley's British Union of Fascists at the end of the 1930s.

Yet the years immediately after the war were good ones for Sisson. His knowledge of historical architecture stood him in fine stead for the extensive amount of restoration work required on bombed-out London churches. He took St John's, Smith Square, the early eighteenth-century masterpiece of Thomas Archer, and rebuilt it almost anew (although it is difficult to tell) as a steel-framed concert hall and broadcasting studio. Restoration of two of Wren's fifty city churches also

came under his direction. Most unusual was his dismantling and re-erection of St Mary's Aldermanbury in Fulton, Missouri. Following this came the restoration of St Andrew-by-the-Wardrobe, the project represented in his Diploma Work. This scheme won him grudging admiration from his peers. Sisson found the structure a burnt-out shell of tower and walls, and he restored it with considered sensitivity, moving pieces from other damaged London churches to replace many of the destroyed furnishings.

The drawing itself is as straightforward as the restoration. Sisson employs only black pen, using the line intensely for horizontal and vertical shading and crosshatching. The sheet is laid out traditionally with plans, elevations and both sections neatly arranged in two tiers.

Architects' Journal, 127, 8 May 1958, p. 686

The Times, obituary, 30 January 1978

James Bettley, 'Marshall Sisson 1897–1978', *Royal Institute of British Architects. Transactions*, 1, 2, 1982, pp. 93–100

South Front

Section

Section

Ground Floor

East Front

Gallery Level

Raymond Erith RA

1904–1973
ARA 23 April 1959
RA 23 April 1964

Bridge over the River Cherwell, Oxford: plans, elevation, section and detail of bridge and plan of Oxford, 1954
Pencil, pen with black and red ink and grey, blue and green washes, 740 × 1300 mm

Raymond Erith's reputation as an architect is that of an old-school classicist who watched the world go modern all around him. Although many of his fellow architects working in the classical tradition at the Royal Academy, such as E. Vincent Harris RA and Donald McMorran RA, pared down the historicist elements in their designs in line with the new modernist aesthetic, Erith maintained the humanist architectural ideals of the past, which were, it can be argued, the very architectural ideals upon which the Royal Academy was founded. Yet today Erith is not best known for his many fine country houses influenced by Sir John Soane RA, but by a clever folly: Jack Straw's Castle on London's Hampstead Heath, a crenellated public house that passers-by usually mistake for an eighteenth-century building.

Erith was a superb draughtsman, as his Diploma Work drawing, presented in 1964, well demonstrates. He had already exhibited the sheet at the Royal Academy in 1954, the year he drew it. The scheme it illustrates, which was not realised, was part of a larger post-war town-planning proposal by the local architect Lawrence Dale to reduce the impact of Oxford's ever-increasing traffic. Erith concentrated on a tree-lined 'Mall' running along the southern edge of Christ Church Meadow. The ornament of the scheme was a bridge crossing the River Cherwell, bisecting the meadow and relieving traffic on Magdalen Bridge. But because of the sensitive location of this proposed new inner ring road, Erith suggested that it be left unlit and the bridge kept low – no easy requirement considering the volume of traffic.

The presentation and layout of the drawing are typical of Erith's fine worked-up sheets. All important aspects of the design are included, both in terms of drawing and text. Erith deals with the architectural engineering of the bridge and its broader context within town planning. Although the sheet is packed, it is neither cramped nor unbalanced by the plans and sections of the bridge, as well as by a large, detailed map of the city of Oxford. And there is even room for a young couple to float beneath the bridge in a punt in what Erith describes on the drawing as a 'Venetian adventure'.

T. Lawrence Dale, 'A Bridge for Oxford', *Architecture and Building*, 29, July 1954, p. 255

Lucy Archer, *Raymond Erith, Architect*, Burford, 1985, pp. 136–37

Lucy Archer, *Raymond Erith: Progressive Classicist, 1904–1973*, exh. cat., Sir John Soane's Museum, London, 2004

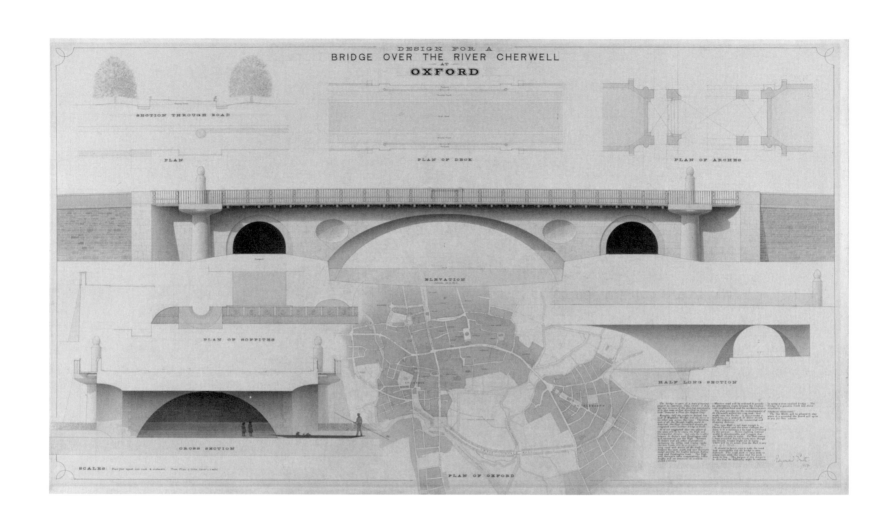

DESIGN FOR A
BRIDGE OVER THE RIVER CHERWELL
AT
OXFORD

William Holford RA, Baron Holford of Kemp Town
1907–1975
ARA 20 April 1961
RA 26 April 1968

Library, Eliot College and Rutherford College, University of Kent, Canterbury: perspective, 1964
Pencil, blue crayon, coloured washes and gouache, 345 × 975 mm

William Holford presented this drawing as his Diploma Work upon his election as a full Royal Academician in 1968. He had exhibited it at the Royal Academy's Summer Exhibition five years earlier when construction was underway on the three buildings represented, the first for the new University of Kent. In fact so fast had the buildings gone up that the university was opened in the autumn of 1965 only two years after Holford had presented his masterplan for the new campus site.

The Library building was set at the heart of the plan, surrounded by a series of colleges in the shape of a cross. The composition is arranged on the ridge of St Thomas's Hill in 260 acres of countryside and with fine views over the city of Canterbury. The campus's picturesque and rigorous planning is indicative of Holford's position as one of Britain's major town planners. His drafting with Lewis Silkin of the 1947 Town and Country Planning Act and with Charles Holden of the 1950-51 City of London Plan transformed the urban landscape of Britain and made him the first town planner to receive a peerage.

Holford was trained in the Beaux-Arts tradition at Liverpool University under Charles Reilly during the 1920s, before carrying out research into urban development at the British School at Rome. So particular was Holford about axial alignment, a foundation of his Beaux-Arts values, that when it came to designing the University of Kent, he set the High Table in the dining hall of Eliot College against a backdrop of a large window with the great cathedral of Canterbury as the climactic focal point in the far distance. This was a dramatic use of *mise en scène*, stage placement planning.

The traditional formality of the completed University of Kent buildings was criticised at the time, a work of 'bleakness and curiously old-fashioned attempted grandeur and formality,' with the internal quadrangles 'a dead place' (*Architects' Journal*). Hasty construction, forced through by the university, led to a falling out between Holford and his client. William Henderson of Farmer & Dark replaced Holford as master architect-planner in 1966 and Holford's cohesive overall plan was abandoned, to the regret of many who saw the subsequent outcome as jumbled.

Any architectural weaknesses within the scheme are sublimated in Holford's Diploma Work by the picturesque qualities of the drawing. A lazy herd of cows graze in the open fields. And where in the past a handsome country house would have nestled on the wooded hillside, here instead are small rectilinear modernist buildings. The dark sky swirls, the day is grey, but intense sunlight, drawn in streaks of white gouache, illuminates the buildings. Although the grouping appears to be a single unit, the Library building is in the centre with the two colleges flanking. In the background on the left is the proposed Sciences building.

Architects' Journal, 142, 17 November 1965, pp. 1141-52

T. Birks, *Building the New Universities*, Newton Abbott, 1972

Graham Martin, *From Vision to Reality: The Making of the University of Kent at Canterbury*, Canterbury, 1990

**Sir Frederick
Gibberd RA**
1908–1984
ARA 20 April 1961
RA 25 February 1969

Metropolitan Cathedral of Christ the King,
Liverpool: part-nave plan, part-roof plan,
part-elevation and part-section, *c.* 1963
Pencil, 1065 × 724 mm

The Metropolitan Cathedral of Christ the King, Liverpool, was consecrated on 14 May 1967. Although construction was swift, taking only five years, the design and building processes had been long drawn out. The foundation stone was laid in 1933 for a spectacular and ambitious design by Sir Edwin Lutyens PRA, whose Roman Catholic cathedral was to have rivalled in size and richness the city's nearby Anglican cathedral, then in its third decade of construction to the designs of Sir Giles Gilbert Scott RA, who presented a drawing of his cathedral as his Diploma Work (see pp. 106–07).

The Second World War and the economic necessities of peacetime reconstruction led to the abandonment of the Lutyens scheme. Only the large and very fine crypt had been completed, and the integration of this underground space was part of the brief in the invited competition of 1960 to find a design for a cathedral that would be modern and in tune with the new liturgical movement. Frederick Gibberd's winning design met these criteria. Its conical plan and unusual, tent-like silhouette were striking, and loosely derived from the recently completed and widely admired Brasilia Cathedral by the Brazilian architect Oscar Niemeyer. The novel placement of the high altar at the centre of the building – a practice that in fact dated from ancient Roman churches – allowed the congregation to view the ritual in the round.

Although Liverpool's Catholic Cathedral was Sir Frederick Gibberd's finest architectural work, it proved to suffer from some of the problems that came to plague post-war construction. Infamously, it leaked and shed badly. Although these failings somewhat troubled Gibberd's architectural reputation, his standing as a town planner was never questioned. Not only did he write the classic textbook *Town Design*, which went into many editions after its publication in 1953, but he also drew the masterplan for one of the most admired post-war new towns, Harlow in Essex, where he lived somewhat like the lord of the manor in a small country house on the edge of his creation. The seven-acre garden, now open to the public, is the setting for the many sculptures that Sir Frederick and Lady Patricia, his second wife, collected.

The bad press that Gibberd received over the cathedral – there was a lawsuit – must have prompted him to submit a working drawing of the project as his Diploma Work in 1970 as proof that his design skills were not the cause of the difficulties. His drawing dates from about 1963, early in the development of the project, when the general design had been finalised. Gibberd chose the sheet from part of a larger set, all of which he had drawn himself, inscribing his Diploma Work as 'one of the 151 Design Drawings of identical size & technique, prepared by Frederick Gibberd'. Sir Michael Hopkins RA, who worked for a time in 'Sir Freddie's' London office in Percy Street, recalls Gibberd's extraordinary ability to take home a new project on Friday night and return on Monday morning with the scheme worked up in as many as twenty or more drawings, all masterfully rendered.

In this large drawing, gently depicted in pencil alone, Gibberd comprehensively includes all the major features of the building in what looks at first glance like a single image. The sheet is, in fact, a composition of quarter drawings, all that is required to represent the whole because the geometry of the building is based on a circle. There is a quarter plan of the nave (lower left), a quarter plan of the roof (lower right), part of the elevation (upper right) and a section (upper left). Gibberd replaced the traditional scale of feet and inches with his own 'golden' ratio of a nine-foot modular, which he has registered, in an example, as 'buttress seven' – in other words, the buttress's length is seven times nine feet, thus 63 feet.

Frederick Gibberd,
*The Metropolitan
Cathedral of Christ
the King, Liverpool*,
London, 1968

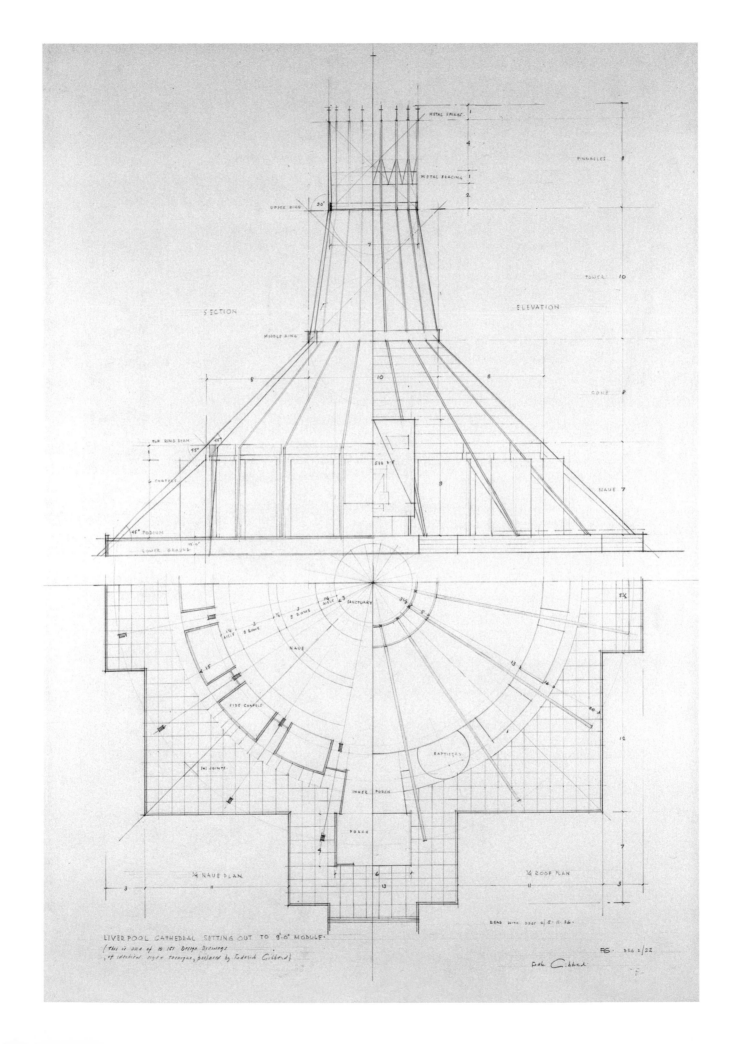

SECTION   ELEVATION

LIVERPOOL CATHEDRAL SETTING OUT TO 8'·0" MODULE·
(This is one of 15 151 Design Drawings
of identical light technique, prepared by Frederick Gibberd)

Sir Hugh Casson PRA
1910–1999
ARA 26 April 1962
RA 23 April 1970

Elephant and Rhinoceros Pavilion,
London Zoo, Regent's Park, London: plan,
perspective elevation and section, c. 1971
Pencil, pen with black ink and coloured
washes on polyester film, 740 × 1030 mm

Sir Hugh Casson's sparkling and winning personality made him a popular Director of Architecture for the 1951 Festival of Britain and a long-serving President of the Royal Academy, from 1976 to 1984. His sprightly spirit spilled over into his architectural drawings and especially the little impressionistic watercolours he made when travelling about. One of his greatest fans was Queen Elizabeth, the Queen Mother. He gave lessons in watercolour to the Prince of Wales, who said that Casson 'on his own admission, sketches with pen and watercolour in the same way that other people hum tunes'.

Casson's architectural partnership with Neville Conder, set up soon after the Second World War, created a substantial body of important commissions, including the Royal College of Art, London (with H. T. Cadbury-Brown RA), faculty buildings for the University of Cambridge, the Ismaili Centre opposite the Victoria & Albert Museum, and Casson Conder's best-known work, the Elephant and Rhinoceros House at London Zoo (1964–65). In his collaboration with Casson on the Zoo project, Conder commented: 'of all the major partnership buildings, the one that is most absolutely Hugh's is the Elephant House. I detailed it, but the main lines had been set because I was engaged elsewhere when the concept was worked out by him' (Manser, p. 225).

The commission for the new Elephant and Rhinoceros House had come out of the masterplan that Casson had made for the Zoological Society of London in 1956, working in close association with the noted zoologist and television personality Desmond Morris. The building lodged four elephants and the same number of rhinoceroses.

This Diploma Work drawing, created and presented to the Royal Academy by Casson in 1971, the year after his election as a full Royal Academician, is a record of a project completed six years before. The representational layout is straightforward: the top half of the drawing is an impressive elevation, with below left a section and a small plan at the bottom right. To create the drawing, the architect took a transparent polyester sheet and made pencil tracings of the three views from previous drawings. He then filled these in with black pen and added coloured washes. Nothing is ruled because Casson preferred freehand draughtsmanship. The jolly animals are pure Casson.

The plan gives the organic nature of the structure, a clustering of pods, actually pens for the animals, as well as a bathing pool, set along a large, central public viewing corridor. The elevation shows the jagged-topped pods into which outside light slips through openings in the copper-clad roof. It is said that the rough texture of vertical ribbing on the exterior pick-hammered concrete walls reminded visitors of the crinkly skin of the pachyderms within. Today the building houses camels and bearded pigs.

Architectural Review,
45, July 1965, pp. 13–20

Mary Banham and
Bevis Hillier (eds),
*A Tonic to the Nation:
The Festival of Britain
1951*, London, 1976

José Manser, *Hugh
Casson: A Biography*,
London, 2000

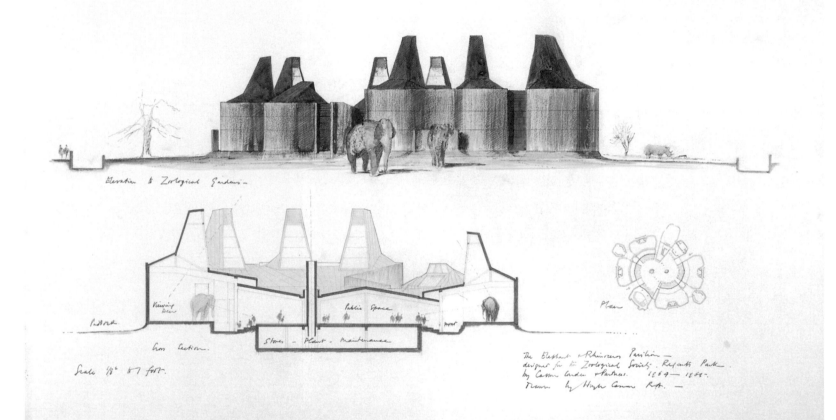

Elevation to Zoological Gardens.

Viewing Dens

Public Space

Stores . Plant . Maintenance

Pit Yard.

Cross Section.

moat

Plan

Scale 1/8" to 7 foot.

The Elephant & Rhinoceros Pavilion —
designed for the Zoological Society, Regents Park
by Casson Conder & Partners. 1964 — 1965.
Drawn by Hugh Casson R.A. —

E. Maxwell Fry RA
1899–1987
ARA 29 April 1966
RA 15 June 1972

Torbay Hospital, Torquay, Devon:
perspective, 18 February 1970
Pen with black ink and coloured chalks,
472 × 690 mm

When the modern movement in architecture began to take off in Great Britain in the early 1930s, Max Fry was one of its leaders. His houses, devoid of historical styles, flat-roofed, with metal windows and geometrically shaped – such as the Sun House in Frognal Way, Hampstead, and Miramonte House in Coombe, Surrey – were shocking interlopers in the midst of the traditional, upper-middle-class suburbs of the time. These were buildings strongly influenced by the pioneering continental developments of Le Corbusier, Mies van der Rohe and Walter Gropius. Fry was even to help Walter Gropius leave Nazi Germany in 1934, taking the founder of the Bauhaus on as a partner in London. Although Gropius remained in Britain only a few years before moving on to teach at Harvard, Fry and Gropius collaborated on Impington Village College in Cambridgeshire and in so doing established a new light and modern method of designing educational buildings that came to be highly influential after the Second World War.

In 1946 Fry set up in partnership with his new wife, the architect Jane Drew. Theirs was a fruitful collaboration. In India, they joined forces with Le Corbusier on Chandigarh, the new capital city of Punjab, taking on most of the housing projects with Le Corbusier's cousin Pierre Jeanneret. They also worked extensively in West Africa where Fry had served during the Second World War. The buildings by Fry and Drew, mainly schools and colleges including the University of Ibadan, Nigeria, had a profound impact on new architecture in the African tropics.

This drawing for Torbay Hospital was Fry's Diploma Work, presented upon his election in 1972. It is dated February 1970, eight months before the building opened.

Torbay Hospital had been a collaborative design effort with Jane Drew, and this is underlined by an article she wrote in celebration of Woman's Year in 1975, in which she discussed staying in the Nurses' Residence at Torbay and learning much about hospital design from the experienced matron. This drawing, however, is clearly in Fry's distinctive and typical stylistic hand. He uses black felt-tip pen with coloured chalks and shows the building in an extenuated profile with a boldness of line and little concern for architectural detailing.

The view looks up the north slope of the hospital site, masking the original buildings by Adams, Holden and Pearson from the 1920s. To the left, three elongated boxes, each an operating theatre, curve with the landscape. The connecting corridor with its long line of windows gives views over the parkland setting. Behind, the eight-storey ward block rises on a two-storey podium.

Hospital, January 1968, pp. 22–24

Building, 218, 8 May 1970, p. 73

Hospital Management, July–August 1971, pp. 232–33

Architectural Design, 45, August 1978, pp. 485–86

Torbay Hospital
Fry Drew & Partners

**Sir Richard
Sheppard RA**
1910–1982
ARA 29 April 1966
RA 15 June 1972

Dining Hall, Churchill College, Cambridge:
interior perspective, *c.* 1973
Pencil and pen with black ink on tracing
paper, 700 × 617 mm

In early 1959 Richard Sheppard, chief partner of the architectural practice Sheppard Robson and Partners, won the limited competition for the new Churchill College, Cambridge (named after Sir Winston Churchill and now holding his personal archive). This was Sheppard's big break, putting him on the path to becoming one of the most important architects of British university buildings during the 1960s and 1970s. With the baby boomers coming of age, the 1963 Robbins Report recommended the expansion of universities and that Colleges of Advanced Technology be given the status of universities. In the wake of this transformation of higher education, Sheppard went on to build for Loughborough, Leicester, Brunel, City, Durham, Manchester and Newcastle Universities and Imperial College, London.

Churchill College has remained Richard Sheppard's most respected work. When its three-stage design was completed in 1964, architectural critics such as Reyner Banham heaped praise on the scheme. The design was unabashed in its modernism, with massive brick walls and exposed concrete framing, and Sheppard reinterpreted the traditional use of courts in a spacious college plan. The largest feature of the project was the dining hall, which the architect chose to revisit pictorially a decade after its completion in his Diploma Work, presented and exhibited in 1973, a year after his election.

The support is tracing paper, suggesting that Sheppard took the general outline from an earlier drawing. The pencil and pen lines are thick, and the whole is drawn freehand. Three horizontal beams representing copper-sheathed lighting tracks traverse the centre space of the drawing. These stretch across the vertical precast concrete mullions beneath the vaulted roof. To the left, the side wall shows the texturing of the panelling in British Columbian red cedar. Silhouetted figures of members of the college are beginning to gather at one of the long refectory tables.

Architectural Review,
136, September 1964,
pp. 174–87

Michael Webb,
'Massive Simplicity
Beside the Cam',
Country Life, 138,
25 November 1965,
pp. 1394–97

Mark Goldie, *Corbusier
Comes to Cambridge:
Post-War Architecture
and the Competition to
Build Churchill College*,
Cambridge, 2009

H. T. Cadbury-Brown RA
1913–2009
ARA 22 April 1971
RA 24 April 1975

A National Museum for the Hashemite
Kingdom of Jordan, Amman, Jordan:
aerial view, view from south and sketches,
October 1975

Pen with black ink, grey wash,
pencil, coloured pencil and inks on
tracing paper, 823 × 570 mm

The home of the late H. T. Cadbury-Brown, 'Jim' to his friends, can be found down a little lane from the seaside parish church of Aldeburgh in Suffolk. Cadbury-Brown purchased the land when his design for an opera house destined for the site fell through. The commission had come from his friend and neighbour the composer Benjamin Britten. So in 1964, Cadbury-Brown designed a low and flat-roofed house, lit by expansive glass windows and skylights, all lovingly detailed by his architect wife Elizabeth Romeyn Elwyn, 'Betty'. Set in an unmown meadow, Jim and Betty's house was smothered in creepers grown from seedlings that the couple had gathered from sites of antiquity. This sensitive handling of a modern building united with nature was a recurring theme in their architecture.

Betty met Jim when she was his assistant on the two pavilions he created for the 1951 Festival of Britain. As part of the Festival team, they worked closely with Sir Hugh Casson PRA. Later, with Casson as the front man, the couple designed the Royal College of Art building, part of the architectural ensemble of Kensington Gore, set off by the landscaped beauty of Kensington Gardens.

In 1975 Jim, working with the designer Robin Wade, was invited by the Jordanian Ministry of Tourism and Antiquities to present a report on a new Jordan Archaeological Museum atop the historic Citadel site in the capital city of Amman. The proposal – which was to remain unrealised – was forwarded in September. The following month, Cadbury-Brown submitted this presentation drawing for the scheme as his Diploma Work to the Royal Academy.

The Citadel is the location of significant ancient structures, among them the Roman Temple of Hercules and the Islamic Umayyad Palace built by a caliph in the early eighth century. Cadbury-Brown's intention was to create 'not a monumental building imposed on the landscape, but one skilfully integrated into it and playing a secondary visual role to the archaeological remains and the Citadel which is the real monument'. Consequently, the proposed plans extended beyond the museum building and were to include the re-erection of three of the temple's fallen columns, pleasant walks, a picnic area and newly planted trees framing views over the city's landmark mosques and Roman amphitheatre. Other proposed attractions included a giant sundial, a solar-powered machine, *son et lumière* spectacles and a camera obscura in the museum offering views over Amman.

The museum building was intended to create 'free-flowing spaces alternating with courtyards', with a pool and perhaps arcades, suggesting that, although modern, the design embodied elements of traditional Islamic planning. The museum, a cluster of octagonal 'cells', was to have been constructed of concrete and reused stones from the site. In the drawing, the building appears squat and fortress-like, its terrace a continuation of the ancient ramparts.

Jim and Betty Cadbury-Brown's last major work, executed in the late 1980s and early 1990s, was their most beautiful and intimate space, the Library and Print Room of the Royal Academy in Burlington House, a modern jewel in an historic setting.

H. T. Cadbury-Brown
and Robin Wade,
'A Report on
"A National Museum
for the Hashemite
Kingdom of Jordan"',
September 1975

Neil Bingham, 'Out into
the Garden. Architects:
H. T. and Elizabeth
Cadbury-Brown',
*Perspectives in
Architecture*,
December/January
1997–98, pp. 68–71

A NATIONAL MUSEUM for the HASHEMITE KINGDOM of JORDAN
Proposals for the Citadel site Amman

Ernö Goldfinger RA
1902–1987
ARA 14 October 1971
RA 9 December 1975

Trellick Tower, Golborne Road, London:
cut-away perspective showing triple
approach, *c.* 1966 and April 1976
Print in black ink with added coloured
pencil, 778 × 671 mm

At thirty-one storeys, Trellick Tower was
the tallest social-housing structure in
Europe when it was completed in April
1972. Rising as the centrepiece above the
Cheltenham Estate in North Kensington,
its rugged profile still makes it one of the
most noticeable works of the Brutalist
movement on the London skyline.
Trellick Tower has always been one
of those 'love it or hate it' buildings.
Its concrete exterior, muscular massing
and boldly separated service tower rising
like an incinerator chimney, forcefully
remind its critics of all that was miserable
about the British welfare state as it sank
to its knees in the 1970s. Aficionados of
Brutalism, however, are attracted to the
building's external rawness and interior
innovation, hailing it as the finest
high-rise in Britain, authoritative
architecture that has created a lively
social mix of residents.

Its architect, the Hungarian-born
Ernö Goldfinger, grew up in Budapest
and Vienna. In the 1920s he moved to
Paris to study at the Ecole des Beaux-Arts,
acquiring the meticulous drawing and
planning skills for which the school was
then famous. But with Paris being the
epicentre of the artistic *avant-garde*, he
was drawn to new architectural leaders,
especially Le Corbusier. Rebelling
against the straitjacket of period styles
taught at the Ecole, Goldfinger joined a
group of other architectural students to
form an *atelier* that explored emerging
modern methods of design and
construction. They asked Auguste
Perret, the influential innovator in
concrete structure, to be their teacher.
Almost half a century later, Goldfinger's
buildings – like Trellick Tower – are the
development of these early lessons in
the rejection of historical associations
and the power and plasticity of working
in concrete.

Goldfinger and his English wife Ursula
Blackwell moved to England in 1934.
Ernö's progressive convictions and
talent made him a rising star in British
modernism. His first major building
essay, the terrace of three houses at 1–3
Willow Road (he and his family lived at
number 2, now a property of the National
Trust), was constructed with a concrete
frame insert with walls of windows
overlooking Hampstead Heath.

Ernö Goldfinger dated his Diploma
Work 'April 1976', printing off a copy of
one of his drawings created about a
decade earlier and then adding coloured
pencil. A cut-away perspective, it is
somewhat difficult to read at first, but
once understood, the image is as clear and
clever as its subject – the system whereby
residents and visitors navigate around
Trellick Tower, getting to and leaving the
flats. The added colouring is coding:
yellow for 'IN', blue for 'UP' and red for
'DOWN'. These direction indicators are
given in perspective in the lower right,
each coloured appropriately beneath
the feet of the figures circulating in
the skywalk passage and on the stairs.
This circulatory section of the drawing is
then repeated immediately above, with
the figures shown in context within the
building. The floors of the three flats on
each storey have been aptly coloured –
yellow, blue and red – indicating how
figures access flats on three different levels
from one common circulatory space.

Goldfinger translated the colour
coding in his drawing into his design for
Trellick Tower by using coloured wall tiles
on the different floors. He had picked up
this system from the colour markings used
on the trains in Budapest. They would
also be helpful, he joked, for tipsy
residents to find their front door
(Dunnett and Stamp, p. 83).

Architects' Journal, 157,
10 January 1973,
pp. 77–96

James Dunnett and
Gavin Stamp, *Ernö
Goldfinger*, London,
1983

Robert Elwall, *Ernö
Goldfinger*, London,
1996

Nigel Warburton, *Ernö
Goldfinger: A Life of an
Architect*, London,
2004, pp. 162–72

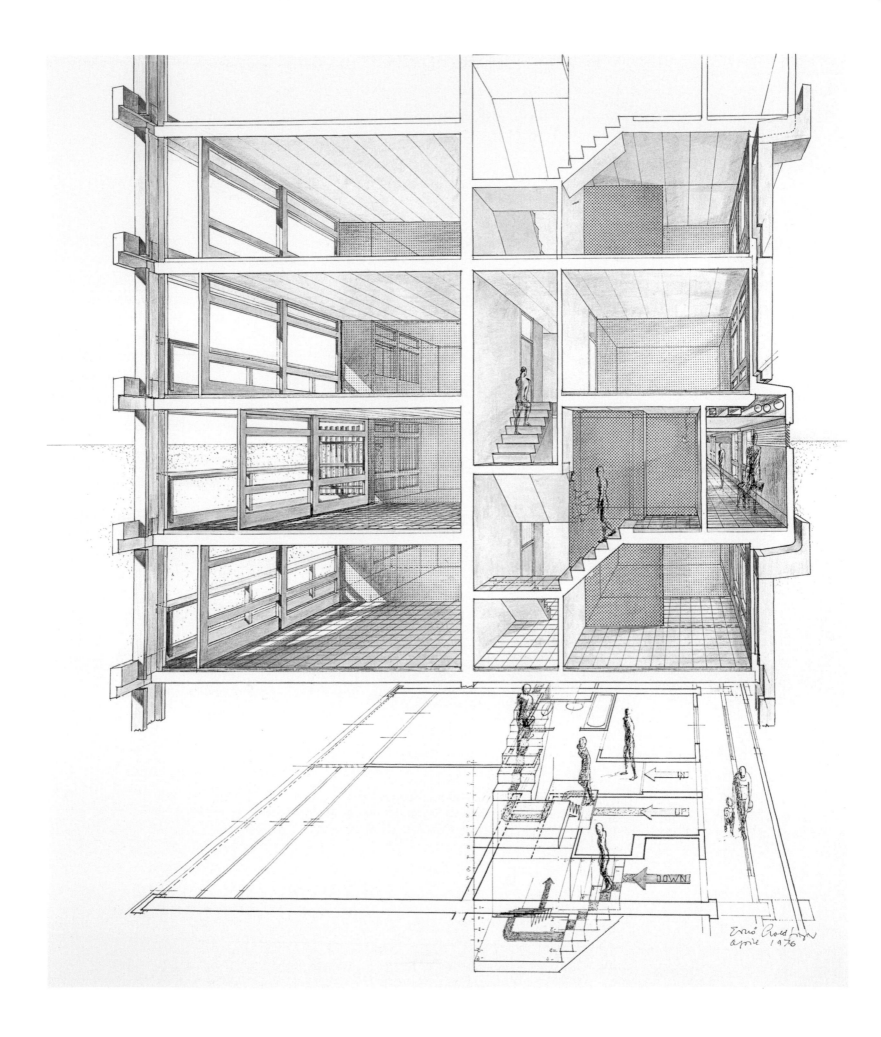

Sir Philip Powell RA
1921–2003
ARA 21 April 1972
RA 1 March 1977

Queen Elizabeth II Conference Centre,
Broad Sanctuary, Westminster, London:
plan at level 6, part-elevation, sectional
perspectives and photomontage
perspective, July 1977

Photograph, pencil and felt-tip pen with
coloured inks on five sheets of tracing
paper, 594 × 840 mm

Sir Philip Powell's Diploma Work drawing is an architectural encryption. When Powell was elected a full Royal Academician in March 1977, he and his partner Hidalgo 'Jacko' Moya had recently received the commission for the Queen Elizabeth II Conference Centre from the government. Powell's drawing, which dates from the early design stage for the project, was made during the summer of 1977 when public disclosure of details of the scheme still carried restrictions. So although the conference centre facilities shown in the drawing are fairly close to what was built and completed by 1986, Powell had to disguise their location and the extracurricular functions that were planned for below ground because of client sensitivities and national security.

The site is in Broad Sanctuary, between the government offices in Whitehall and a battery of historic buildings: Westminster Abbey across the street, the Wesleyan Central Convocation Hall to the southwest, Middlesex Guildhall (now the Supreme Court) immediately to the east, and in the near distance, St Margaret's Church and the Houses of Parliament. Placing a modern building in such a context required sensitive handling. The architects considered the modern style of their building as non-historical but appropriate, with its tough external appearance and its introduction of new materials to the area, such as steel, plate glass and concrete. Margaret Thatcher, whose government inherited the project, did not agree, however, and gave Sir Philip her candid opinion at a Royal Academy dinner when seated next to him. But the die had been cast by then (Powell, p. 113).

Powell, a sprightly and witty man, clearly enjoyed creating an architectural drawing as if it were a jigsaw puzzle, teasingly giving clues to the location of the conference centre, reversing orientation

and scrambling the surroundings. In the upper left, the exterior perspective labelled 'view from west' – actually from the east – is a montage of a photograph of the design model set within a freehand drawing of the site, showing part of the Wesleyan Hall sprouting a tower it does not possess. The section in the upper right of the drawing reveals the massive nature of the development, although Powell suppresses the lower levels for government security reasons and plays the game of sketching in a vista of a make-believe medieval street with a spired church at its termination. The site plan, too, in the lower left of the drawing, showing the large conference halls within the building, hints at the massive outline of the Abbey across the plaza. The details in the lower right, however, are accurate, showing a cutaway and elevation of the overhanging lobbies with black lines representing aluminium louvres that control daylight.

The Queen Elizabeth II Conference Centre was one of Powell and Moya's last great works. They had started extremely young, and were only 23 and 24 years old respectively when in 1946 they won the competition to build Churchill Gardens. This massive social-housing development in Pimlico covered thirty acres along the River Thames and took fifteen years to complete. During the second half of the twentieth century, Powell and Moya created a reputation for modern architecture that was direct and sophisticated, with college buildings for Oxford and Cambridge, the Chichester Festival Theatre and their masterful Museum of London. Their most iconic structure – the Skylon, an attenuated metallic sculpture, a sky pylon that rose above London's South Bank during the 1951 Festival of Britain – proved ephemeral.

Architects' Journal,
167, 14 June 1978,
pp. 1134–35

Construction (London),
46, Spring 1984,
pp. 31–35

Architecture (AIA), 75,
September 1986,
pp. 52–53

Ken Powell, *Powell and
Moya*, London, 2009,
pp. 112–15

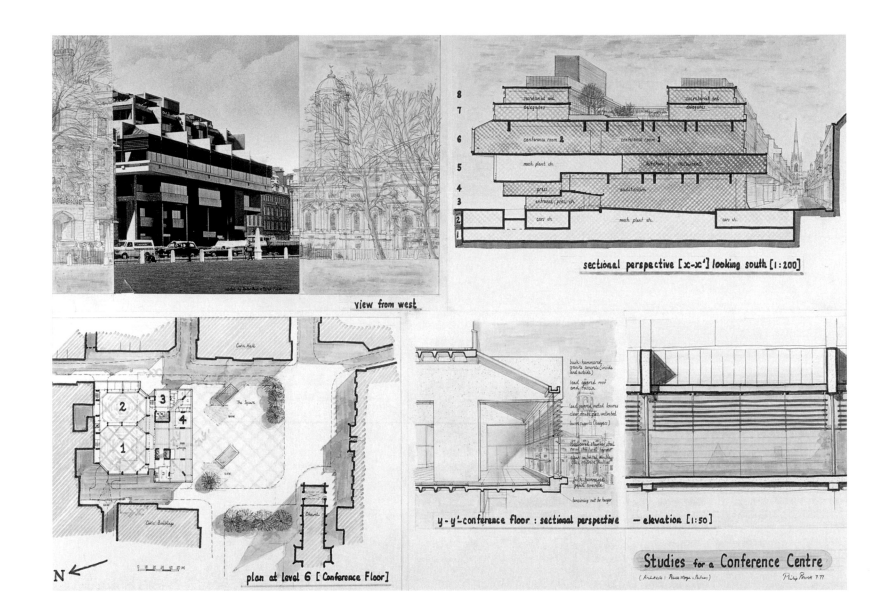

view from west

sectional perspective [x-x'] looking south [1:200]

8
7
6
5
4
3
2
1

secretariat and delegates

secretariat and delegates

conference room 2

conference room 1

mech. plant etc.

kitchens restaurant

press

auditorium

entrance, press etc.

cars etc.

mech. plant etc.

cars etc.

N

plan at level 6 [Conference Floor]

Civic Hall

The Square

Civic Buildings

Church

y-y' conference floor : sectional perspective

— elevation [1:50]

Studies for a **Conference Centre**

(Architects: Powell Moya Partners)

Peter Chamberlin RA
1919–1978
ARA 25 April 1975
RA 11 May 1978

Sketch designs for the Barbican Estate,
London; the Economist Building,
St James's Street, London; and Churchill
College, Cambridge, c. 1959–70

Pencil, pen with black ink and black and
red crayon with black dry transferable
lettering added, on nine sheets of tracing
paper mounted on card, 840 × 592 mm

Peter Chamberlin, known familiarly as
Joe, died on 23 May 1978, less than two
weeks after being elected a full Royal
Academician. His Diploma Work,
therefore, was submitted in his memory.

The work consists of nine sheets of
sketches, carefully arranged and affixed to
one large backing sheet. A trio of schemes
are represented. The three sheets along
the top are sketch designs for the vast
Barbican Estate in the City. The bottom
left sheet is of sketches and extensive
pencilled notes in preparation for the
competition for the Economist Building,
London. And a column of four small
sheets along the bottom right contains
sketches relating to the competition
for Churchill College, Cambridge.

Chamberlin was the most prominent
partner in the architectural practice
Chamberlin, Powell and Bon. He,
Geoffrey Powell and Christoph Bon
had been fellow tutors at Kingston
Polytechnic, banding together in 1952
when Powell won the social-housing
competition for the Golden Lane Estate,
London. Out of this project grew the great
scheme for the Barbican, adjoining
Golden Lane to the south, but
Chamberlin did not live to see this
long-running project completed
in the early 1980s.

The largest image at the top of the
sheet, a site plan of the 40-acre Barbican
site, is dominated by the shapes of the
concert hall and the theatre auditorium,
initial ideas for London's premier arts
complex, which sits at the heart of a series
of low blocks and high-rise towers, 2,000
flats integrated as part of a sculpted urban
landscape. In this Diploma Work, the
three sketches by Chamberlin show more
than two dozen jottings, ranging from
conceptual plans to blocked-out forms

The sheet relating to the Economist
Building dates to about 1959, the time of

the competition. In the end this small
complex of modern, American-style
buildings in London's St James's was
designed by the architects Alison and
Peter Smithson in 1959–64. In his sketch
for the project, Chamberlin emphasises
the didactic as much as the visual,
creating written lists of 'queries',
'advantages' and 'principles' alongside
more than half a dozen plans and views.

The third section of Chamberlin's
memorial drawing is associated with his
firm's competition entry of 1959 for the
new Churchill College, Cambridge.
Chamberlin's idea of using a traditional
college court with an extended,
semicircular end is indicated in the top
of the four sketches. Although the firm
did not win this competition – the
commission went to Sheppard Robson
(Richard Sheppard RA gave his design
for the dining hall as his Diploma Work;
see pp. 156–57) – Chamberlin, Powell and
Bon went on to become the principal
architects of extensive building projects at
the University of Leeds during the 1960s
and 1970s.

David Heathcote,
*Barbican: Penthouse
Over the City*,
Chichester, 2004

William Whyte, 'The
Modernist Movement
at the University of
Leeds, 1957–1977',
The Historical Journal
(Cambridge), 51, 2008,
pp. 169–93

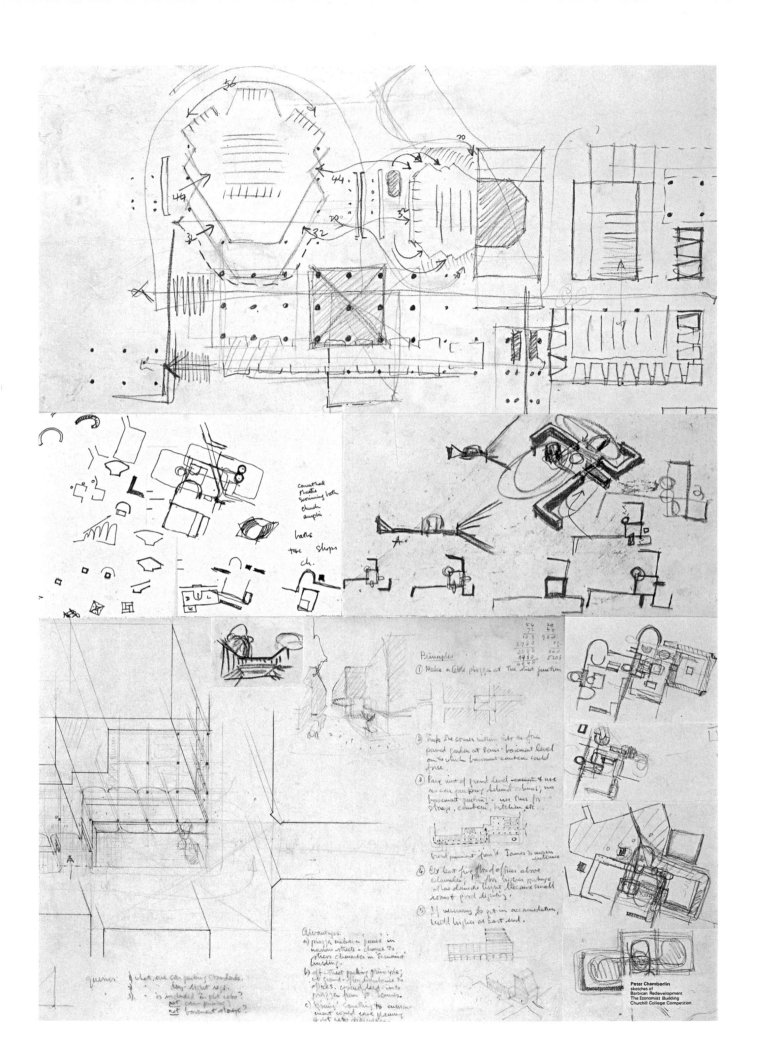

Peter Chamberlin
sketches of
Barbican Redevelopment
The Economist Building
Churchill College Competition

Leonard Manasseh RA
b. 1916
ARA 30 April 1976
RA 9 May 1979

Design for Lake Radipole pumping station, for Weymouth and Portland Borough Council, Weymouth, Dorset: plan, elevations and section, 9 April 1979

Print in black ink with added pencil and coloured pencil and two paper labels printed with black ink, 800 × 950 mm

Leonard Manasseh, a man of great charm and humour, enjoys telling the anecdote about his first major commission. He had been chosen to design the luxury restaurant for the 1951 Festival of Britain, but the undertaking was cancelled and all he ended up creating were the public lavatories with the little '51 Bar' on top

This incident boded well for Manasseh, as his architectural practice developed a fine reputation for creating public 'infrastructure facilities' on sensitive sites; in other words, buildings that we all need but often do not especially want to see. In such cases, the best solution is obviously to design, as Manasseh did, pleasing buildings that are carefully placed in their setting. His Diploma Work drawing illustrates just such an example: a sewage pumping station in a nature reserve.

Leonard Manasseh began site-sensitive work in the 1950s as a response to post-war reconstruction that often tended to trample over the past in the name of progress. Teaching at the Architectural Association, the independent school of architecture in Bedford Square in London that he had attended in the 1930s before serving in the Fleet Air Arm during the war, Manasseh formed a long and fruitful collaboration with his fellow student Dame Elizabeth Chesterton, who became his teaching colleague. As Chesterton became an increasingly strong force in planning, and especially in the conservation and public enjoyment of historic buildings within areas of natural beauty, Manasseh acted as architect. Following her study of King's Lynn, Norfolk, in which she rejected the planned motorway through the medieval heart of the town, Manasseh worked on retaining the historic fabric of King's Lynn while making sensitive additions,

such as a new Law Courts building.

In the late 1960s and early 1970s, following another of Chesterton's advisory reports, Manasseh developed the historic Beaulieu estate in the New Forest as a popular tourist destination by creating an ensemble of buildings for the National Motor Museum. Other heritage projects ensued, including work on the Royal Mews at Windsor, the Royal Greenwich Observatory and historic country houses such as Kingston Lacy in Dorset. Manasseh's skill in designing amenity buildings in sympathy with the landscape gained him increasingly large commissions in the 1980s, most notably in his design for a prototype power station that resulted in such examples as Killingholme in Lincolnshire.

The siting of a pumping station on the shores of Lake Radipole, near the centre of the Dorset town of Weymouth, called for Manasseh's considerable powers of persuasion in convincing openly hostile local officials of the possibility of adding to rather than marring the beauty of the area. The drawing that he presented as his Diploma Work, a copy print to which the architect has added intense pencil shading and lively colouring in blue and turquoise crayon, played a key role in making the successful bid. The aspect is a fusion of plan and elevations. The long elevation of the station is set near the top centre of the sheet, its rectangular outline edging the lake and mirrored in the water. In the centre of the elevation is a stylised letter 'W' (for Weymouth), and beside it '1981', the date of expected completion, which was changed to '1982' when the building was opened.

The lower three-quarters of the sheet contain a site plan, showing the ground floor of the pumping station set in its wooded location. As a light touch, Manasseh has drawn in a line of cars,

parked badly. Inserted, but in scale, are, at the left edge of the sheet, a side elevation showing the distinctively shaped roof running the whole length of the building and, on the right, a section through the pumping station that illustrates the water held in the wet well and the bell-like pump of the dry well with the motor-room above.

RIBA Journal, 88, March 1981, p. 61

Timothy Brittain-Catlin, *Leonard Manasseh & Partners*, London, 2010

WEYMOUTH & PORTLAND BOROUGH COUNCIL Main Drainage Scheme: RADIPOLE LAKE PUMPING STATION

J.R. KEMBLE BSc(Eng) MICE FIMunE FInstHE
Borough Engineer

L.G. MOUCHEL & PARTNERS
Consulting Engineers

Leonard MANASSEH & Partners
Chartered Architects and Planning Consultants
The Old Brewery, Freshford, Bath BA3 6EU.

Trevor Dannatt RA
b. 1920
ARA 13 May 1977
RA 18 May 1983

Ambassador's Residence, HM British
Embassy, Riyadh, Saudi Arabia:
ground- and first-floor plans, west and
east elevations and two sections, 1984
Pencil and coloured pencil on polyester
film, 595 × 840 mm

In the mid-1970s the architect Trevor Dannatt completed the King Faisal Conference Centre and adjoining Intercontinental Hotel and mosque in Riyadh, capital of Saudi Arabia. Less than a decade later, when the Saudi Arabian government offices were moved from Jeddah to Riyadh, obliging foreign embassies also to relocate, Dannatt was given the commission to build a new British Embassy. He designed offices and recreational facilities, the ambassador's residence and 35 houses for staff.

It was at this time too that Dannatt was elected a full Royal Academician, choosing to submit as his Diploma Work a drawing he had made for the ambassador's house in Riyadh. 'The Residence', although only two storeys in height, is substantial, spacious and ideally suited to social occasions. The coloured crayon of the drawing shows off the intended warm-coloured exterior cladding of Saudi granite infilled with beige Riyadh limestone. In keeping with traditional Arab domestic building types, Dannatt's design is made for a desert climate: the house is internalised to avoid the sun as much as possible and is landscaped with a cool, scented garden within a high enclosed wall. And with no windows facing the road, security was increased.

The drawing's presentation is straightforward and beautiful. The two plans cover more than half of the sheet, a scaled indication of the substantial size of the house, with its principal elevations shown at the top. There are two sections, one placed lower right and the other along the right edge in traditional orthogonal projection of a cut-through laid out parallel to the adjoining plan. Interestingly, the arrangement for the furniture is also shown. The focus is the principal reception room, measuring

10 by 7 metres beneath an atrium roof. Gathered near a grand piano there are five seating areas, including one around a fireplace and another of seating inset into the semicircular bay window that overlooks the garden.

Dannatt's drawing of the ambassador's residence is a summation of his long career in domestic architecture. Since the late 1940s, he has built houses of calm and comfort. His preference is for geometric forms, symmetry and light. He makes spaces flow and merge: vistas open while intimate areas can be enclosed, and public can be detached from private. And with their furnishings often set in place at planning stage, Dannatt's designs are thought out from the outset as homes, scaled for living, rather than mere shells to be filled and occupied.

After his work in Saudi Arabia, Dannatt undertook a series of major projects, many of them in his native southeast London. He was brought up in Blackheath, and one of his earliest buildings was the Congregational Church there (1957). In the late 1980s Dannatt's practice was appointed as consultant architects to the nearby University of Greenwich. The university had acquired Wren's historic Royal Hospital and Dannatt converted and refurbished this national monument and several of its ancillary buildings with gentle sensitivity and a cultured approach.

Construction, 54, Spring 1986, pp. 63–68

Roger Stonehouse, *Trevor Dannatt: Works and Words*, London, 2008, pp. 207–21

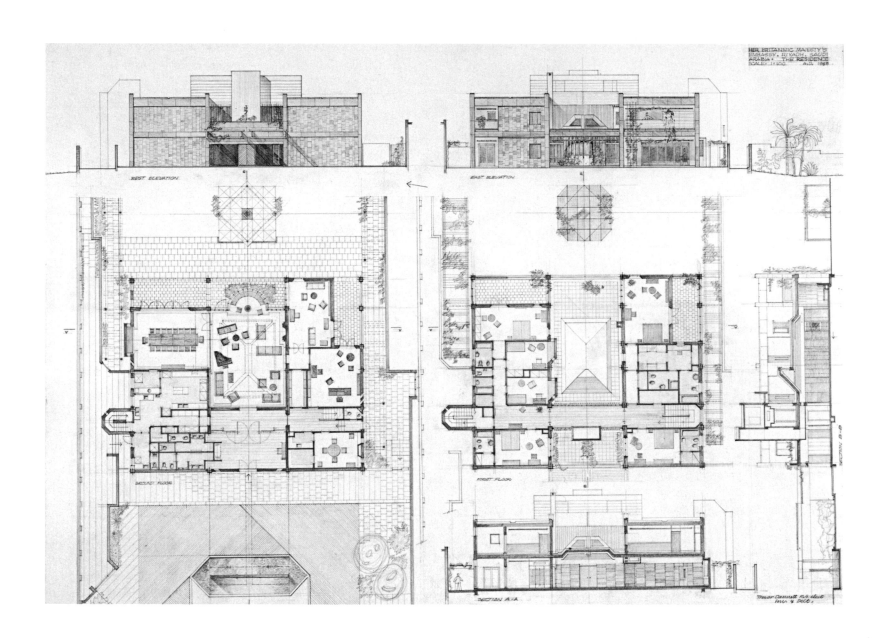

HER BRITANNIC MAJESTY'S
EMBASSY, RIYADH, SAUDI
ARABIA · THE RESIDENCE
SCALE 1:100   A.D. 1985

WEST ELEVATION

EAST ELEVATION

GROUND FLOOR

FIRST FLOOR

SECTION A-A

SECTION B-B

Trevor Dannatt R.A. Architect
Inv. & Delt.

Richard Rogers RA, Baron Rogers of Riverside
b. 1933
ARA 11 May 1978
RA 9 May 1984

Inmos Microprocessor Factory, Newport, Gwent: section perspective, 1980 (detail opposite, full drawing overleaf)

Print in red ink with pen and red ink added, 440 × 1067 mm
Drawn by Mike Davis

Richard Rogers, Lord Rogers of Riverside, has been a leading player on the world's architectural stage since he and the Italian architect-engineer Renzo Piano HON RA completed the Centre Georges Pompidou in Paris in 1977, a gallery-museum in a glass box hung within an exoskeletal steel frame. Here was a new way of building – playfully called 'inside-out architecture' – with engineering that was exposed, beautifully detailed and practical, enabling wide unsupported spans. Over the next several decades Rogers, together with his former architectural partner Norman Foster RA, became leaders of the growing group of architects who made Britain the acknowledged centre of the major architectural movement known as high tech.

As its name implies, this movement went hand in hand with the rise of new technology. Buildings by Richard Rogers epitomised the aesthetic bridge between the digital age and architecture. His Lloyd's of London Building, completed in 1986, with its exterior glass lifts, gleaming stainless-steel modules and vast glazed atrium, mirrored the growth of British business in a bull market. However, technology for Rogers also serves to enhance the planning and social aspects of his buildings. Many of his large commissions – for instance his airport structures at Madrid Brajas (2006) and Heathrow Terminal 5 (2008); the Millennium Dome (today called The O2); and the Senedd, the Welsh National Assembly Building, in Cardiff, completed in 2006 with its transparent walls – encourage a sense of participation, of public activity in building types that, in other hands, can seem busy yet lifeless.

Design on the Inmos factory began in 1980, the date of the striking line drawing that Rogers gave as his Diploma Work.

The project was a perfect coupling of the cutting-edge technology of Rogers's highly engineered architecture with the building's function as a factory headquarters of the government's flagship initiative in the manufacturing of microprocessors. The drawing is by Mike Davis – the tiny initials 'MD' with the date are sequestered in the mechanics of the roof, mid-right. Davis, an architect who joined Rogers's office on the Centre Pompidou and became a founding partner of the Richard Rogers Partnership in 1977, was project manager of the Inmos scheme (and many projects since, including the Millennium Dome). No doubt part of the reason for the blood-red ink colouring of the drawing is that Davis is known for his love of the colour red and is always seen wearing red clothing.

The drawing's aspect is a hybrid, part-perspective and part-section. The building appears like a battleship. The long, lower section is seen in perspective, a view through the single storey of offices and laboratories where microchips are designed and made. Down the centre runs a 'street', a continuous corridor of seating and visitor reception. But it is the roof structure that attracts most attention, with guide wires, trusses and high masts running the length of the building above the central corridor. Along the factory's tall spine are large containers housing services. Pipes snake along the roof. As with the Centre Pompidou and the Lloyd's of London Building, flexibility and adaptability were essential elements of the design. The spine, for example, can be extended, or the services in the containers exchanged or replaced at convenience.

'Richard Rogers & Architects', *Architectural Monographs*, 10, London, 1985, pp. 60–63

Richard Burdett (ed.), *Richard Rogers Partnership: Works and Projects*, New York, 1995, pp. 78–83

Kenneth Powell, *Richard Rogers: Complete Works. Volume 1*, London, 1999, pp. 228–35

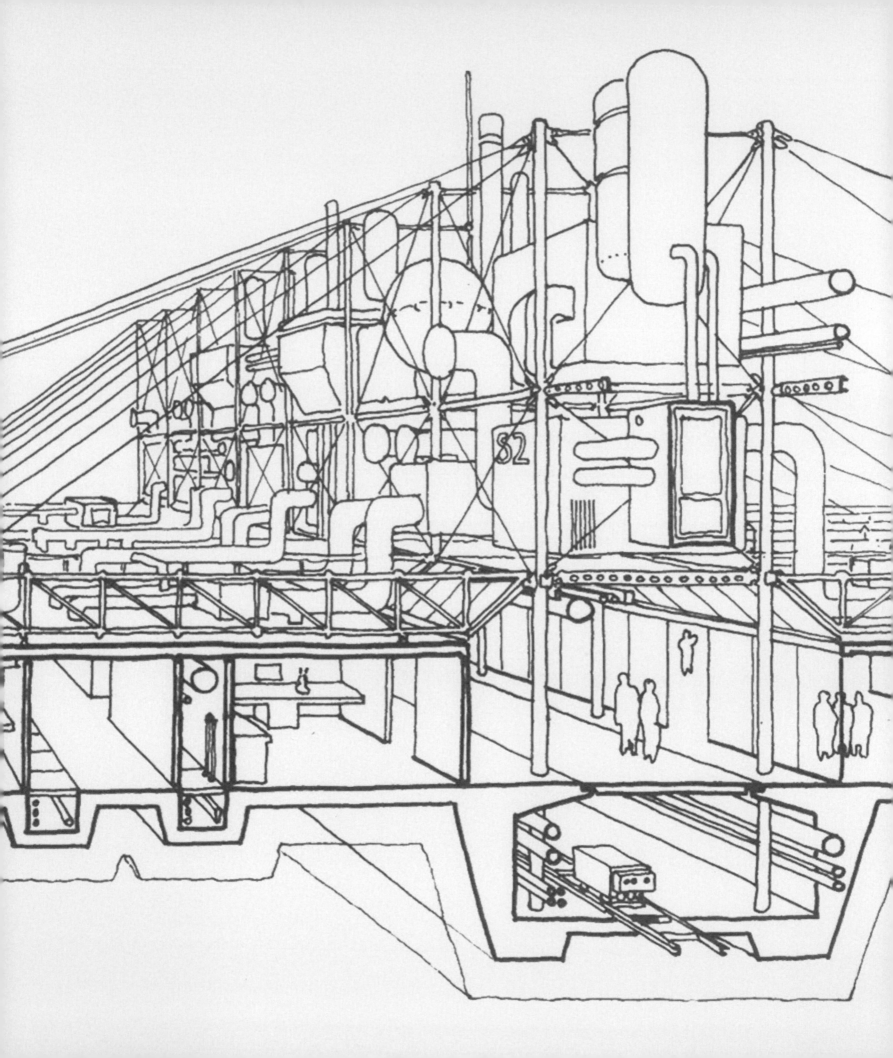

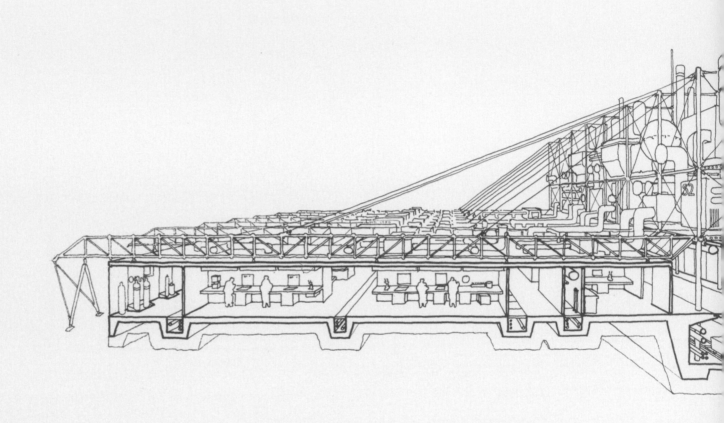

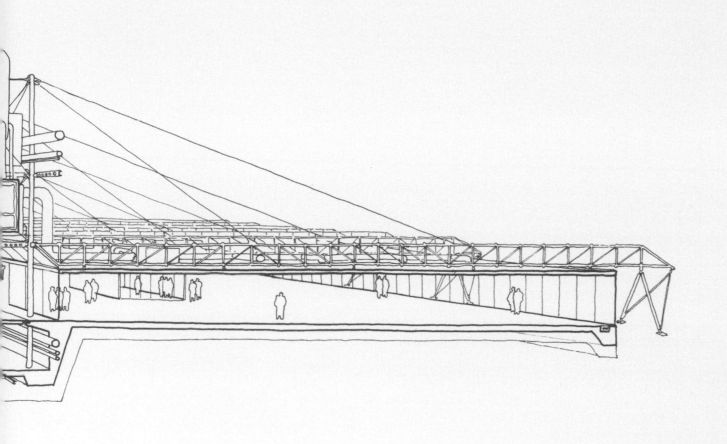

Sir Leslie Martin RA
1908–2000
RA 20 May 1985

Centre of Modern Art, Calouste Gulbenkian
Foundation, Lisbon, Portugal: perspective
of entrance and sectional perspective
through main gallery along south side,
c. 1985

Pencil on polyester film, 730 × 1187 mm

As architect, town planner and teacher,
Sir Leslie Martin had a profound
influence on many generations of British
designers. At the age of just 26, he was
head of the then small school of
architecture at Hull, and able to attract
such international stars as Marcel Breuer
to lecture to his students. Twenty years
later, he became the first Professor
of Architecture at the University of
Cambridge, eventually setting up the
University's Centre for Land Use and
Form, which has since been renamed the
Martin Centre. A natural and respected
leader, Martin was appointed as principal
group architect of one of Britain's most
prestigious post-war buildings: the Royal
Festival Hall on London's South Bank,
opened at the 1951 Festival of Britain.
Two years after its completion, he was
running the largest architectural office in
Europe as Chief Architect of the London
County Council, a powerful position
that required him to oversee a massive
social-housing programme. His designs
were uncompromisingly modern,
concerned with architecture that was
formal, linear and based upon his
'geometrical principles'. At times,
as among the colleges of Oxford and
Cambridge, where he often built, Martin's
concrete buildings appear like lions
among gazelles.

Martin often designed in conjunction
with his associates, including Colin St
John Wilson RA and Patrick Hodgkinson,
and in the case of the Gulbenkian Centre
of Modern Art with Ivor Richards.
The commission, in 1979, was for a
new gallery building within the growing
ensemble of the Calouste Gulbenkian
Foundation and Museum in Lisbon.
The Foundation had been created out
of the wealth and collections of paintings
and objects amassed by the Armenian
Constantinople-born Gulbenkian,

who had died in 1955. Martin's art centre
was created mainly for exhibiting newer
works, particularly those by Portuguese
artists, as well as the Foundation's
extensive holdings of modern works
of art from Armenia and Britain.

The setting for the building is a park
with an old stone-wall enclosure of
rustication and turrets. These features are
clearly highlighted in the Diploma Work
that Martin submitted in 1985 upon
his election as a Royal Academician.
The drawing, executed in pencil alone,
shows a perspective of the building viewed
from the street entrance, cleanly drawn,
almost transparent. Typical of Martin's
later work, the structure is impressively
exposed, here in the straight massing of
concrete post and beam. The emphasis in
the perspective is on the centre's entrance,
an open continuation of the structure
out onto the street. Below is a sectional
perspective looking through the building;
the dotted lines show the structure
removed in order to reveal the stepped
roof that gives the galleries their different
ceiling heights.

Leslie Martin, *Buildings
and Ideas 1933-83
from the Studio of
Leslie Martin and
His Associates.*
Cambridge, 1983,
pp. 100–14

Architects' Journal,
178, 5 October 1983,
pp. 46–53

Architectural Review,
178, September 1985,
pp. 22–31

The Entrance Portico. Centre of Modern Art.
The Calouste Gulbenkian Foundation. Lisbon.
Leslie Martin.

Sir Philip Dowson PRA
b. 1924
ARA 9 May 1979
RA 14 November 1985

Forbes Mellon Library, Clare College,
Cambridge: site plan and section, *c.* 1986
Pencil, 512 × 839 mm

Forty years after completing his postgraduate studies at Clare College, Cambridge, Philip Dowson returned to his old college to design a new library building. In the intervening years, he had used his successive degrees in mathematics, art and architecture to cultivate a rational and imaginative approach to design. The Forbes Mellon Library, which opened in 1986, is one of Dowson's purest examples of an aesthetic formed as a result of his mathematician's love of logic and his architect's love of form.

Early in his career, Dowson joined the office of Britain's leading civil engineer Sir Ove Arup RA. In 1963 Dowson led the firm as founding partner into becoming Arup Associates, integrating the services of architects, engineers, planners, consultants and project managers. Today this design conglomerate, perceptively in touch with a modern, multi-disciplinary world, is named simply Arup and boasts an international staff of many thousands scattered across dozens of countries. During his high-profile career, Dowson has gained many honours, including a knighthood in 1980, the RIBA Royal Gold Medal in Architecture the following year, and between 1993 and 1999 the presidency of the Royal Academy.

Dowson has been involved in many famous building projects, not least among them Sydney Opera House in Australia. He came to excel in a distinctive approach to building within the context of historical British settings. Like many architects during the 1960s and 1970s, he designed new buildings in a clear, strong and even downright tough modernist style whose robustness was particularly noticeable in the many Arup-designed college buildings created under his direction, in which mathematical grids of engineered concrete and glass were slipped in among old brick and stone quadrangles. And there were gentler examples, such as his conversion in 1967 of a Victorian malthouse at Snape in Suffolk into a concert hall for the composer Benjamin Britten.

The Forbes Mellon Library at Clare College shows Dowson engaging in an historic context without abandoning the formal elements of modernism. In his Diploma Work drawing, presented following his election as a full Royal Academician in 1985, he shows in the lower half a site plan of the library within the courtyard of the neo-Georgian Memorial Court, built between 1923 and 1934 by Sir Giles Gilbert Scott RA. In the long horizontal segment at the top of the drawing, Dowson illustrates a section through the library. Figures of staff and readers are seen in the two-level space, the shelves crammed with books. At the heart of the scheme is the octagon, evocative of the eighteenth-century octagonal antechapel in the college's Old Court. The façade elevation of the new building, which is not illustrated in the drawing, is a contemporary interpretation of the entrance front of the Pazzi Chapel, Brunelleschi's Renaissance masterpiece at Santa Croce in Florence.

Dowson made this pencil drawing especially for presentation to the Royal Academy. Creating such presentation drawings was, he said in conversation with the author, 'untypical'. For him, drawing meant sketching, spontaneous and rapid, just as Ove Arup did, on long rolls of paper, uncoiling towards a design solution.

Michael Brawne,
*Arup Associates:
The Biography of an
Architectural Practice,*
London, 1983

ARUP Journal, 22,
Autumn 1987, pp. 7–12

Michael Brawne,
Library Builders,
London, 1997, pp. 32–33

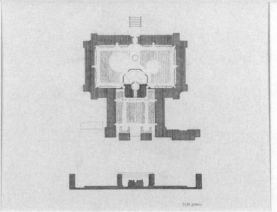

CLARE COLLEGE LIBRARY

Sir Ove Arup RA
1895–1988
RA 20 November 1986

Kingsgate Bridge, Durham: plan,
north elevation and detail, 1987
Print with black ink with added pencil,
blue pencil and black dry transferable
lettering, 568 × 760 mm
Drawn by 'KNY'

As Britain's leading civil and structural engineer, Sir Ove Arup created the global firm of consulting engineers, planners and project managers responsible for such modern architectural icons as the Sydney Opera House and the Barbican in the City of London. Yet despite the multitude of mega-projects his company created, Arup's favourite scheme always remained a small pedestrian bridge for which he had taken personal responsibility. Kingsgate Bridge, which he designed in 1963, is a slip of reinforced concrete pathway strung high above the River Wear, in the shadow of Durham Cathedral. It was from his beloved bridge that Ove Arup chose to have his cremated ashes scattered.

Arup's fine drawing of Kingsgate Bridge was made specifically as his Royal Academy Diploma Work by a draughtsperson identified only by the initials 'KNY'. The work is a polished exercise based upon design and presentation drawings made more than twenty years before, when the project was underway. Arup considered the formality of this type of representation more suitable for a Diploma Work than his customary 'doodles' of caricature and sketches, dashed off one after another in a 'spirited and vigorous' manner, as Sir Hugh Casson PRA said of them.

The mood of the drawing is studied and reflective. The misty, pencil-shaded silhouette of the great Norman cathedral looms over the view from its high promontory. Kingsgate Bridge lies below. The elevation in the centre of the sheet bleeds into the plan beneath by means of the confluence of the blue pencil colouring, taking the viewer from looking down onto the water to seeing straight through it. The striking elegance of the design is evident in the spidery legs of the clustering V-shaped supports on either side of the riverbank that capture the attenuated line of the walkway. The detail at the top of the drawing is over-scaled in relationship to the plan and elevation, emphasising the sculptural engineering of a bronze expansion joint.

The architect Peter Ahrends said of Kingsgate Bridge that it was the work of 'a man who had decided, as a student, to become a good engineer rather than a mediocre architect. In making this bridge, and in establishing the underlying spirit of his engineering practice, he imaginatively blurred all conventional edges between engineering and architecture, between art and science' (*Ove Arup 1895–1988*, p. 53).

Sir Ove Arup is the only engineer to have been elected a Royal Academician.

Ove Nyquist Arup,
Doodles and Doggerel,
introduction by Hugh
Casson, Ove Arup
Partnership, London,
n.d. (c. 1989)

Ove Arup 1895–1988,
The Institution of Civil
Engineers, London,
1995

Kingsgate Bridge at Durham

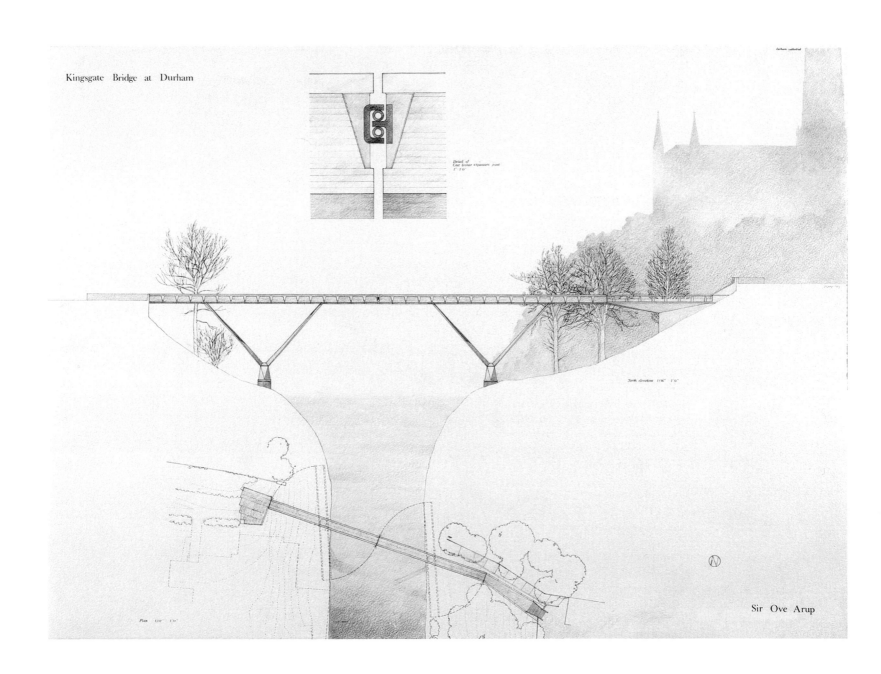

Detail of
Cast bronze expansion joint
1" 1'0"

North elevation 1/16" 1'0"

Plan 1/32" 1'0"

Sir Ove Arup

John Partridge RA
b. 1924
ARA 21 May 1980
RA 8 December 1988

Crown and County Courthouse,
Legh Street, Warrington, Cheshire:
south elevation, c. 1989

Pencil, pen with black ink, coloured
washes, blue pencil and black dry
transferable lettering, 445 × 940 mm

John Partridge was a partner in a celebrated quartet of British architects who had first met and worked in the architects' department of the London County Council. In 1959, with Bill Howell, John Killick and Stanley Amis, Partridge created Alton West on London's Roehampton Estate: five concrete tower blocks based on Le Corbusier's single apartment block of Unité d'Habitation in Marseilles. Their bold scheme proved very influential in social housing and the clustering of multi-storey slab blocks was much emulated over the next several decades.

The partners of HKPA worked closely together during the 1960s until the tragically early deaths of Killick in 1972 and Howell in 1974. Many of HKPA's large and important buildings were for universities, especially Oxford and Cambridge, usually in a geometric modernism built in pre-cast concrete. Yet their architecture was sensitive and in touch with historic settings. At Downing College, Cambridge, HKPA created a pavilion in witty allusion to the temple form of the adjoining Greek Revival hall by William Wilkins RA.

By the time John Partridge was elected an Associate Royal Academician in 1980, HKPA was moving in new directions. Having designed the county courts for Basildon and Haywards Heath, Partridge was beginning to specialise in such building types. His largest was in Port of Spain, the Hall of Justice building for the Supreme Court of Trinidad and Tobago, with 28 courtrooms. In these later buildings, Partridge maintained the powerful and sharp forms for which HKPA was known, although concrete now often gave way to brick. The drawing of the Warrington courts that Partridge presented as his Diploma Work illustrates this development: the hard-edged,

unsculpted line of the building's brick brutalism is set within the expansive glazing of the façades, clerestories and skylights. In planning, the complex issue of the four separate routes required by the public, defendants, jury members and judges – who should only meet upon entering the courtroom – was resolved by the architect using 'discrete circulation' (conversation with the author).

Partridge's use of red brick relates to the nearby walls of the glorious historic country house once known as Bank Hall, designed in 1750 by James Gibbs. Bank Hall is now Warrington's town hall and Partridge's Crown and County Courthouse is sited in the corner of the remains of the historic landscape of its park, now part of the town centre.

Sherban Cantacuzino,
*Howell, Killick,
Partridge and Amis:
Architecture*, London,
1981

SOUTH ELEVATION

SCALE 1·100

WARRINGTON CROWN & COUNTY COURTHOUSE

DESIGNED FOR PSA
HKPA ARCHITECTS

JOHN PARTRIDGE

Theo Crosby RA
1925–1994
ARA 5 May 1982
RA 13 December 1990

Battle of Britain Monument, Surrey Docks,
Southwark, London: elevation, *c.* 1987
Print with black ink, with added
coloured washes, 998 × 653 mm

Theo Crosby was an important facilitator of architecture and design. In 1956 he organised the 'This Is Tomorrow' exhibition at the Whitechapel Gallery, London, bringing together members of the Independent Group of writers, thinkers and creative practitioners in what proved to be the most influential British gallery show of the post-war period. For more than a decade he edited the monthly journal *Architectural Design*, and then set up Pentagram, a design company comprising mainly graphic designers who created corporate identities through graphics such as logos. Pentagram went global. Although Crosby is not generally known for his own works of architecture, his re-creation of Shakespeare's famous Globe Theatre in Southwark is a most significant and winningly popular building.

In 1987 Crosby's ongoing visionary search for identity within the contemporary city found expression in his unrealised proposal for a dramatic monument in southeast London. Working with artist-collaborators Michael Sandle RA and Pedro Guedes, Crosby maintained that London lacked memorials because 'modernist thinking' disapproved. He proposed a monument, surrealist in its form, commemorating the aerial Battle of Britain during the Second World War. The suggested site was near the River Thames at Surrey Docks, Rotherhithe. In the late 1980s the area, which had been heavily bombed by German aircraft in the war, was beginning to undergo enormous changes as part of the regeneration and gentrification of the London Docklands. Crosby recommended that this landmark structure be positioned midway between St Paul's Cathedral and the Royal Hospital at Greenwich.

Crosby deposited a coloured-up print of his monument design as his Royal Academy Diploma Work. The structure's silhouette was postmodern, a style incorporating exaggerated classical elements whose popularity was at its zenith at around the time of Crosby's design. A great pyramid forms the foundation, where visitors enter through a Doric-columned portal. A continuous frieze around the base bears the inspirational words of Sir Winston Churchill: FORTH TO THE RESCUE AND LIBERATION OF THE OLD and WE SHALL FIGHT ON THE BEACHES. Above rises a column, with four glass lifts taking visitors to the spooky installation on the upper viewing platform. At each corner sarcophagi eerily emit searchlights, scanning the sky. Then 'the visitor goes on foot,' the designers directed, 'up the perimeter stairs to the final experience, the sacred place high in the vast sky, at the peak of this artificial mountain. Here is the crowning sculpture: a circular pit with chairs and a table set with a simple meal, a corpse laid out. Crashing down on this is a huge Heinkel bomber with a Spitfire beside it.'

Raw commemoration or macabre funfair attraction? Reaction to the monument was mixed. The architectural historian and critic Gavin Stamp certainly agreed about the lack of new monuments in Britain, but compared Crosby's Battle of Britain unfavourably to the intensely moving works of commemoration by the British War Graves Commission, thinking especially of the simple, monumental and moving Thiepval Memorial to the Missing of the Somme designed by Sir Edwin Lutyens PRA. Stamp's article in the *Daily Telegraph* on 15 September 1987 bore the heading 'How to go monumentally wrong'.

Theo Crosby, *Let's Build a Monument*, London, 1987

Michael Sandle, Theo Crosby and Pedro Guedes, *The Battle of Britain Monument*, London, 1987

BATTLE OF BRITAIN
MONUMENT

Sir Geoffrey Jellicoe RA
1900–1996
RA 29 May 1991

The Secret Garden, St Paul's Walden Bury, Hertfordshire: plan of garden and elevation of green arch, 26 November 1990 (print) and *Completed / autumn 1991* (added)

Print with black ink with added felt-tip pen with red and blue ink and coloured pencil, 491 × 359 mm

Sir Geoffrey Jellicoe was the Capability Brown of modernism, Britain's foremost landscape designer of the twentieth century. His interest in landscape was kindled while he was researching *Italian Gardens of the Renaissance*, the influential study that he and J. C. Shepherd published in 1925. Jellicoe's approach to garden design became a spiritual journey, influenced by the writings of Carl Jung, as he explored landscape through psychology and the subconscious. Reflecting upon memory and allegory, Jellicoe created such projects as the Surrealist Garden at Sutton Place in Surrey, and the nearby President John F. Kennedy Memorial. One of Jellicoe's last major commissions, although it was never realised, was a summation of his journey through the evolution of humankind and landscape, a sequential history of world gardens destined for the Moody Gardens in Galveston, Texas.

Jellicoe was elected a Royal Academician in the senior order in 1991 and deposited this drawing for a 'secret garden' at St Paul's Walden Bury in Hertfordshire as his Diploma Work. The large estate with its fine house has been owned by the Bowes-Lyon family since 1725. The wooded park was the setting for the future King George VI's marriage proposal to Lady Elizabeth Bowes-Lyon, later Queen Elizabeth, the Queen Mother. Jellicoe began to add to the rich, French-inspired landscape of St Paul's Walden Bury as early as 1936, by prolonging and creating vistas and inserting picturesque garden buildings. One long glade he humorously nicknamed 'the running footman garden'. He sculpted the landscape at St Paul's Walden Bury intermittently for over half a century, and the gardens there have been called Jellicoe's 'permanent laboratory' (Spens, 1994, p. 22).

Jellicoe's Diploma Work is a print of a drawing that he worked up with coloured pen and crayons. It is a characteristic example of his freehand style, which gives the lines movement and liveliness. The scheme, which was realised, presents the client with a small garden entered from the drawing room of the house through a trio of French windows. The garden, paved and ornamented with plants in tubs, leads to grass and brick paths around rectangles of free planting, a classic example of Jellicoe's fondness for reminding us of mankind's attempts to balance disorder with order. The central axis is a vista terminating in a small semicircular pool with a fountain glimpsed through a green arch that is elaborated in the upper-left corner of the drawing by an elevation with a standing figure.

Jellicoe dated the original drawing from which this print is taken: '26.11.90 / Highpoint'. After his wife Susan died, the architect moved up Highgate Hill in London from their family home to a flat in Highpoint, the modernist apartment block by Berthold Lubetkin RA. There Jellicoe displayed his fine collection of British paintings and drawings in a crowded hang on his sitting-room wall as if they were colourful plants in one of his garden designs.

Michael Spens, *Gardens of the Mind: The Genius of Geoffrey Jellicoe*, Woodbridge, 1992

Michael Spens, *The Complete Landscape Designs and Gardens of Geoffrey Jellicoe*, London, 1994 (the drawing illustrated on page 25 is a variant of the Royal Academy's Diploma Work)

Geoffrey and Susan Jellicoe, *The Landscape of Man: Shaping the Environment from Prehistory to the Present*, third edition, London, 1995

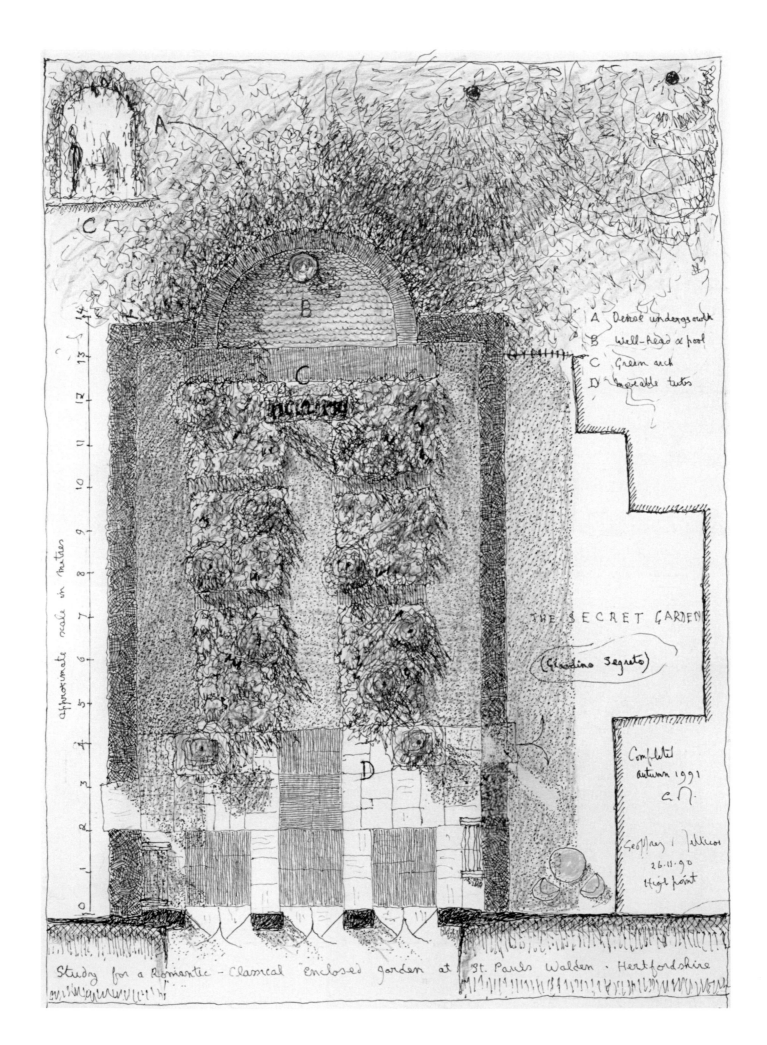

A Dense undergrowth
B Well-head & pool
C Green arch
D moveable tubs

A

C

B

C

THE SECRET GARDEN

(Giardino Segreto)

D

Completed
autumn 1991
G.J.

Geoffrey Jellicoe
26·11·90
High point

approximate scale in metres

Study for a Romantic-Classical Enclosed garden at St. Pauls Walden · Hertfordshire

Sir Denys Lasdun RA
1914–2001
RA 29 May 1991

'Models in Dialogue'. The National Theatre, South Bank, London, 1991

Photograph of room with models, with added autograph perspective drawing in pen with black ink and white correction fluid, 611 × 611 mm
Photograph by Arnold Behr

For his Diploma Work, Sir Denys Lasdun presented this black-and-white photograph of a tumbling pile of wooden architectural models for his National Theatre project. The work's apparently simple format, instead of a real model or a design drawing of the scheme, belies the architect's desire to abstract objects of representation from his built architecture. The design process is finished and over, Lasdun implies, leaving beautiful but broken objects.

The photograph was taken in a corner of Lasdun's office at 50 Queen Anne Street, London, by the architectural photographer Arnold Behr in about 1967, the year the National Theatre opened. Illustrated in *A Language and a Theme: The Architecture of Denys Lasdun & Partners* (p. 96, fig. 87), the photograph is captioned 'Models in Dialogue' and became an iconic image. The short text written by Lasdun that accompanies the section of the book headed with this title begins with a quotation from the fifteenth-century Italian architect Alberti, about the benefit of using models. Lasdun then continues (p. 99): 'Models have a social function as a basis of dialogue … The "strata" of the National Theatre underwent lengthy study on models of different scales examining form, profile, texture, so that the structure might be harmonised with the guiding ideas of the design … When the building has been constructed, the models reach the end of their useful life and become removed from their original meaning as historical makers in a series of transactions which have involved user and architect. Nevertheless, [the modelmaker] Philip Wood's craftsmanship has given them such tautness and elegance that they take on the status of works of art in their own right.'

In the white space of the photograph, in the top left corner, Lasdun has added a drawing of his own right hand holding the pen creating a memory sketch-view of the National Theatre. This was done at the request of the Council of the Royal Academy in order to render the photograph autographic and unique. The theatre is seen from the River Thames, the water twinkling in a series of short marks, Waterloo Bridge on the right, the building a study in horizontal lines. Dots along the lines represent a festive crowd.

The self-portrait of a pen in a hand making a drawing is a conceit with a long tradition in Western art. The most famous architect to have drawn his own hand is the Renaissance master Andrea Palladio, who did so on a sheet of façade sketches in the Drawings Collection of the Royal Institute of British Architects, with which Lasdun was familiar as a council member on the Architectural Drawings Committee.

As a young architect in the late 1930s, Denys Lasdun was an early British modernist. After the war, he created a series of social-housing cluster blocks in concrete, a material with which he became increasingly identified as he developed into a leader of the Brutalist movement with such later buildings as the ziggurat-shaped terraces of the University of East Anglia (1968) and the bold form of the Institute of Education for the University of London (1976). In 1997 he was given a major retrospective exhibition at the Royal Academy.

Denys Lasdun, *A Language and a Theme: The Architecture of Denys Lasdun & Partners*, London, 1976

Colin Amery (ed.), *The National Theatre: 'The Architectural Review' Guide*, London, 1977

William J. R. Curtis, *Denys Lasdun: Architecture, City, Landscape*, London, 1994

Edward Cullinan RA
b. 1931
ARA 31 May 1989
RA 26 June 1991

Lycée Privé (private secondary school),
Lagny, France: competition design,
aerial view, 1992
Pen with black ink on tracing paper,
614 × 726 mm

In Jungian psychology, dreams about flying represent exhilarating freedom. In this charming perspective, a group of picnicking hot-air balloonists float leisurely over Edward Cullinan's proposed school building. And those baguettes and bottles of wine make the location instantly recognisable as France, the village of Lagny. Drawn in freehand, the cheerful characters are typical of the way Cullinan populates his presentation drawings, a visual allusion to his humanist approach to architecture. The jovial expression of this unbuilt competition design – entered by Cullinan in conjunction with the Parisian architectural firm of Hutchinson Associates – also reflects the relaxed and imaginative path he has taken in planning educational buildings.

Cullinan's vision of architecture and education was formed early. After training at the University of Cambridge and the Architectural Association in London, Cullinan worked on and off in the late 1950s and early 1960s for Sir Denys Lasdun RA on such projects as the student buildings at the University of East Anglia with their famous ziggurat forms. He made several extended visits to America, where the liberal atmosphere of the University of California at Berkeley, a hothouse of the counter-culture movement, especially appealed to him. From an early stage of private practice, the breadth of his approach created buildings that although they did not eschew the high technological developments of his contemporaries nevertheless incorporated contextual and sustainable tactics, such as local building materials and energy performance systems, issues that came to be of global concern in later years.

Cullinan's energy strategies go hand-in-glove with an architecture that is sensitive to site. For the Weald and Downland Open Air Museum, a collection of historic rural buildings in the Sussex countryside, Cullinan built the principal collections and administration building, the Downland Gridshell, a lightweight oak and lath structure emulating but not imitating the traditional framed building type. His Fountains Abbey Visitor Centre fitted neatly into a World Heritage Site. As Cullinan continues to explore unusual and novel solutions for the educational community in schools, universities and libraries, he creates fine works even in regenerated industrial landscapes, such as the Royal Albert Dock with his campus for the University of East London, exemplifying the colour and life that can be brought to such large-scale developments.

Edward Robbins,
'Edward Cullinan,'
Why Architects Draw,
Cambridge, Mass.,
and London, 1994,
pp. 56–78

Kenneth Powell,
*Edward Cullinan
Architects*, London,
1995

Jonathan Hale, *Ends
middles beginnings:
Edward Cullinan
Architects*, London,
2005

**Norman Foster RA,
Baron Foster of
Thames Bank**
b. 1935
ARA 19 May 1983
RA 26 June 1991

Carré d'Art, Nîmes, France: perspective
with cut-away section, 2009
(detail opposite, full drawing overleaf)
Pencil and green and blue coloured pencil,
530 × 1080 mm

Asked to name influences on his drawing style, Norman Foster replies: 'Paul Rudolph, Louis Kahn and Hugh Casson' – all of them architects and, of course, all superlative draughtsmen (conversation with the author). When Foster was a postgraduate at Yale University in the early 1960s, Paul Rudolph was his teacher. And, for a short time, Rudolph took Foster on in his office to make presentation drawings, where the use of straight-edge drawing tools was favoured. Foster also encountered Kahn at Yale, where Khan was a visiting critic. Both these great architects drew in a cool, rectilinear hand, using colour sparingly, as is appropriate for design drawings of their monumental concrete buildings. In contrast, Sir Hugh Casson PRA drew freehand, in a jolly and light-hearted way, in the English picturesque tradition. As a student, Foster had spent a summer working for Casson.

Hints of all three architects are especially strong in the architectural drawing that Foster submitted as his Diploma Work. The subject is the Carré d'Art in Nîmes, a building that contains a library, media centre and art gallery. The aspect is ruled in slender pencil lines softened by gentle green crayon, the scene enlivened with people and vehicles. Foster calls it 'an explanatory drawing, not a presentation. I wanted to encapsulate in the view a wider civic order, not just the building, but the procession, the street, the quality of the visitor.'

Right from the outset of the project in 1984, Foster had sought to link his building not only to the ancient Roman temple of the Maison Carrée sited opposite, but to the city as a whole, a link based, as is exemplified in this drawing, on order and social activity. Foster is a prolific sketcher, often on-site, using drawings as an introspective means of understanding and interpretation. So, for example, when he presented his ideas for the Nîmes scheme to the panel of judges, he showed his drawings and made spontaneous sketches on the spot. The dynamic mayor Jean Bousquet said that when Foster did this 'with two pencil strokes I knew he understood the city' (*Works* 2, p. 358).

As his Diploma Work, Foster chose to fine-tune a drawing, now lost but published, that he had first made in August 1985. The drawing represents a point in the design when all the principal elements were in place although not fully developed. The form of the building is a grid of bays of equal length, the geometry imitating the order of the Maison Carrée (in French *carré* means square, as in geometry) and the order of the underlying urban grid plan of Roman Nîmes. A flat-canopied roof overhangs the front of the structure, poised on slender columns (five were used when built), echoing the portico of the temple. The translucent quality of the finished building, which is encased on all four sides by clear glass (with louvers on the sunny front, as shown), eradicates size and scale, and is here suggested by the lack of walls as the drawing reveals a cut-away view of the interior. Running through the centre is the grand ceremonial staircase, an internal court lit by skylights. The space is layered, 'like the terraced towns', says Foster, that surround the city of Nîmes.

Norman Foster selected the Carré d'Art project to present to the Royal Academy because he believes it is a transitional scheme, a moment poised between his early and later works. The building does indeed show affinities with his earlier well-known buildings, like the Sainsbury Arts Centre at the University of East Anglia, as well as later works, like Stansted Airport and his light-filled inner court of the Royal Academy's own Sackler Wing of Galleries at Burlington House. The French commission also signalled the moment when Foster stepped onto the world stage in the role of architectural superstar. Today his reputation grows ever stronger as he and his large team at Foster + Partners design building after building of international acclaim – the restored Reichstag in Berlin, Chep Lap Kok Airport in Hong Kong, the Hearst Tower in New York City, and the affectionately nicknamed 'Gherkin' in London, to name but a few from their extensive international portfolio.

Werner Blaser (ed.), *Norman Foster. Sketches*, Basel, 1992

Norman Foster, 'Carré d'Art, Nîmes' in Michael Brawne (ed.), *The Architecture of Information: British Pavilion, Venice Biennale 1996*, London, 1996, pp. 18–27

Malcom Quantrill, *Norman Foster Studio: Consistency through Diversity*, London, 1999, pp. 142–51, drawings pp. 68–69

David Jenkins (ed.), *Norman Foster. Works* 2, Munich and London, 2005, pp. 346–407

Deyan Sudjic, *Norman Foster: A Life in Architecture*, London, 2010

Paul Koralek RA
b. 1933
ARA 19 May 1986
RA 26 June 1991

Competition design for the Royal Library,
Copenhagen, Denmark: plans, elevations,
sections and perspectives, 1993
(detail opposite, full drawing overleaf)

Computer-generated print on electrostatic
plotter paper with added pen with black
ink, crayon and Pantone-coloured
overlay film on five panels, 1165 × 795 mm
(each of 5 panels)

When discussing architecture,
Paul Koralek is fond of quoting the
philosopher and art historian Ananda
Coomaraswamy (1877–1947), who
reflected that 'styles are the accident, by
no means the essence of art'. Architecture
is not something therefore you put on like
a suit of clothes, explains Koralek, but
a search for technical and practical
principles within design, which may
also be symbolic of the way we live.
For example, a library may house books
and be a place for reading them, but a
library is also the symbol of learning and
knowledge. Link these principles, Koralek
believes, and 'we can make buildings
which will be satisfactory and fulfilling in
relation to all levels and aspects of human
life and activity' (*Ahrends Burton and
Koralek*, 1991, pp. 32–33).

Koralek is one of three partners who
founded the architectural practice of
Ahrends Burton and Koralek (ABK) in
1961. A decade earlier, Peter Ahrends,
Richard Burton and Koralek had been
students together at the Architectural
Association in London. Upon
graduation, Koralek worked for Powell
and Moya (the practice of Sir Philip
Powell RA and Hidalgo Moya) and then
spent a period in America under the
great modern master Marcel Breuer,
student and teacher at the Bauhaus in
the 1920s. An understanding of Breuer's
powerful manner of massing concrete
was instrumental in Koralek's winning
design in the international competition
for the Berkeley Library at Trinity
College Dublin in 1960. This was ABK's
first major project, a true *tour de force* and
a taste of many successes that saw the
practice flourish, to great critical
acclaim, with such works as their
residential building at Keble College,
Oxford, notable for its fortress-like
exterior walls in brick and its transparent
interior walls, completed in three phases
between 1972 and 1980. During the same
period, the practice also designed a
number of industrial buildings, early
examples of the high-tech style, such as
the Habitat warehouses and showroom
at Wallingford, Oxfordshire, created
from 1972 to 1974 and designed with
a rippling steel casing and internally
exposed trusses and joints as part of
the aesthetic.

The practice suffered a significant
setback at the moment that should have
been its greatest triumph, when they
won the competition in 1982 to build an
extension onto the National Gallery in
Trafalgar Square in London. Their
scheme, publicly criticised by Charles,
Prince of Wales, was subsequently set
aside. But with substantial projects on
the drawing board such as the John
Lewis department store in Kingston-
upon-Thames, and by their strength of
talent, ABK slowly progressed to triumph
once again with such fine work as the
British Embassy in Moscow, completed
in 2000.

Paul Koralek headed the practice's
1993 competition entry for the new
Royal Library building in Copenhagen.
Although the Danish architects Schmidt,
Hammer & Lassen were the eventual
winners, Koralek chose to submit his
magisterial entry drawing, done in
mixed media, as his Diploma Work.
The sheet measures an impressive four
metres in length. It is cut into five panels
of equal size for ease of transport and
storage, each in an acrylic box frame
so that the group can be hung as a
continuous whole.

Koralek's drawing was the first
architectural Diploma Work to use
computer-generated imagery. The use
of computers in architects' offices was
relatively new at the time and this
drawing is a highly sophisticated
example for the period of design and
graphic printing using programming
confined to lines, circles, arcs and text.
Printing was carried out on a large-
format electrostatic plotter, a piece of
equipment introduced to the market in
the late 1980s that was soon replaced by
inkjet and laser printers. The printing
paper, on long rolls, was negatively
charged as it passed through a line of
tiny electrode wires thus attracting the
positively charged black toner. Colours
were added by hand afterwards.

The site chosen for the Royal Library
was on Copenhagen's harbour front,
near the city centre. Koralek proposed a
long, sleek structure with an undulating
roof, like a billowing wave, low and
unobtrusive. The building is in two
sections: the attenuated waterside form
and the inland block. These are linked
by a large rotunda, which straddles the
waterfront of Christians Brygge.

The design is comprehensive and
detailed, arranged in three horizontal
bands. The upper band, on a white
background, shows a site plan, an
elevation of the library building against
the skyline of Copenhagen, and many
floor plans and sections. In the centre
band, against a blue background,
a coloured-up perspective appears on
the left; to balance on the right, a colour
crayon perspective of the scheme seen
from across the water has been affixed to
the panel. The bottom section contains
a line of twenty-five small attachments
of explanatory texts and drawings.

194

*Ahrends Burton and
Koralek*, introduction
by Peter Blundell-
Jones, London and
New York, 1991

Kenneth Powell,
*Collaborations: The
Architecture of ABK*,
London, 2002

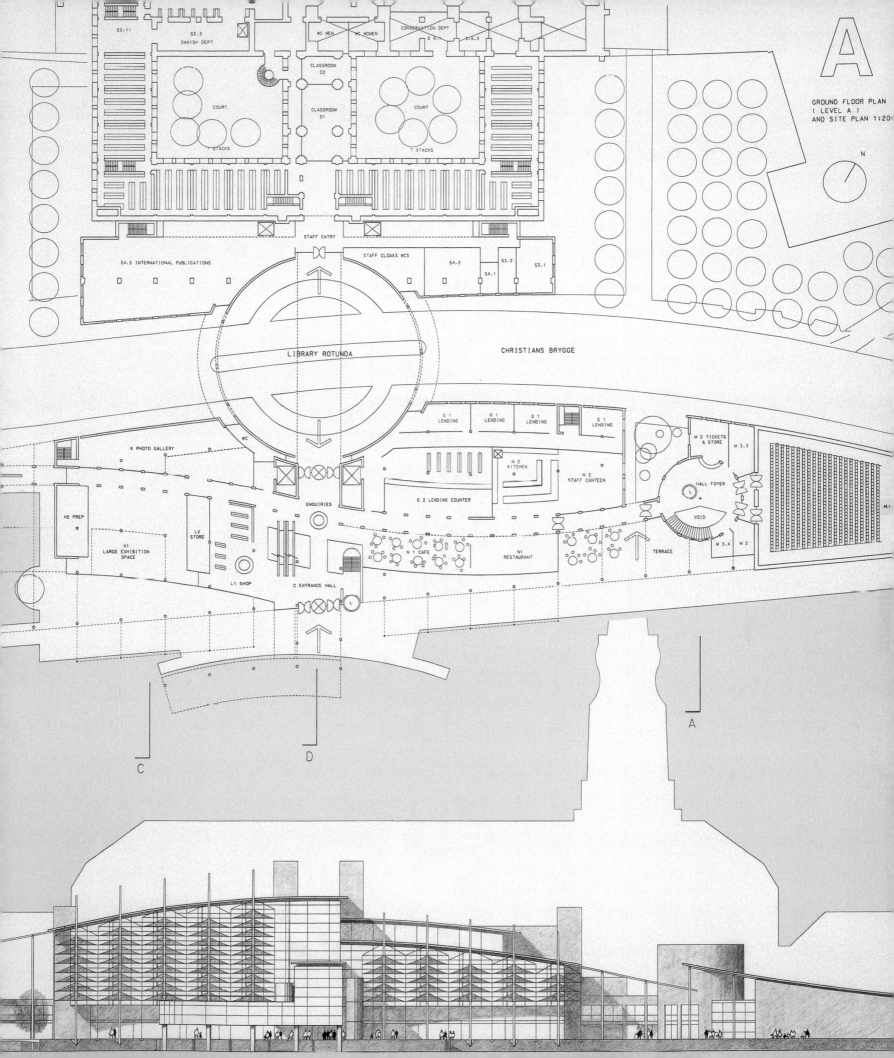

N

S2.11

DANISH DEPT
S2.3

CLASSROOM
D2

WC MEN   WC WOMEN   CONSERVATION DEPT

S 6.1   S.6.2

CLASSROOM
D1

COURT

COURT

T STACKS

T STACKS

STAFF ENTRY

S4.3 INTERNATIONAL PUBLICATIONS

STAFF CLOAKS WCS

S4.2   S3.2   S3.1

S4.1

LIBRARY ROTUNDA

CHRISTIANS BRYGGE

K PHOTO GALLERY

WC

G 1
LENDING   G 1
LENDING   G 1
LENDING   G 1
LENDING

M 2 TICKETS
& STORE   M 3.3

N 2
KITCHEN   N 2
STAFF CANTEEN

HALL FOYER

ENQUIRIES

G 2 LENDING COUNTER

VOID

M 3.4   M 2

H2 PREP

L2
STORE

L
N 1 CAFE   N1
RESTAURANT   TERRACE   M1

H1
LARGE EXHIBITION
SPACE

L1 SHOP

C ENTRANCE HALL

L

A

A

C

D

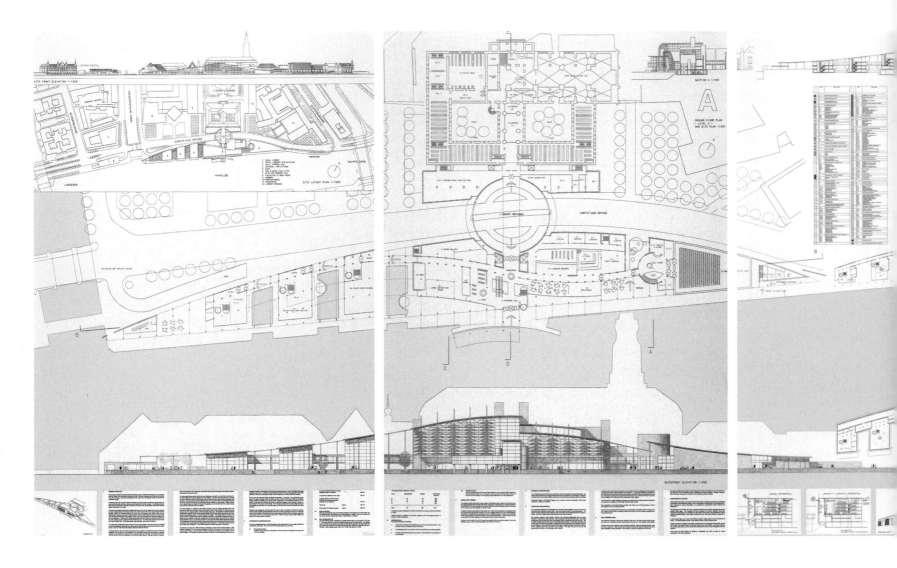

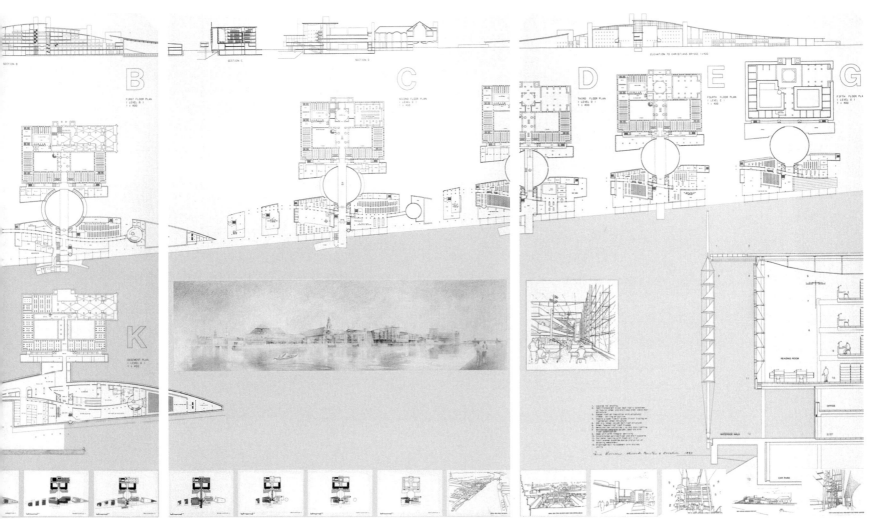

The British Library, St Pancras, London:
longitudinal section from south
(entrance hall) to north, 1995
(detail opposite, full drawing overleaf)

Pencil, pen with black ink and coloured
washes, 756 × 2891 mm
Drawn by Dennis R. Dornan

Sir Colin St John Wilson described the battle to get his design for the new British Library built at St Pancras as his 'thirty years' war'. Although he received the commission in 1962, his vision for the new library did not become a reality until the 1990s, following decades of bitter debate regarding every aspect of the project, from the building's location and budget to its scale and form. The end result, however, was a triumph: the nation's library housed in the largest public building constructed in Britain in the twentieth century, its architecture one of soaring spaces, intimate study areas, bright offices and kilometres of underground storage for the collections.

Like many young architects in the post-war years, Wilson – 'Sandy' to family and friends – was an idealist. His hero was Le Corbusier, whom he zealously defended in debates and articles. Joining the London County Council Housing Division in 1950 gave Wilson the opportunity to put words into action. Taking Le Corbusier's methodology as a model, he designed high-rise council estates such as Bentham Road in Hackney with modular units, a concrete frame and piloti supports. But all this was to change when in 1956, Sir Leslie Martin RA, the first Professor of Architecture at the University of Cambridge, asked Wilson to join his staff.

Martin's zeal for reform was stirring up a younger generation eager to change the academic approach to teaching architecture, and Wilson soon became caught up in this. The study of historical styles that had traditionally dominated architectural training gave way, under Martin and Wilson, to theoretical research based upon the way people use buildings and how this could be standardised in geometric forms, a so-called 'pattern of needs'. Wilson rejected his early adherence to modernism, seeing it as dogmatic and limiting, and pursued the 'humanist' approach as practised mainly by Scandinavian architects, most notably the Finn Alvar Aalto. Wilson went on to create – sometimes with Martin and his Cambridge colleagues, sometimes independently – a highly respected collection of college buildings and private houses.

It was with Martin that Wilson landed the job for the British Library, following the success of their grouping of three libraries, the St Cross Faculty Libraries, Oxford, in a large single building. At first, the British Library was projected to spread across a considerable stretch of Bloomsbury in front of the British Museum. Martin and Wilson created a design for an immense building intersected by malls and squares that focused upon Nicholas Hawksmoor's baroque church of St George. But public outcry at the destruction of so much of this historic area shifted the project in 1975 to a disused railway depot next to the mighty neo-gothic silhouette of George Gilbert Scott RA's St Pancras railway station. Wilson, now working with his own team, crafted scheme after scheme as governments changed, budgets were cut and decisions deferred. Work began on the site in 1982, but it was start-stop until, finally, the building was opened in phases between 1997 and 1999.

Colin St John Wilson's Diploma Work is a section through the part of the British Library building that stretches from the great sloping entrance hall concourse, with its grand staircase, through to the dense grid of the tower, which houses the King's Library, the historic book collection of King George III, then across public and staff areas to the trellised roof terrace at the northern end.

The intensity of the draughtsmanship and the size of the drawing, on a single sheet nearly three metres (nine feet) long, capture the analytical quality and sheer scale of the project. The drawing is the work of Dennis R. Dornan (b. 1956), one of Wilson's students at Cambridge in the late 1970s during his time as Professor of Architecture. Dornan joined Wilson's office as an architect in 1988 and remained there until the British Library was completed and the practice was dissolved. In discussing the drawing, Dornan gives an insight into the practice's process of design and making: 'As is usually the case in these types of drawing, we don't just "finish" the design and then make representations of it. All drawings are part of the design process and give the designer (or design team) an opportunity to view/evaluate/investigate/develop certain aspects of the design. Such was the case with this long section and I remember it evolving over a period of about four to six weeks. I would say that the actual drafting and watercolouring was probably about eighty hours of my time' (correspondence with the author).

The large square form glimpsed in the entrance hall at the left of the drawing is a tapestry based on a painting by R. B. Kitaj RA, one of many works of art especially commissioned for the building at Wilson's instigation. Wilson was a passionate collector, friend and champion of contemporary artists. One of his last projects, carried out in collaboration with his architect-wife Mary Jane Long, was to design an extension to Pallant House Gallery in Chichester, West Sussex; he donated his own important collection of twentieth-century British art to the gallery's collection.

Roger Stonehouse and
Gerhard Stromberg,
*The Architecture of the
British Library at St
Pancras*, London, 2004

Sarah Menin and
Stephen Kite,
*An Architecture of
Invitation: Colin
St John Wilson*,
Aldershot, 2005,
pp. 169–219

Roger Stonehouse,
*Colin St John Wilson:
Buildings and Projects*,
London, 2007,
pp. 318–99

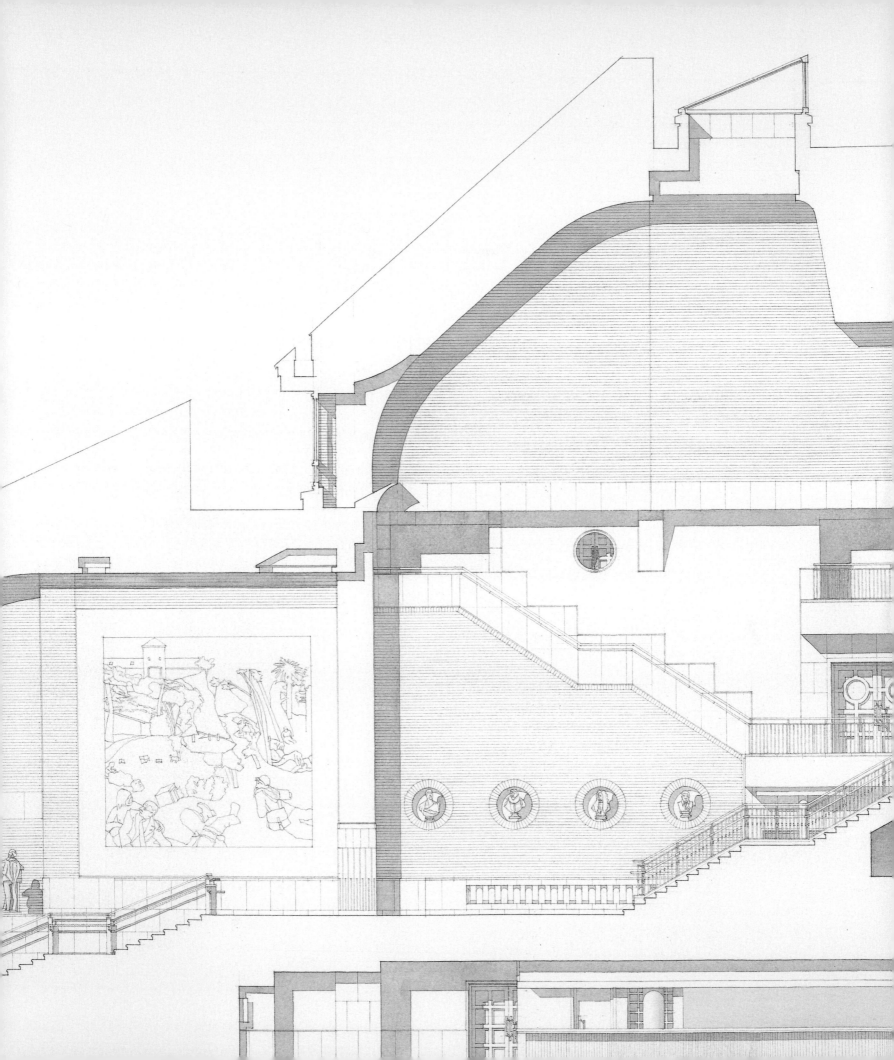

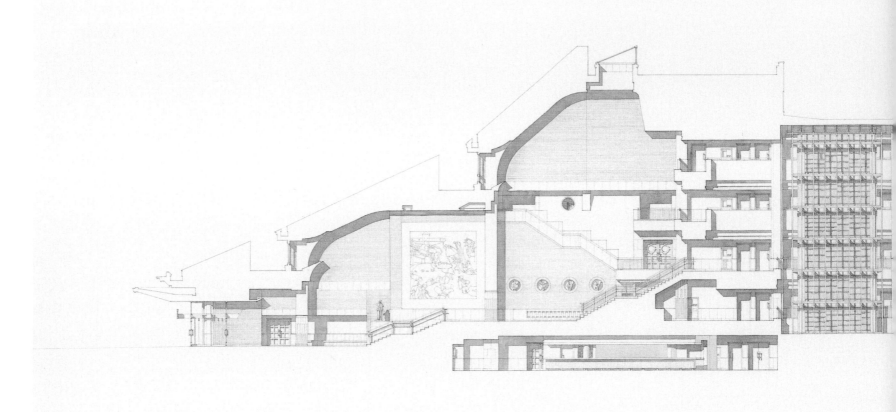

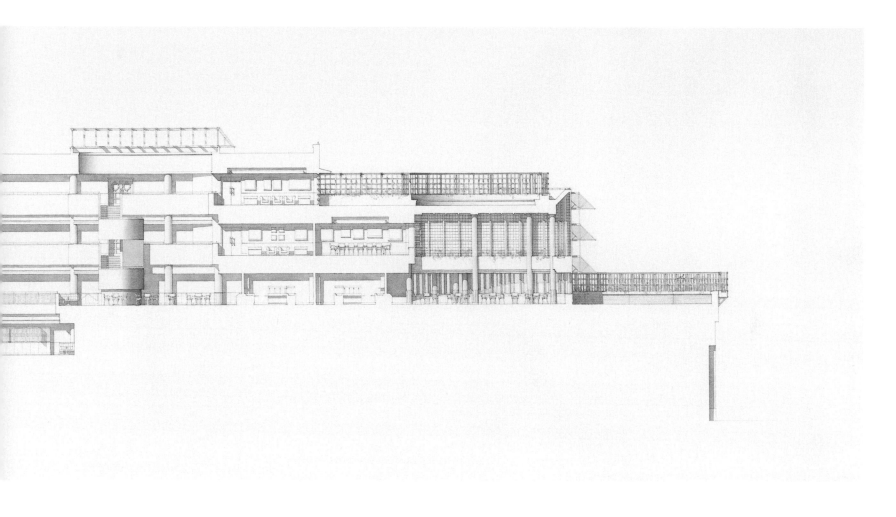

Sir James Stirling RA
1926–1992
ARA 20 May 1985
RA 26 June 1991

Channel 4 Headquarters, Horseferry Road, London: exterior (top) and interior (bottom) worm's-eye axonometrics, 1990

Pen with black ink, pencil and blue and brown coloured pencil on tracing paper, 356 × 430 mm; pen with black ink and blue and brown coloured pencil on tracing paper, 258 × 380 mm

Following Sir James Stirling's untimely death two days before the first anniversary of his election as a Royal Academician and twelve days after the announcement of his knighthood, this delicately beautiful pair of drawings was presented to the Royal Academy by his wife Mary and his long-time architectural partner Michael Wilford. The drawings represent two highly unusual views of a scheme for a new London headquarters for the Channel 4 Television Company. Channel 4, then known for arts and culture programming, had initiated a limited competition in 1990 inviting three firms to design its building: Stirling Wilford, Bennett Associates, and the eventual winner, the Richard Rogers Partnership.

Stirling's design is presented in dramatic worm's-eye view – one for the exterior, the other for the interior – looking up into the building as if it were floating in space above the viewer. In the exterior view, the criss-crossing building frame and glass walls form a rim around the perimeter. Tiny round brown points mark sets of revolving doors on either side of the covered walk-through that is lit by natural light from the circular form of the cone-shaped opening above. The interior drawing shows the cone, on the left, rising through the building; a similar lighting cone also houses the lifts.

From the beginning of his architectural practice in the early 1950s, James Stirling showed a fondness for drawing axonometrics, developing them until they became a trademark of his working methods and presentational style. An axonometric projection, set at an angle of 45 degrees, keeps the length of the lines true to the plan and thus creates an accurate three-dimensional representation. The image is usually pulled upwards, so that the building is seen from above, the so-called bird's-eye

or aerial axonometric. This is how Stirling first used the axonometric in drawing his early schemes, showing aerial observations of his flats at Ham Common, London, designed in the late 1950s with his then partner James Gowan, followed by his most famous projects of the 1960s, the Leicester University Engineering Building (also with Gowan) and the Cambridge University History Faculty Building, completed in 1968. However, by the early 1970s, Stirling was frequently pulling the image downwards to create a worm's-eye axonometric. His most famous buildings, such as his major addition to the Staatsgalerie in Stuttgart and the triangular No. 1 Poultry, in the heart of the City of London at Bank, completed posthumously, were the subjects of a whole series of axonometric views, swinging the buildings around, down and then up in a worm's-eye prospect.

Michael Wilford, who joined Stirling in 1960 and became a partner in 1971, relates how, as the practice grew, the whole office would take part in the drawing operation, gradually reducing the image on tracing paper to its minimum while conveying the maximum amount of useful information. 'We make use of three-dimensional exploratory drawings to study details or special elements of construction because by using single, simplified images we can grasp the essence of an idea in a way which normal orthographic projection can only achieve using several images, and often with far less clarity' (*Buildings and Projects 1975–1992*, p. 5). This pair of drawings for the Channel 4 Headquarters is an example of this collaborative clarification. Control of the design nevertheless remained with Stirling who, at the end of the process, added his own distinctive soft colouring and intense blue dotted background.

James Stirling was a large, affable man who earned the affectionate nickname of 'Big Jim'. He was held in such respect by the architectural community that in 1996 the Royal Institute of British Architects created in his honour the Stirling Prize – Britain's highest-profile architectural award for the most significant building of the year by a member of the RIBA. The much-anticipated presentation ceremony is broadcast annually on Channel 4.

James Stirling: Buildings and Projects, introduction by Colin Rowe, London, 1984

James Stirling Michael Wilford and Associates: Building and Projects, 1975–1992, London, 1994, pp. 268–71

Mark Girouard, *Big Jim: The Life and Work of James Stirling*, London, 1998

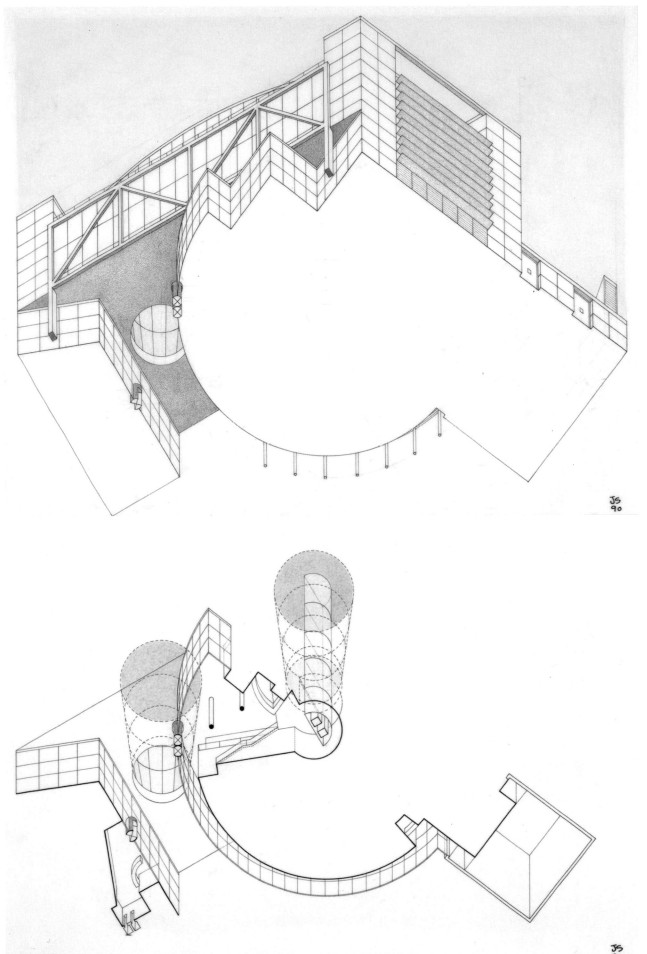

Sir Michael Hopkins RA
b. 1935
RA 28 May 1992

Model of a masterplan for the Royal Academy of Arts, linking 6 Burlington Gardens with Burlington House, Piccadilly, London, 2003 (detail opposite, full model overleaf)

Wood, acrylic, red paint, resin figures and cork and metal tree, 1070 × 950 × 270 mm

'I miss it,' says Sir Michael Hopkins. For many years the architectural model of his project for Burlington House, home of the Royal Academy, greeted him as he entered the practice office, residing in place of honour upon a plinth right near the doorway. Although the scheme was only very partially carried out, he finds some consolation now that he has presented the model to the Royal Academy as his Diploma Work, saying wryly: 'Everyone will be reminded of a lost opportunity' (conversation with author).

Hopkins's proposal for replanning and extending Burlington House was halted in 2003 by a lack of success in raising the necessary funds. The commission had commenced in 1999 with the anticipation of the purchase of 6 Burlington Gardens, the former administrative headquarters of the University of London, built in the late 1860s by the architect James Pennethorne. When the Royal Academy first moved to Burlington House in 1867, Pennethorne's Victorian pile was being raised over the far northern end of the house's garden. At the same time, on the middle ground of the garden, near the house, the Academy was adding the present grand suite of exhibition galleries and accommodation for the Royal Academy Schools beneath to the designs of Sydney Smirke RA. Hopkins's scheme would have knitted together the whole site by creating a central corridor linking and opening up the non-exhibition spaces and adapting Pennethorne's building to provide much-needed office accommodation.

The wooden model, made in the Hopkins office, is both beautiful and intriguing. It is in three sections. Down the centre is a large representation of the whole site. At the Piccadilly entrance (shown at the top of the model, pp. 206–07), the Victorian courtyard buildings are the only part left untouched, as they contain the neighbouring learned institutions. Next in sequence is Burlington House, a town mansion dating mainly from the early eighteenth century. Behind this is Smirke's gallery building, with a new door leading into the 'forum', Hopkins's proposed covered atrium on the site of the current service yard. And finally comes Pennethorne's building, its attic storey removed and replaced by a glass roof between the towers.

Running the length of the right side of the model is the ground-floor plan, which clarifies the axial alignment of the proposed connection that would have allowed visitors to walk straight through from one end of either building to the other via the vaulted undercroft of the Main Galleries and the forum. And along the other side of the model, laser-cut into the wooden block, is a section through the principal part of the scheme (see p. 205, opposite).

For Michael Hopkins, the Royal Academy project highlights the major shift in direction that his practice has taken in recent years. In the 1970s and early 1980s, Hopkins had earned a reputation as one of the leaders of the high-tech movement. Having practised for a time with Norman Foster RA, Hopkins began to develop innovative lightweight structures that were cheap to build, flexible and made of standard component parts. Then in 1976 he set up in private practice with his architect-wife Patty, and together they designed their own house, which became an instant classic: a two-storey industrial box with metal sheeting for interior walls and floors, steel lattice trusses, and the exterior walls entirely made of glass.

Hopkins used the engineered aesthetic of his own house as the basis for a similar series of buildings, usually in characterless areas such as industrial parks, until a moment when he found himself having to confront buildings and urban settings of historical interest. His response, as is evident from the Burlington House project, was sympathy not servility, modernism in touch with its historic setting. He was thus able to move on to creating such fine buildings as Glyndebourne Opera House in Sussex, which is attached to a country house, and the tented structures of such venerable British sporting venues as Lord's Cricket Ground and Goodwood Race Course. One of his most prominent buildings set in a historical setting is Portcullis House, beside Sir Charles Barry RA's Houses of Parliament on the Thames embankment at the foot of Westminster Bridge. Here the splayed ribs of the rooftop and the black chimney-pot ventilators complement the nearby gothic fenestration of Westminster Abbey. And below street level, in Westminster Underground station, the travelling public experiences the sensation of moving through the monumentally cavernous spaces of a Piranesi etching, escalators in place of stairs.

At Burlington House, the only part of Hopkins's grand scheme to have been completed was the courtyard approach. The entrance porch was modified, glazed over and ramped. And with parking now banned, Hopkins made the courtyard into an enjoyable public space. The central area was set with grey Cornish granite flags, a base for a changing display of large works of sculpture. In the centre, in alliance with the adjacent Royal Astronomical Society, is a constellation of fountains re-creating the pattern of the stars on the night of 16 July 1723, when the founding president of the Royal Academy Sir Joshua Reynolds was born.

Colin Davies, *Hopkins: The Work of Michael Hopkins and Partners*, London, 1993

Colin Davies, *Hopkins 2: The Work of Michael Hopkins and Partners*, London, 2001, pp. 178–81

Cristina Donati, *Michael Hopkins*, Milan, 2006, pp. 202–03

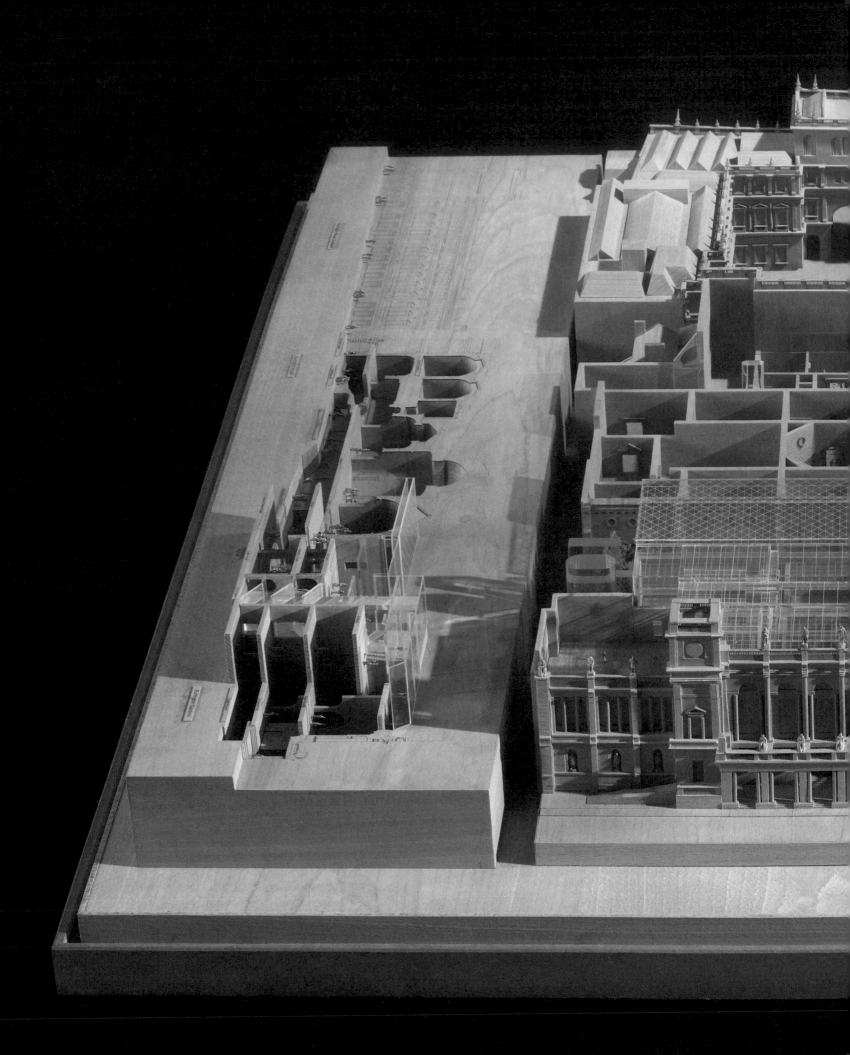

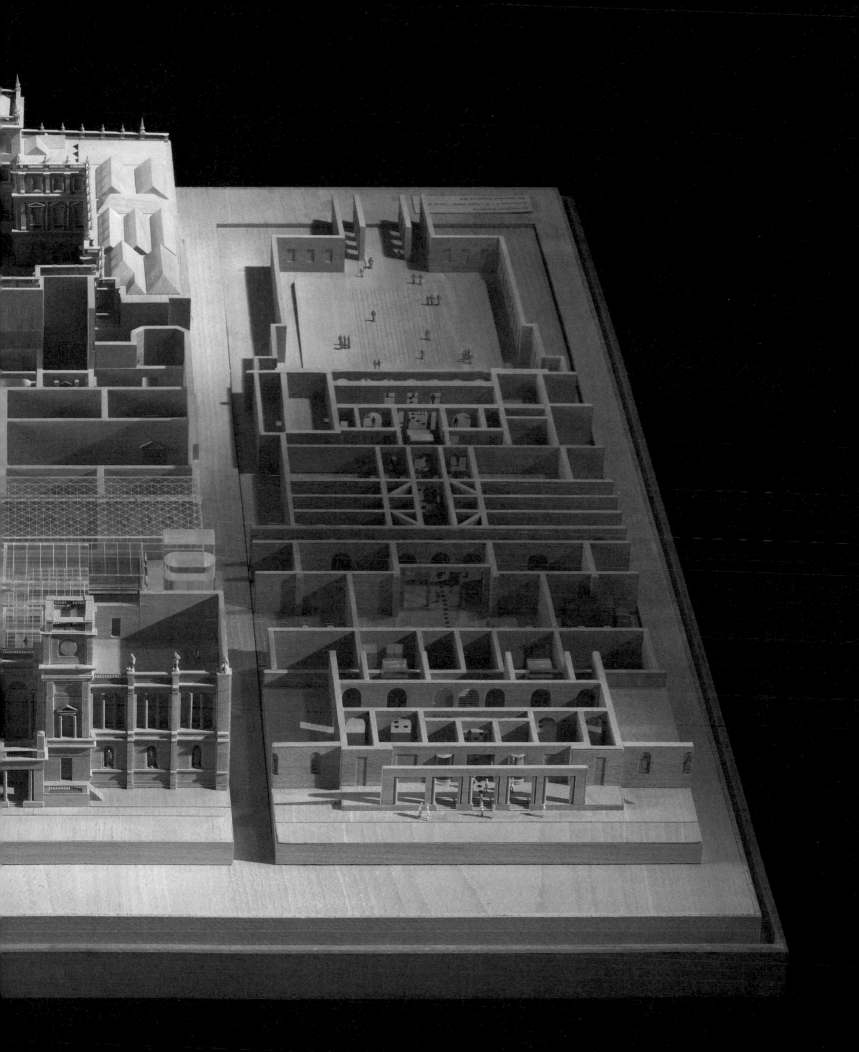

Sir Richard MacCormac RA

b. 1938

RA 24 May 1993

Ruskin Library, Lancaster University:
ground-floor plan, first-floor plan
and model, 1996
Ground- and first-floor plans: prints with
black ink with added colour crayon,
570 × 844 mm each

Model: wood, acrylic and other plastics
and electrical parts, 407 × 545 × 894 mm
(case), made by Thorp Modelmakers
(London)

The architecture of Sir Richard MacCormac mediates between history, the modern movement and contemporary demands. The claims of a brave new world made by the modern movement never fully convinced Richard MacCormac when he encountered them as an architecture student at Cambridge University and London's Bartlett School during the late 1950s and early 1960s. Driven by such factors as technology and engineering, modernism had arisen in response to the traditional forms based upon the history of period styles, breaking with this past and developing its own language, supposedly stripped of the rhetoric of tradition, ornament and symbolism. MacCormac, in response, gravitated towards architectural design that balanced the past with the present. When he became leading partner in MacCormac Jamieson Prichard from 1972 – today called MJP Architects – MacCormac began to pursue a course in architecture that, he says, speaks of the past as 'collective memory' that incorporates 'present experience' (Brawne, p. 40).

Many of MJP's major projects have been in town planning and for universities, areas of design that focus upon developing new architectural solutions in conjunction with listed historic buildings. In Coventry, a city first war-ravaged then scourged by post-war rebuilding, MacCormac created an extensive regeneration scheme that included using buildings both old and new to articulate public spaces, and commissioning works of art from contemporary artists.

It would seem that the more historic influences and pressures are put upon a project, the more balanced MacCormac's architectural solutions become. The colleges of Oxford and

Cambridge have afforded him ample opportunities to find sensitive solutions to historic contexts. The beautiful, contemporary space of Fitzwilliam College Chapel (1991), for example, emerged out of its combined setting of a Georgian house and garden and modern buildings by Sir Denys Lasdun RA, with references to Sir John Soane's architecture – a true mix of past and near-present enfolded into the present.

The strongest discourse that Richard MacCormac has had with history and architectural continuity is his Ruskin Library for the University of Lancaster. MacCormac was deeply drawn to this project to house the Whitehouse Collection of archives and collections of John Ruskin, one of the most influential polemicists on art and architecture of the nineteenth century. The design became, MacCormac says, 'a struggle to see if it was possible to fulfil historical architecture without resorting to pastiche' (interview with the author), a situation that John Ruskin himself was unable to avoid as he watched the gothic revival that he had so championed descend into suburban Victorian sprawl.

MacCormac shows his Ruskinian sensibilities woven into the abstraction of modernism in the set of drawings and an architectural model for the Ruskin Library that he submitted as his Diploma Work. He speaks of the building metaphorically as being like a 'keep', a fortified medieval tower, while also literally being a place to *keep* Ruskin's heritage. The elliptical walls, constructed of stone with horizontal stripes, are windowless. Glazing is reserved for the sliced gap between the side walls. In the ground plan, the entrance is seen crossing a dry moat, with the building cast as a stronghold, a Venetian island in its lagoon, a reference to Ruskin's *The Stones of Venice* (1853), a work that influenced late nineteenth-century art and architecture. Within the building, the archives are sealed in a 'treasury', which is shown coloured in red crayon in the drawings to simulate the polished plasterwork in 'Venetian red'. MacCormac has enshrined the memory of Ruskin in the great Victorian's beloved Venice in a truly modern way.

Richard MacCormac, 'Ruskin Library, Lancaster University', in Michael Brawne (ed.), *The Architecture of Information: British Pavilion, Venice Biennale 1996*, London, 1996, pp. 38–46

Richard MacCormac, 'Architecture, Art and Accountability', in Nicholas Ray, *Architecture and Its Architectural Dilemmas*, London, 2005, pp. 49–54

Richard MacCormac, *Building Ideas – MJP Architects: Essays and Speculations by Richard MacCormac*, London, 2010

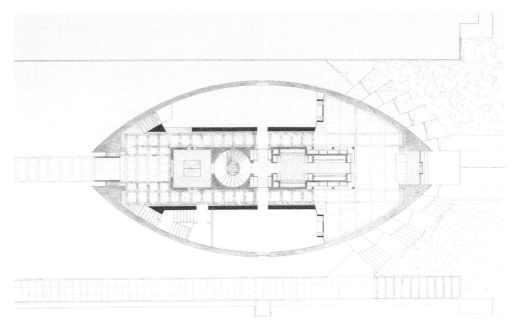

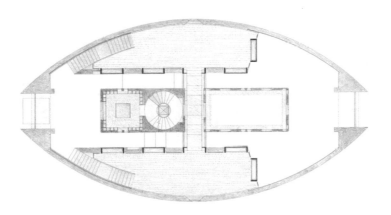

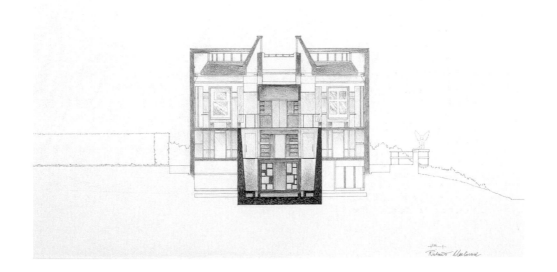

Sir Nicholas Grimshaw PRA
b. 1939
RA 23 May 1994

Waterloo International Railway Terminal, London: plan at platform level, west elevation and details, 1 June 1997 (detail opposite, full drawing overleaf) Print with black ink with added blue and grey coloured pencil, 749 × 1756 mm

Sir Nicholas Grimshaw's buildings are characterised by industrially inspired design, with beautifully engineered components to create large, open-span spaces cloaked in metal and glass. His architecture is often described as 'high tech'. He prefers the term 'engineering-based'.

Grimshaw began his building experiments by using readily available cladding systems attached to or suspended from bespoke fixings. The lightweight insulated enclosure of his Oxford Ice Rink (completed in 1984), for example, was suspended on guide wires from a pair of masts. From such a methodology Grimshaw developed sophisticated structures based upon the elegant precision and visibility of materials and technological elements. The columns of his Financial Times Print Works on the edge of London's Docklands not only support the roof beams but also the massive glazed wall. And his British Pavilion was the hit of Expo '92 at Seville as everyone rushed out of the sun-baked heat into a space cooled by a whole wall of falling water and by billowing façades of steel masts with fabric sails based on yacht technology.

Grimshaw's interest in building ecology, accompanied by a fascination with the geodesic domes of Buckminster Fuller, the visionary American architect who paid an admiring visit to Grimshaw's first built project, came together in the Eden Project in Cornwall. To create the world's largest plant enclosure, Grimshaw designed eight interlinking 'biomes', spheres with skeletons of steel tubes layered with cushioned synthetic material shaped with channels for collecting rainwater for the plants. Since its first stage of opening in 2000, the Eden Project has become one of Britain's top-ranking attractions.

As a designer at the cutting edge of building technology, it seems appropriate that Sir Nicholas Grimshaw submitted a computer-aided drawing as his Diploma Work. Dating from 1997, the work is a record drawing of his completed international terminal building at Waterloo Station, opened, as is noted on the sheet, by Her Majesty The Queen in May 1993. The drawing was created and printed in his office, and Grimshaw added shades of blue and grey crayon, a nice touch in the hand of an architect known for his sketches, who makes, as the artist Stephen Farthing RA has observed, 'a steady flow of drawings that relate directly to a controlled design process' (*Sketchbooks*, p. 9).

Grimshaw's terminus along the western edge of Waterloo Station was an instant success with travellers using the high-speed Eurostar passenger trains linking London with the continent via the newly constructed Channel Tunnel. The building's engineered construction, fine detailing and sinuous shape captured the public's love affair with the novelty of the international train service. Thus there was some sadness when the news emerged that continental services were to transfer from Waterloo to St Pancras Station in November 2007 to improve high-speed links and capacity.

'Although you couldn't build from this one drawing,' said Grimshaw in an interview with the author, 'you can understand the building from it.' The principal aspects stretch across the centre: the platform plan at the top, the waiting trains with their carriages in plan, complete with seating, bars and lavatories; the roof plan in the centre, with its snake-like body and showing the shed covering, one of the most spectacular parts of the project; and, below, the west elevation with arriving and departing passengers and vehicle drop-off points beneath. Around the sheet, to left and right, appear sections through the building and such all-important Grimshaw engineering details as, in the lower left, glazing details of the western façade, showing the anti-vibration cladding fixtures necessary because of train movement.

Rowan Moore (ed.), *Structure, Space and Skin: The Work of Nicholas Grimshaw & Partners*, with an introduction by Kenneth Powell, London, 1993, pp. 24–55

Peter Davey and Stephen Farthing RA, *The Sketchbooks of Nicholas Grimshaw*, London, 2009

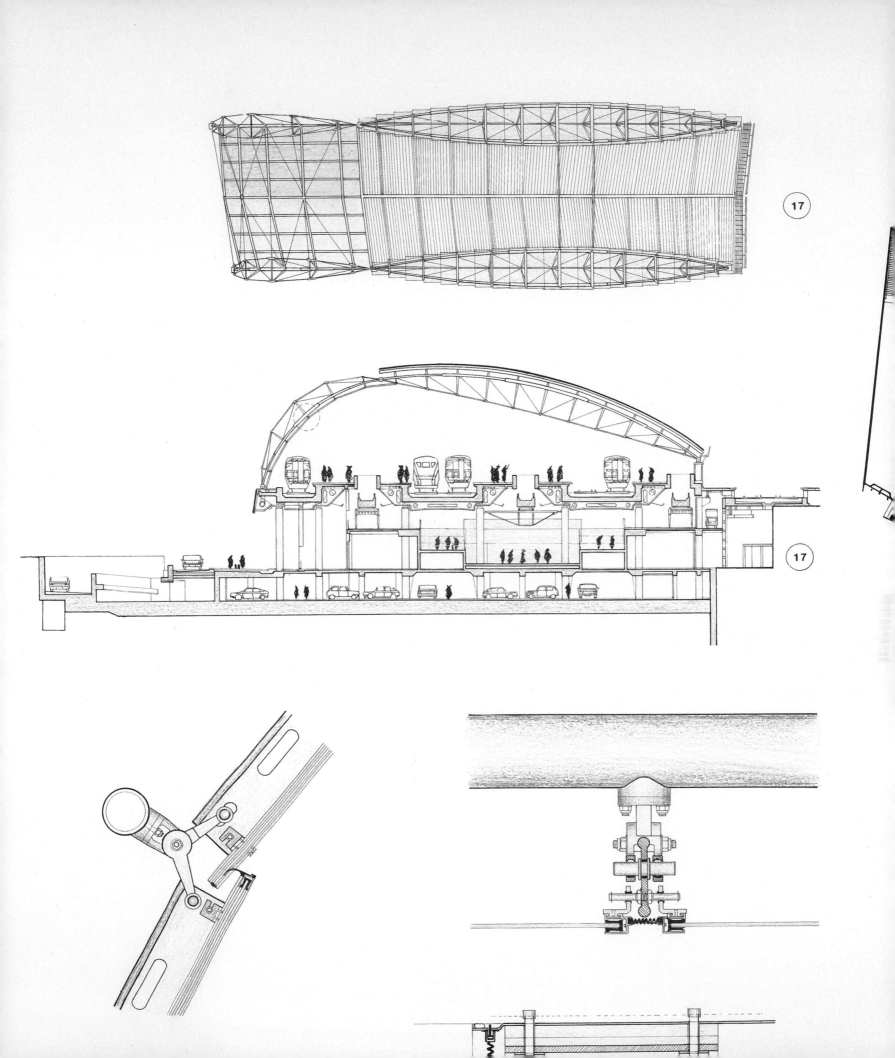

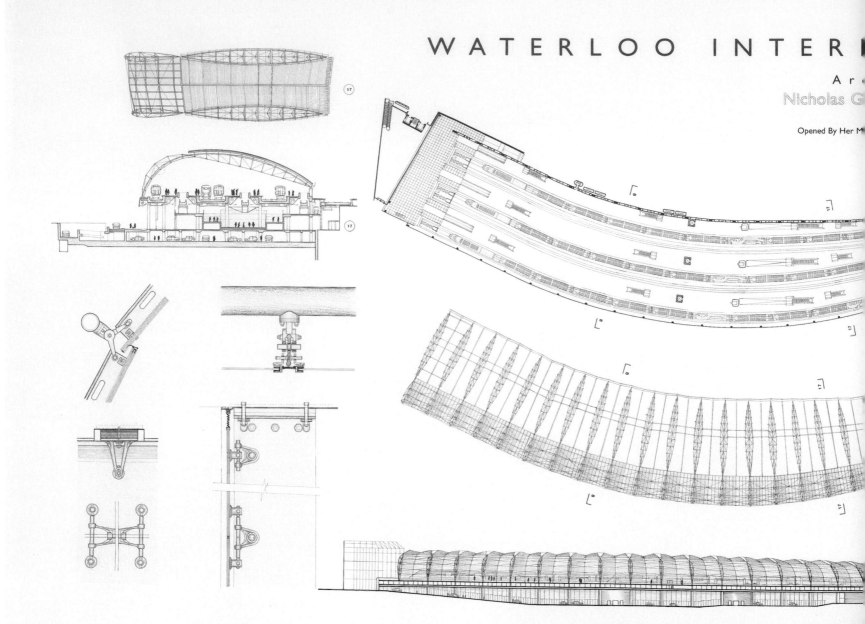

ATIONAL TERMINAL

tects

haw & Partners

een Elizabeth II - May 1993

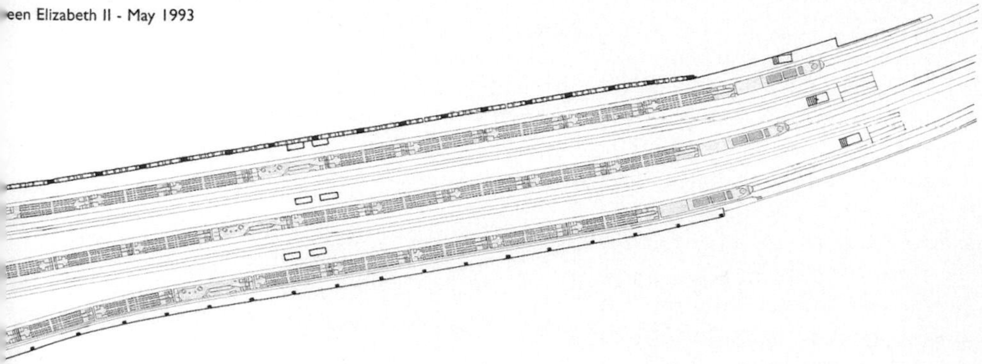

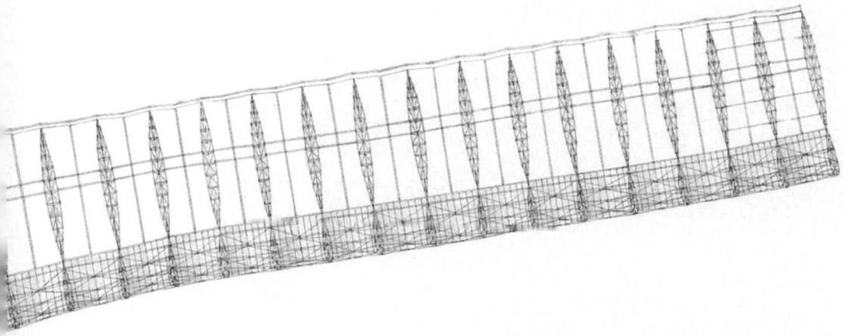

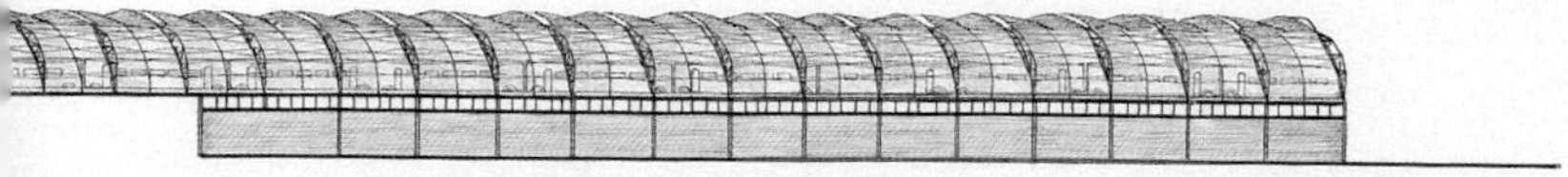

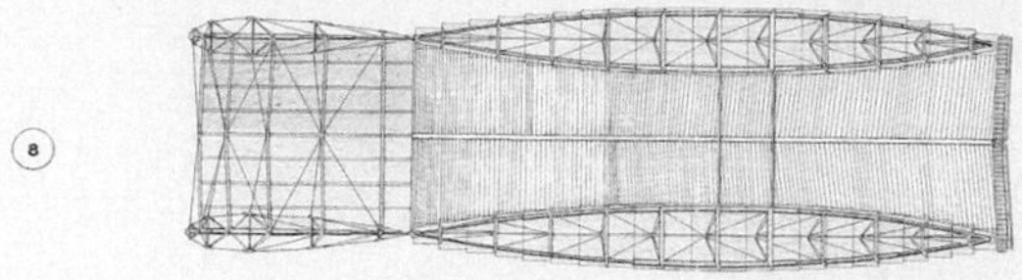

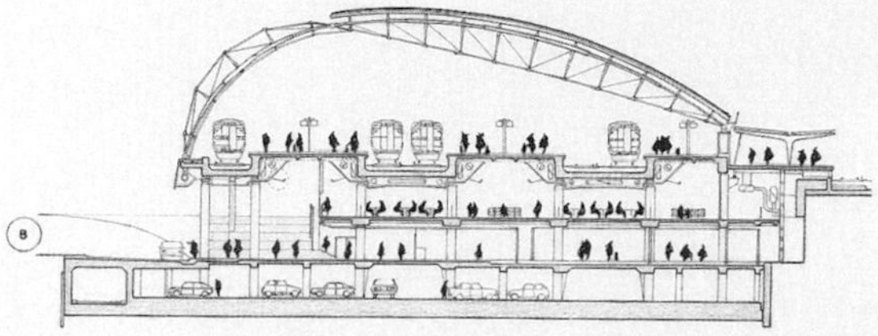

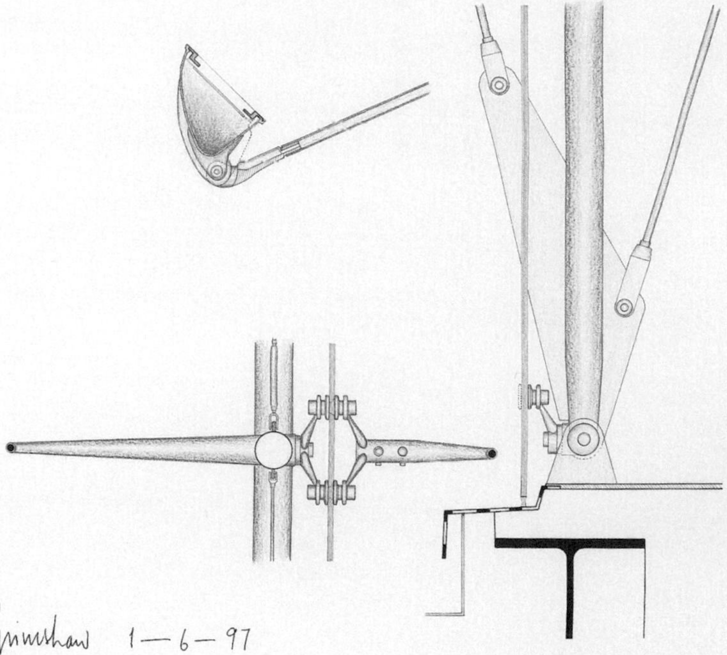

Nick Grimshaw 1—6—97

Michael Manser RA
b. 1929
RA 8 November 1994

Office extension building for Vokes Limited, Henley Park, Normandy, Surrey, c. 1983 Model made by Kondor Modelmakers (London): new building of mirrored perspex and polystyrene sheeting; old building of spray-painted timber; grass texture of cork granules, painted; trees of cork granules on twisted wire stems; cars and people of metal, painted; on timber base, dimensions 207 × 706 × 555 mm (case)

In 1984 Michael Manser, as President of the Royal Institute of British Architects, was seated beside Charles, Prince of Wales, at a ceremony at Hampton Court celebrating the 150th anniversary of the RIBA when the prince rose and made his famously controversial speech attacking modern architecture. As a consequence, a deeply embarrassed Manser found himself drawn into the most public controversy over the nature of architecture that had taken place in Britain since the Battle of Styles in the mid-nineteenth century, when the classical style had been pitted against the gothic revival. In the late twentieth century, the modern movement was pitted against a return to traditionalism, or more simply put, new versus old.

Manser took a strong line in the ensuing debate, evoking the ideals of William Morris that had formed the basis of the British conservation movement a hundred years earlier, seeing no necessity for a new building to be 'in keeping' or stylistically to imitate the old when the two found themselves neighbours. 'The old is always demeaned by imitation,' Manser argued, stating, 'conversely a new building, using new materials and stretching its techniques to their technical limits to serve new purposes, will always complement the old. That is how the old buildings were generally built. If a building is ever to achieve timelessness it first has to be of its own time' (AD Profile).

There can be no better illustration of Manser's own response to fusing the modern with the traditional than his Diploma Work: an architectural model of an unexecuted project for placing a long and elegant new office building alongside a venerable country mansion. In terms of building types, the work mingled Manser's two specialities: stylish glass and steel houses in the country and large-scale commercial buildings. In the early 1980s, Michael Manser received the commission to add a new building to Henley Park for extra office space. The client, Vokes Limited, was a company specialising in fuel and oil filtration. In the midst of the Second World War, Vokes had moved from London to this country house in Surrey, using it as their factory until the 1950s, when they built a separate factory building in the grounds and made the house their headquarters.

Manser's new-meets-old solution was a separate structure lightly attached to the northern elevation of the house by a small, enclosed bridge spanning a large reflective pool between the two buildings. The proposed new structure would have been of considerable size: 26,500 square feet. Placing the office building at an angle to the house and encasing it in mirror-glazing would have achieved a harmony, says Manser, because 'wherever you were, it was doing a disappearing act' (interview with the author).

Manser has had a long association with incorporating modern buildings into rural settings, having first made his reputation in the early 1960s with a series of elegant, glass-walled houses that sat lightly in their landscaping. As in the Vokes design, Manser used glass as a transitional skin between architecture and nature. Similarly, his 1990 design for the Hilton Hotel alongside Heathrow's Terminal 4, with its vast, six-storey glass wall, was extolled by the novelist J. G. Ballard as the airport's 'centrepiece and most inspiring in England … Its vast atrium resembles a planetarium in the way that it salutes the skies above its roof.'

In 2001 the prestigious Manser Medal was established in Manser's honour, an annual award for the best one-off house or major extension designed by an architect in the United Kingdom.

Michael Manser, 'The Prince and the Architects', AD Profile 79: Prince Charles and the Architectural Debate, London, 1989, pp. 17–19

J. G. Ballard, 'Airports', The Observer, 14 September 1997

The Orangery, Prague Castle, Czech
Republic, 1998

Six colour photographic transparencies
mounted on a lightbox (sheet glass,
stainless steel, medium-density fibreboard
and electrical parts), 695 × 944 × 75 mm
Photographs by Richard Bryant

In 1997, 229 years after the foundation of the Royal Academy, Eva Jiricna was the first female architect to be elected an Academician. For her Diploma Work she chose to create a lightbox with six photographic transparencies showing various views of the Orangery she had designed for Prague Castle. As an object, it cleverly combines representations of the conservatory with the distinctive materials (glass and stainless steel) and structural elements of her designs that are used to such fine effect in the commission. Moreover, the Czech connection alludes to Eva Jiricna's personal and architectural origins.

Jiricna was born in Zlín, the Czech city famous for its early modern architecture centred on the futuristic ideals of the shoe-manufacturing company Bata. Having trained at the University of Prague and the Prague Academy of Fine Arts, Jiricna suddenly found herself a refugee in Britain when, during her short-stay work placement in 1968, the Soviets invaded her home country. Befriended by such architects as the Hungarian-born Ernö Goldfinger RA, she spent more than a decade as project architect on the large Brighton Marina scheme for the Louis de Soissons Partnership. Her move to work with Richard Rogers RA, carrying out interiors for Lloyd's of London, and then collaborating with Jan Kaplicky and his Future Systems on the influential Way In store at Harrods, drew her into the centre of the new high tech movement.

In 1982 Jiricna established her own private practice and quickly gained a reputation as the mistress of structural glass and stainless-steel fixings. Her staircases – light, transparent and dazzling – became a signature feature in the many shop interiors she designed, especially for Joseph Ettedgui and his Joseph boutiques. From trendy nightclubs, such as Legends and Browns, to bespoke apartments, Jiricna's engineered interiors, beautifully detailed and shimmering with elegance, were all the vogue.

Larger-scale projects came in the 1990s with projects such as the glass-encased bus station at Canada Water as part of the Jubilee Line Underground extension and a new library at Leicester's De Montfort University. And although she continues to create jewel-like interiors elsewhere – quite literally in the case of her 2008 Jewellery Gallery at the Victoria and Albert Museum – it was Eva Jiricna's return to the Czech Republic following the Velvet Revolution in 1989 that presented the most significant new opportunities for this prodigal daughter. To the modernism of her hometown she has added a library building at the Tomas Bata University. And in keeping with high fashion, her Hotel Josef is Prague's most stylish boutique hotel.

Eva Jiricna's Diploma Work is a poignant reminder of her architectural homecoming. The project was instigated by the respected first President of the Czech Republic (and last President of Czechoslovakia), the poet Václav Havel. Suffering from lung problems due to chain smoking, Havel often sat in the decrepit old conservatory that supplied plants for Prague Castle, the humid atmosphere easing his breathing while he was writing speeches. Jiricna made this modern replacement both for the plants and for the president.

Jiricna's new Orangery resides in the historic hillside setting of the castle, dominated by the spires of St Vitus Cathedral. A 100-metre long conservatory, the Orangery's semicircular shell is designed in signature Jiricna materials: suspended laminated glass panels over a diagonal mesh of metal tubes and cross-frames. 'You can't call it high tech,' teases the architect when speaking of her building in an interview with the author, 'as we are using low-tech methods – everything is handmade. It's more about trying to minimise materials with finishes that are honest.'

The presentation method of her Diploma Work is characteristic of Eva Jiricna. Almost every year since she began exhibiting at the Royal Academy, she has shown her projects on the lightboxes that she first used in her revelatory début exhibition in 1987 at the Architectural Association: 'Eva Jiricna Designs'.

Martin Pawley, *Eva
Jiricna: Design in Exile*,
London, 1990

José Manser, *The
Joseph Shops, London,
1979–1988: Eva Jiricna*,
London, 1991

Eva Jiricna, *Staircases*,
London, 2001

Dennis Crompton (ed.),
with Annie Bridges and
Zuzanna Lipinska, *In/
Exterior: The Works of
Eva Jiricna*, Prague,
2005, pp. 145–51

Ian Ritchie RA
b. 1947
RA 10 December 1998

Cultural Greenhouse Terrasson, 2001
Etching, 130 × 370 mm
Crystal Palace Concert Platform, 2001
Etching, 130 × 370 mm

Dreaming of a Project, 2009
Etching, 298 × 316 mm
Alba di Milano, April 2000
Etching, 260 × 260 mm

As with the Book of Genesis, so too with the architect Ian Ritchie: in the beginning is the word. Whereas most architects find inspiration for their initial designs by sketching on paper, or by working on a computer, even perhaps by modelling in card or clay, Ritchie uses words: 'Writing is essentially an act of discovery,' he says, 'and through it one discovers oneself a little more as well as finding potential answers to the design challenges at hand' (unpublished MS, 2008). And rather than long-winded explanatory texts, Ritchie plays with writing short and stimulating aphorisms and, also with greater concentration, poetry, connecting dreams and thoughts as he explores how to communicate and construct.

Next, having avoided the ubiquitous succession of architectural sketches at this early stage of design, so as to avoid a mental image becoming too quickly embedded in the collective consciousness, Ritchie will suddenly make a small graphite or brush mark in his notebook to capture the essential thoughts from his written investigations. He then takes up a brush and sugar lift or a soft-ground block to draw directly onto the copper plate, or draws through paper onto a prepared soft-ground plate, etches, and finally makes a printed proof. So emerges an initial visual impression, sometimes, but not always, an idea of the form of the project.

Since his election as a Royal Academician in 1998, Ritchie has chosen to submit an ongoing selection of these impressionistic prints with their accompanying poetic texts. Illustrated here are four representative prints, each relating to a project. Three are like calligraphic brush strokes. The white streak on the dark background is *Alba di Milano* – the Dawn in Milan – a sculpture

of light. Winner of an international competition, this work was erected in front of Milan's central train station in 2000 (and abruptly removed in 2002): a thirty-metre high and ten-metre wide floating fabric made from optic fibres and stainless-steel wire that created flowing, scintillating colour. The stroke in the print is the sloping light seen from the side. For Ritchie, the image *Alba di Milano* raised as many questions as it answered. Is the line falling to earth? Is it still rising from the earth? Is it searching for an equilibrium between levitas and gravitas? Hot or cold? Previously Ritchie had explored luminous reflections with his Monument of Light, also known as the Spire of Dublin, a stainless-steel pointed spire completed in 2003 and rising 120 metres over the heart of the Irish capital.

The long drawing *Crystal Palace Concert Platform* is also the gestation of a project created through a print showing a section through the site's topography, its scale and balance. At the far right of the image is the outdoor stage, its roof precariously inclined to project sound to the performers and across Paxton's landscape bowl within Crystal Palace Park in south London. As built, the canopy structure was constructed of Corten steel, which has rusted to a mottled red-gold patina like autumn leaves. The venue sits in a small lake, for beauty and resonance.

The calligraphic line and swirl of the other long drawing, *Cultural Greenhouse, Terrasson*, captures the idea of building as landscape – a curved outer stone wall and the virtual lake of glass of a garden building in the Dordogne as it nestles into the flat side of a hill.

The random interconnected pattern in *Dreaming of a Project* represents simulations of stimulations of neurons and dendrite brain cells, the prelude to Ritchie's design for the Sainsbury

Wellcome Centre for Neural Circuits and Behaviour, University College, London.

'Now I am designing with the mind in mind,' the architect says in his accompanying poem.

'Design and Innovation Culture', lecture delivered in Moscow, 8 April 2005, www. ianritchiearchitects. co.uk

Ian Ritchie, *Lines*, London, 2010

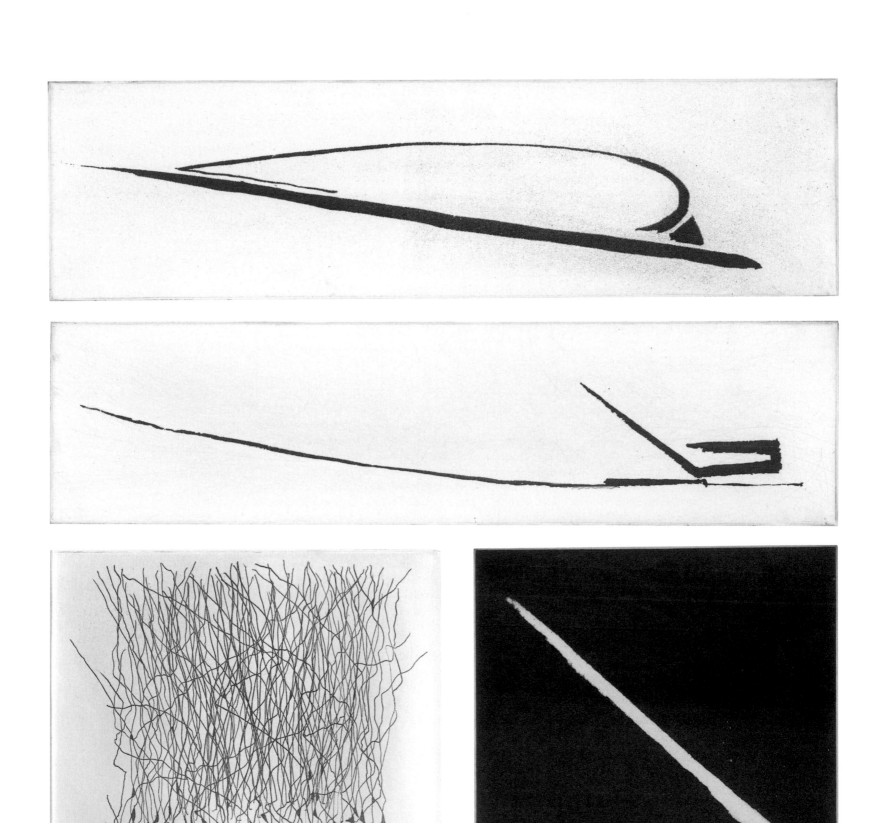

Will Alsop RA
b. 1947
RA 25 May 2000

Fog Is an Urban Experience, c. 2007
Acrylic over pencil on two layers of wove
paper with attached collage pieces,
1694 × 1386 mm

Just as Will Alsop pushes back boundaries in architecture, so too his Diploma Work has ventured into areas hitherto unexplored in architectural presentation in the Royal Academy's collections. Fluorescent and iridescent colours are drawn and painted on a large sheet of paper of shredded cuts folded back off the surface. Collaged strips of laid and folded paper are stuck on with studied abandon. Elongated forms cluster, some of them almost looking like the sculptural shapes of Alsop's own buildings. It is a drawing that blurs the frontiers between painting, sculpture and architecture, the three arts that Alsop practises and teaches. After all, as he says with a shrug of the shoulders, 'It's all out of one soup' (interview with author).

Fog Is an Urban Experience relates to a project from 2007 that Alsop had been working on in Toronto, Canada, for redeveloping – 'without destroying', he adds – the lively Kensington Market district of the city. The drawing is one of a series that he made exploring urbanism, architecture and people. 'I paint to learn, to exercise my brain and my imagination,' he wrote when exhibiting his drawings (Olga Korper Gallery, Toronto, 8 June – 28 July 2007). 'Cultural Fog is my musing on the possibilities for Kensington Market and the real nature of community.'

But why fog? Because it can obscure, hide and add complexity. And that, Alsop contends, is an experience that most people enjoy. Alsop likes to confront the modern obsession with perfection, non-committal buildings that are too straightforward, too precise and crisp in their design and detail. Real life is messy, diverse and should be enjoyed. 'The clarity of reading a city', he said about the Kensington Market project in a lecture, is 'full out with many urban designers; they try to make things clear when I think

things should become unclear. I think that's absolutely vital.'

At the Royal Academy, Will Alsop once had a group of teenage students paint a sheet of paper the size of a small wall by lunchtime so that they could then all go for a good lunch. Daunted at first, but encouraged by Alsop, the students did just that, to their great delight. That is the role of an architect, says Alsop: to encourage people to have belief in themselves and enjoy life.

When he was in his teens in the 1960s, Alsop worked for a local architect in his native Northampton while finishing his schooling. For a time he turned to studying art, and then took up architectural training at the Architectural Association. In 1971, while still a student, he came second out of the 500 entrants in the competition for the Centre Georges Pompidou in Paris. Setting out in practice, he spent a brief time with Maxwell Fry RA and Jane Drew before a very important four years with Cedric Price, the visionary architect who built little but whose projects were influential not only on Alsop but on generations of designers seeking fun and flexibility in building. One of Alsop's first major buildings struck just such a light-hearted chord: modelled on his disposable cigarette lighter, the temporary visitors' centre for Cardiff Bay proved so popular that it became permanent.

For a time in the 1990s much of his work was in Germany, where he worked with his then partner Jan Störmer, creating extraordinary forms, most notably in their Hamburg Ferry Terminal and then with a commission for the Hôtel du Département des Bouches du Rhône in Marseilles, a whale-shaped building, deep blue in colour. Alsop finally and triumphantly broke through the conservatism of British clients and

planners with his first major building in London: Peckham Library, completed in 1999, brought a renewed joy and community belief to a struggling urban area and won him the RIBA Stirling Prize for best building of the year.

Like his Diploma Work drawing, Will Alsop's many buildings on the international stage are generally colourful, patterned and of unusual composition. In Toronto, just before he received the Kensington Market commission, Alsop had built the Sharp Centre for Design at Ontario College of Art and Design, a building that the city heartily embraced for its cheerful countenance and challenge to convention. Affectionately nicknamed 'The Tabletop', its flat white form, covered in a surface pattern of random black squares, perches on a dozen angled legs, high above its neighbours.

Alsop's Diploma Work also marks another new departure: in the very upper left corner of the drawing is the red crescent moon of a stain from a wine glass.

Kenneth Powell, *Will Alsop: Book 1*, London, 2001

Kenneth Powell, *Will Alsop 1990–2000: Book 2*, London, 2002

'Street Creatures', lecture by Will Alsop at the Canadian Centre of Architecture, Montreal, 2 October 2008, www. cca.qc.ca

Tom Porter, *Will Alsop – The Noise*, New York and London, 2011

Gordon Benson RA
b. 1944
RA 25 May 2000

Museum of Scotland, Chambers Street,
Edinburgh, 1998: plan of first floor,
1536 × 1434 mm; longitudinal section
through Enlightenment Gallery,
994 × 1435 mm

Printed copy of original drawings
with black ink, to scale, with added
coloured pen

In the age of the computer-generated architectural drawing, Gordon Benson maintains the tradition of drawing his projects by hand. Having been chosen in the 1991 competition to build the Museum of Scotland – from an overwhelming 347 anonymous entries – the Glasgow-born Benson, his architectural partner Alan Forsyth and their small office team at Benson + Forsyth produced a staggering 27,000 drawings for the project over the next eight years. Many were drawn by hand before being translated into digital format for contractual purposes. For his Diploma Work, Benson presented two key drawings from the hand-drawn set in pristine copy form, as the originals had become so worn from constant use. Both sheets are of impressive size, having been drawn at 1:50.

Benson's museum building, which met with critical acclaim when it opened in 1998, is sited in Edinburgh's Old Town, where it is linked to the Royal Museum, a Victorian building of 1861 styled in a sombre Italian neo-renaissance style by Captain Francis Fowke, Royal Engineer. United, the old and the new buildings are known as the National Museum of Scotland, housing a collection of objects related to Scottish history and culture arranged in thematic galleries.

The plan is upside down, having been drawn the opposite way round with north correctly positioned at the top; but logically Benson has presented the drawing with the main façade on Chambers Street at the bottom of the sheet. The drawing illustrates the four principal parts of the building: the circular entrance block, the long angled reception area, the large block of main galleries and amenities, and, in the triangular space in between, a covered atrium. Benson has emphasised three strategic lines running horizontally across the plan in different colours. In green, the lower one between the reception area and main block denotes alignment of his building with the long gallery of cast iron and glass in the adjacent, older museum and, in the opposite direction, to the historic Greyfriars Church across the street. In blue, another line runs through the central axis of the galleries, through the middle of the four plans of the large exhibits that dominate the space. And, near the top, a red line is inscribed 'line of City "Flodden wall"', referring to the section of the early sixteenth-century wall with its main entrance gate to the city that originally stood on the site.

The spirit of an old wall anchors this museum of history to its historical site. Throughout the building – in its fabric, design and orientation – Benson + Forsyth resolutely make reference to Scotland and the city of Edinburgh. The very fabric of the main façades shimmers in a smooth honey-coloured sandstone hewn from the northeastern district of Moray, which harmonises with Scotland's stone-built capital. The cylindrical entrance tower, set apart, forms a bastion modelled on an ancient Scottish broch, an Iron Age stone tower with hollow, double skinned-walls. The rounded end of the gallery block, which contains the principal staircase, clearly seen in the plan, is a direct reference to the famous Half Moon battery that juts out from Edinburgh Castle. The castle itself is framed throughout the museum from many angles, one of numerous panoramas and pinpoint glimpses of city and country landmarks viewed through the museum's broad windows and tall, narrow slot arrowslits (in yet another historic allusion) and from rooftop terraces.

In fact, although every opening is calculated for its views, the natural light that the windows and an abundance of skylights bring in is used strategically to illuminate and set up reflections in the large gallery spaces and to penetrate into the deepest corners of the building. The architect Sir Colin St John Wilson RA commented upon this achievement: 'What is technically admirable … is that, in a large volume of space, both natural light and artificial light meld together as one – even the areas limited to levels of 50 lux', the museum standard for sensitive objects, and they 'somehow manage to convey the impression of no constraint. That is no mean feat!' (*Museum of Scotland*, p. 5).

The sectional drawing shows the five levels of the galleries. The exhibits are drawn in very fine detail, with a Newcomen atmospheric steam engine rising most prominently in the centre.

Gordon Benson's use of meticulous hand drawings extended beyond the Museum of Scotland into Benson + Forsyth's next major commission, the Millennium Wing of the National Gallery of Ireland in Dublin, which opened in 2002. Benson observes that he 'has always, and continues to draw the building, and all visible components – internal and external – by hand, thereby ensuring seamless continuity, conscious and unconscious between thought, imagination and product' (correspondence with the author).

Museum of Scotland,
London, 1999

Architects' Journal,
209, 25 February 1999,
pp. 26–35

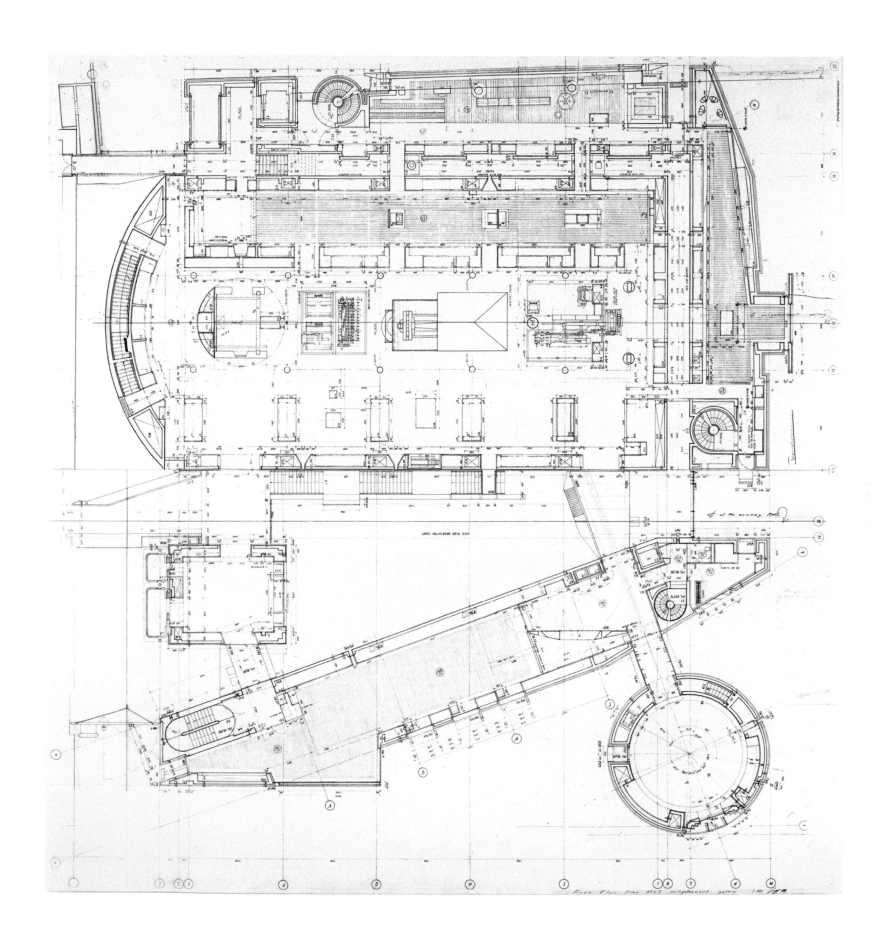

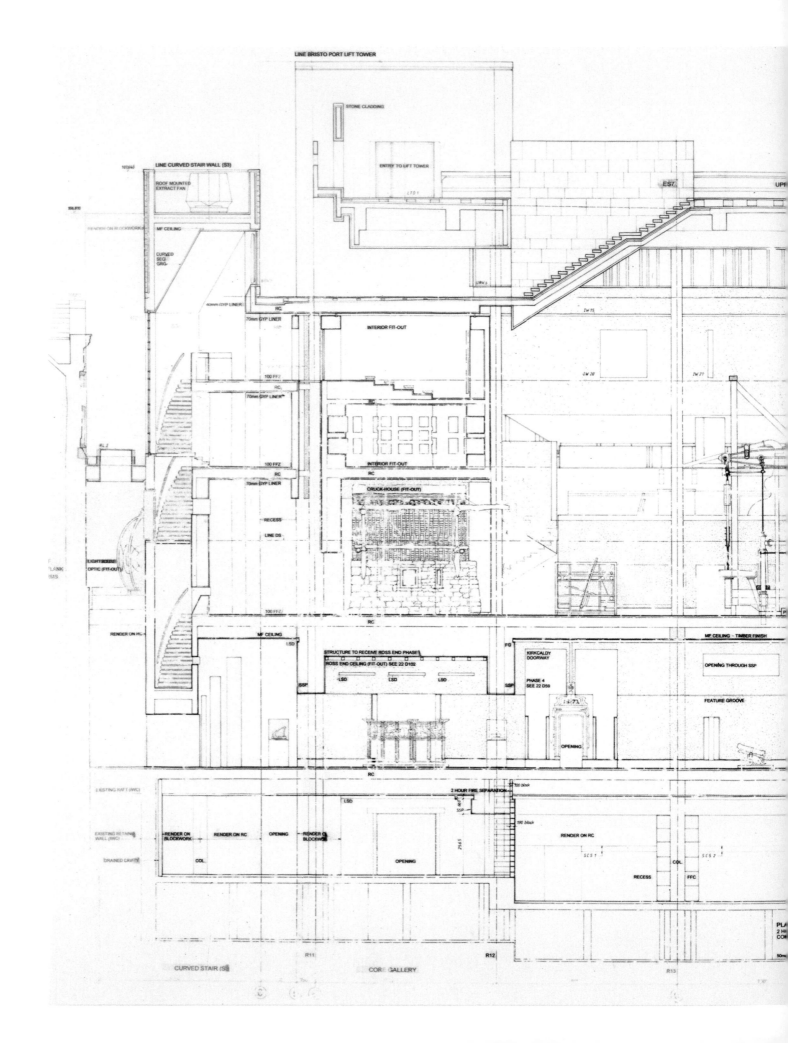

LINE BRISTO PORT LIFT TOWER

STONE CLADDING

ENTRY TO LIFT TOWER

LINE CURVED STAIR WALL (S3)

ROOF MOUNTED
EXTRACT FAN

MF CEILING

CURVED
SEG
GRG

RENDER ON BLOCKWORK

40mm GYP LINER

70mm GYP LINER

INTERIOR FIT-OUT

100 FFZ

RC

70mm GYP LINER

100 FFZ

RC

70mm GYP LINER

INTERIOR FIT-OUT

RC

CRUCK-HOUSE (FIT-OUT)

RECESS

LINE DS

LIGHT
OPTIC (FIT-OUT)

PLANK

100 FFZ

RC

RENDER ON RC

MF CEILING

LSD

STRUCTURE TO RECEIVE ROSS END PHASE
ROSS END CEILING (FIT-OUT) SEE 22 D102

LSD   LSD   LSD

SSP

MF CEILING - TIMBER FINISH

FG

KIRKCALDY
DOORWAY

OPENING THROUGH SSP

PHASE 4
SEE 22 D59

SSP

FEATURE GROOVE

OPENING

RC

RC

EXISTING RAFT (IWC)

LSD

2 HOUR FIRE SEPARATION   700 block

SSP   190 block

EXISTING RETAINING
WALL (IWC)

RENDER ON
BLOCKWORK

RENDER ON RC

OPENING

RENDER ON
BLOCKWORK

RENDER ON RC

DRAINED CAVITY

COL

OPENING

2765

SCS 1   SCS 2

COL

RECESS   FFC

R11   CURVED STAIR (S3)   CORE GALLERY   R12   R13

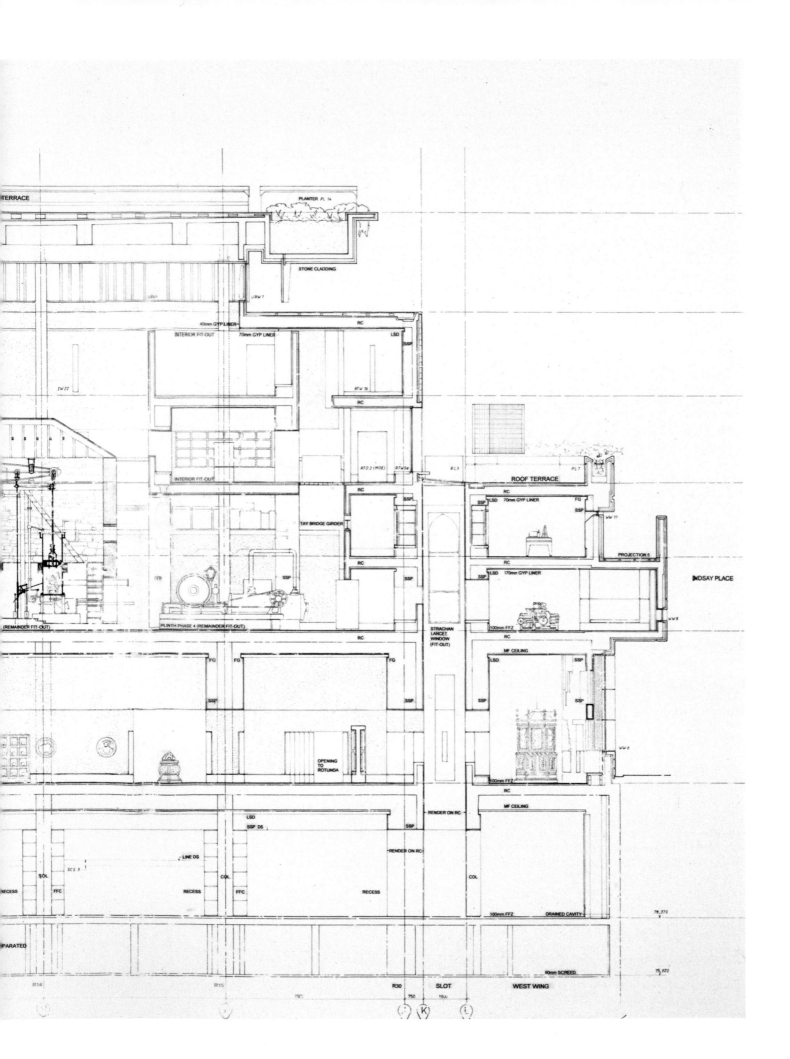

TERRACE

PLANTER *PL 14*

STONE CLADDING

JRW 1

40mm GYP LINER

INTERIOR FIT-OUT

70mm GYP LINER

RC

LSD

SSP

IW 22

RTW 38

RC

INTERIOR FIT-OUT

ROOF TERRACE

RC

LSD

70mm GYP LINER

FG

SSP

SSP

WW 11

RTD 2 (MOE)   RTW9a   RL3

TAY BRIDGE GIRDER

RC

RC

SSP

SSP

PROJECTION 5

LSD

LINDSAY PLACE

RC

LSD

170mm GYP LINER

SSP

SSP

WW 6

RC

SSP

PLINTH PHASE 4 (REMAINDER FIT-OUT)

(REMAINDER FIT-OUT)

STRACHAN LANCET WINDOW (FIT-OUT)

100mm FFZ

RC

RC

MF CEILING

FG

FG

FG

LSD

SSP

SSP

SSP

SSP

SSP

OPENING TO ROTUNDA

WW 5

100mm FFZ

RC

MF CEILING

LSD

RENDER ON RC

SSP

SSP DS

RENDER ON RC

LINE DS

SOL

SCS 3

COL

COL

RECESS

FFC

RECESS

FFC

RECESS

100mm FFZ

DRAINED CAVITY

79 370

PARATED

50mm SCREED

75 920

R14   R15   R30   SLOT   WEST WING

750   750   180

K

Piers Gough RA
b. 1946
RA 5 December 2001

Bling Bling Building, Hanover Street and
School Lane, Liverpool, June 2009
Pencil, 560 × 760 mm

Piers Gough says he is an architect who likes to 'cheer up ordinary locations. My buildings are celebratory.' He even gives cheery names to his buildings, such as Love Bites in Brighton and Bling Bling, one of the buildings represented by this architectural drawing that Gough drew and submitted as part of a trio for his Diploma Work. Completed in 2006, in the regenerated Paradise Street area of Liverpool, the building looks like a brash piece of jewellery, bling-bling. Large sculpted bronze forms hanging off and traversing the shiny black glass walls resemble, he remarked in an interview with the author, a boxed 'necklace' worn with a 'big ring' jutting out over the street. Down around the entrance, the surround imitates 'a blonde woman's haircut' in playful caricature of the building's main tenant, the flamboyant hairdresser Herbert Howe of Herbert of Liverpool.

But Gough's building is obviously more than just a fashion accessory. Rightly, the architect says that he is 'suspicious of fashion'. The Bling Bling Building, he points out, enjoys wearing accessories just as much as do its older neighbours, commercial blocks from around 1900 that drip with 'Edwardian bling in their big bags of cornices and window surrounds'.

Piers Gough seems to bring a *joie de vivre* to the sometimes hard urbanity of life. A founder member of the architectural practice CZWG, with partners Nicholas Campbell, Roger Zogolovitch and Rex Wilkinson, Gough has created many striking residential buildings in East London's Docklands development. Irregular in shape and often not shy of colour, Gough's buildings add great visual entertainment to this post-industrial landscape. Water passengers on the Thames, circling the Isle of Dogs, cruise past Cascades, one of Gough's riverside apartment buildings:

a great twenty-storey tumbling form, with a backdrop of the sleek glass towers of Canary Wharf in the near distance.

Style in architecture has a history of being very serious, from the classical orders to today's sleekly engineered skyscrapers. But Gough is of a movement in architecture that believes in radical fun. He first saw this in action when studying at the Architectural Association, London, in the 1960s when he encountered his teacher Peter Cook RA, member of Archigram, a recently formed group that brought all the fun of Pop Art to visionary architecture (see pp. 228–29). In private practice, one of Gough's first major jobs was to build a brick house near London's Smithfield Market to match the bubbly, outspoken personality of his former classmate at the AA, the journalist and broadcaster Janet Street-Porter. He made her a modern witch's hut, spun with quirkily shaped windows, a scenic balcony fit for Juliet, and terrifying great sheets of grid-metal as if to ward off evil spirits.

Gough was the appropriate architect to design hugely successful exhibitions about two architect-Academicians: Sir Edwin Lutyens PRA and Sir John Soane RA. Both architects, like Gough, knew a thing or two about adding delightful little twists of novelty to their designs.

Gough recognises that he is the last of a generation of architects trained in design through hand drawing – 'a privilege', he says. Around him in the CZWG office, the younger generation have been raised using computers in 'non-conversational engagement'. He understands, but feels that so many of them are missing out on the enjoyment of the 'physical presence' that a drawing gives. But then, even today Gough only finds time to make presentation drawings when he is obliged, as with his Diploma Work. The pencil

drawing of the Bling Bling Building, he remarks, is 'dark', a move away from his earlier 'sweeter dry style'. Indeed, there is a dark humour about this representation that captures the architecture of 'polite swaggering vulgarity' that Gough believes is appropriate for this site in this city.

English Extremists: The Architecture of Campbell Zogolovitch Wilkinson Gough, with essays by Deyan Sudjic, Peter Cook and Jonathan Meades, London, 1988

Max Thompson, 'CZWG Bedazzles in Liverpool', *Architects' Journal*, 226, 5 August 2007, pp. 14–15

CZWG, London, n.d. (c. 2009)

Sir Peter Cook RA
b. 1936
RA 17 March 2003

Medina Circle Towers, Tel Aviv, Israel:
elevation, 1997
Print with added coloured washes and
red plastic film, 1422 × 522 mm

Peter Cook is a member of the Archigram Group that was formed in the early 1960s to create architectural designs based on technological considerations infused with all the fun of the Pop Art movement. Members of Archigram were celebrated for their 'paper architecture' because so many of their exuberant drawings seemed unbuildable. They created a science-fiction world in which mankind lived, worked and enjoyed the freedom of moving about the planet in giant walking pods, or burrowed down into the earth. Yet within this visionary message, Archigram produced serious ideas about mechanised building production and design that enabled the next generation of architects to develop new forms of building, most notably in the emergence of high-tech architecture.

A working independence exists among the loose association of the group members even today, as their influence endures and inspires others. Peter Cook has become important as a teacher and spokesperson of the group's experiences. And he has begun to build. One of his most notable works, made in conjunction with Colin Fournier, has been the Kunsthaus in Graz, Austria, a contemporary art museum completed in 2003, so unusually shaped – like an inflated bag with bright blue skin that beats with studded light from fluorescent rings – that it is affectionately called the 'friendly alien'.

Peter Cook was elected in 2003, submitting as his Diploma Work this design for a block of flats. He undertook the project in the late 1990s with Christine Hawley, who had been a pupil of Cook's at the Architectural Association, London, and later a partner in his practice. The drawing is in the style of the Archigram Group: flamboyant, quirky, vibrant. The concept is reminiscent of one of the group's early schemes that was introduced by Cook in 1964, *Plug-In City*, which featured a megalopolitan city-structure, like a space station on earth, with a gigantic crane that moved mobile sections around for different facets of human living.

In 2008 Peter Cook published *Drawing: The Motive Force of Architecture*, a poetic, questioning and personal philosophy about architectural drawing by a master in the art. The book features drawings by Archigram colleagues and admired contemporaries as well as Cook's own work. His Diploma Work is illustrated as a presentation drawing for client and public, a 'propositional work'. Cook explains:

'... I could not have imagined making the project of the Medina Circle Tower in Tel Aviv (1997) without the extensive use of colour. It is not that the sky in Tel Aviv is red; rather that the warmth of the climate and the wish to articulate the profile ran together with a semi-conscious statement about the volatility and entrepreneurship of the locals. Moreover, the red colour establishes a palette that can incorporate shades of blue, purple and a kind of pink that serve to illustrate key constituents: windows, screens, sun blinds and shadowy interior forms.

'The basic position is of three towers to occupy the upmarket location of the Medina Circle in North Tel Aviv. It was originally designed with the co-operation of Oscar Niemeyer, whose intention was always that the big circle of shops and apartments contain some towers within it. So far this has not happened. My composition is of a housing tower (discretely in the rear, in pink), the vegetated racking of a parking tower and a primary tower made up of 10 different categories of entrepreneurial activity: offices, showrooms, hotels, consultancies etc. Each type with differing requirements and differing façade characteristics. Each articulated from the other and threaded together like a vertical kebab.

'There are some local incidents, deviations and appendages ... There is an emphasis on the glassy quality of much of the building, and the basic line drawing is mostly coloured in watercolour, which I always find to be both highly controllable and capable of reconsideration as one proceeds. It enables one to gauge the degree of contrast or the degree of "filming" over the preceding layer of colour.

'Such a drawing is therefore quite conventionalised, as befits a propositional work. It is in some ways slightly overstating the situation, drawing attention to the relation between programme and form.'

Dennis Crompton (ed.), *Concerning Archigram*, London, 1998

Neil Bingham, Clare Carolin, Peter Cook and Rob Wilson, *Fantasy Architecture, 1500–2036*, exh. cat., Hayward Gallery, London, 2004

Peter Cook, *Drawing: The Motive Force of Architecture*, Chichester, 2008, pp. 163, 165–66

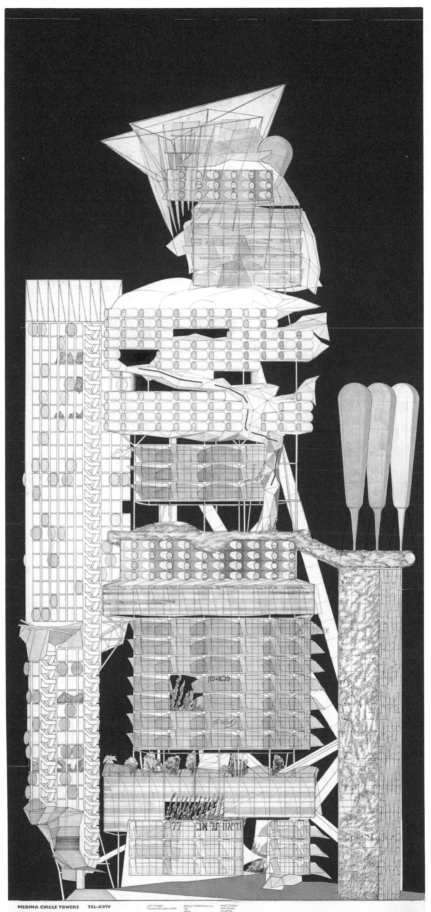

MEDINA CIRCLE TOWERS   TEL-AVIV

LEFT TOWER
housing with cafes outside

MIDDLE TOWER (backing)
club
offices
club bedrooms
hotel
stadia offices
garden
day hotel
garden
day hotel
offices
shopex/markets/theatres
garden
offices
showers/clinics/dorm

RIGHT TOWER
water storage
car parking

PETER COOK
COOK
AND
HAWLEY
ARCHITECTS

ELEVATION 1: 200

MAXXI: National Museum of XXI Century
Arts, Rome, Italy: aerial view, 2010

Ink and automobile paint sprayed on
gelatine and chrome-polyester mounted
on DI-BOND (composite sandwich-type
of O_2 aluminium sheets with polyethylene
core), 2000 × 900 mm

Zaha Hadid's highly distinctive style
of drawing is intimately linked to her
architecture. In fact, it was through her
drawings with their dramatic, exploding
fragmentary forms that she first came to
prominence in her early career. But, so
different were they from the norm that her
projects appeared unbuildable and Hadid
received few commissions. The major
turning point came in 1994 with the
opening of the fire station that she
designed for Vitra, the contemporary
furniture design and manufacturing
company, at their complex in Weil am
Rhein, Germany. Shaped by shattered
geometry and lines of energy, with angled
walls and a sharp tipped roof, this small
concrete building won international
recognition, injecting a new force into
architecture. Large and prestigious
commissions followed, with such notable
works as the Rosenthal Center for
Contemporary Art, Cincinnati, in 2003,
and in 2005 two projects in Germany, the
Phaeno Science Center, Wolfsburg, and
the BMW Central Building in Leipzig.
Zaha Hadid is one of today's most
celebrated architects.

The MAXXI in Rome opened in 2010
after an extended gestation period.
Developed in conjunction with her
long-time co-designer Patrik Schumacher,
Hadid's building won the competition in
1999 out of 273 entrants; but funding was
slow in coming. Hadid's electrifying 'silver
painting' shows the scheme as it was
projected in 2003, close to its eventual
realisation. The view is from above, the
building integrated into its urban setting,
the old army barracks with their red roofs
retained for museum use and wrapped
into the sinuous form of the new structure.
The museum slips and slides over the site,
in layers, like the ancient city in which it is
found. Hadid speaks of the circulation as
having 'directional drifts', with the

intertwining spaces leading the visitor
'experimentally' through the tubes of
galleries. Metal-finned louvers controlling
light and for hanging pictures can clearly
be seen in the painting, running like
tracks in the glazed surfaces of the roof.

This painting, its glistening
appearance resembling a mirror of
polished metal, was one of the first of the
silver series that Hadid directed. The work
is painted on a polyester skin treated with
a chrome-like paint overlaid with
transparent gelatine that enables the
surface to absorb water-based colours.
The image is first laid down very lightly
through a sequence of digitally generated
images. Then, with masking tape to
control the edges, the paint is applied,
mainly automobile acrylic, but also
coloured inks, approximately 80% of
it with a spray gun and 20% with an
airbrush. Finally, the surface is varnished
with a UV-resistant coat. The result is
a silver painting of three-dimensional
intensity, with the reflective MAXXI
building snaking in lines of movement
against the opaque city background.

Zahah Hadid's silver paintings are
rooted in her early research of using
drawing and painting to create radical
architectural forms. Born in Baghdad,
Hadid moved to London in the 1970s and
studied at the Architectural Association.
Her thesis project from 1976-77, entitled
Malevich's Tektonik, was a hotel on
London's Hungerford Bridge in which she
derived her use of multiple perspective
and fluid abstract space from the Russian
Suprematists, such as Kasimir Malevich
(1879-1935), and Constructivist artists
(thus earning Hadid's style the term
'deconstructivist'). In 2004, when
accepting the Pritzker Architecture Prize,
Hadid spoke of the association between
her paintings and architectural space:
'One concrete result of my fascination with

Malevich in particular was that I took up
painting as a design tool. This medium
became my first domain of spatial
invention. I felt limited by the poverty
of the traditional system of drawing in
architecture and was searching for new
means of representation.

The obsessive use of isometric and
perspective projection led to the idea that
space itself might be warped and distorted
to gain in dynamism and complexity
without losing its coherence and
continuity. Despite its abstractness – this
work was always aimed at architectural
reality and real life.'

Joseph Giovannini,
'In the Nature of
Design Materials:
The Instruments of
Zaha Hadid's Vision',
in *Zaha Hadid*, exh.
cat., Solomon R.
Guggenheim Museum,
New York, 3 June
– 25 October 2006,
pp. 23–32

MAXXI museum
website: www.
fondazionemaxxi.it

Zaha Hadid's Pritzker
Architecture Prize
acceptance speech:
www.pritzkerprize.
com/laureates/2004/
ceremony_speech1.
html

Chris Wilkinson RA
b. 1945
RA 27 March 2006

Mary Rose Museum, Portsmouth Historic
Dockyard, Hampshire, 2006
Model: acrylic and photopolymer resin;
figures: polystyrene; case dimensions
380 × 560 × 560 mm

'It's like an oyster enclosing the pearl,'
observes Chris Wilkinson of his new
Mary Rose Museum, designed to house
the remains of the Tudor warship. The
exterior of the museum building, elliptical
in shape, does indeed resemble an oyster
or a mussel shell. However, in the concept
model that Wilkinson presented as his
Diploma Work, the 'shell' of the building
has been shucked, revealing the
delectable morsel of the interior.

The *Mary Rose* sank in the Solent just
off Portsmouth harbour on 19 July 1545
during an engagement with the French
fleet. From the shore, King Henry VIII
watched in despair as the pride of his
navy, the flagship of the Royal High
Admiral, went down with great loss of life.
In the seabed ooze the Mary Rose rotted
away until its surviving carcase, and
thousands of objects, were recovered
in 1982. Put into dry dock, near Lord
Nelson's famous HMS *Victory*, and
carefully dried out, the ship and a small
selection of its contents went on display
in temporary quarters until the architects
Wilkinson Eyre were commissioned to
design a new museum to house them.

Chris Wilkinson, founding member
with Chris Eyre of the architectural
practice Wilkinson Eyre, created this
design model for the new Mary Rose
Museum in 2006. It was made to be shown
to Charles, Prince of Wales, president
of the trustees for the project, at a
fundraising dinner around the time
of Wilkinson's election as a Royal
Academician. The jewel-like quality
of Wilkinson Eyre's work shines through
in the model. Wilkinson and his team
are known for dynamic structures of
technological elegance, such as their
Gateshead Millennium Bridge of 2001.
Today, Wilkinson Eyre have achieved
celebrity status with a broad portfolio.
In China, for example, they have created
the country's tallest skyscraper, the
shimmering Guangzhou International
Finance Centre.

The Mary Rose Museum model is
moulded in two segments: one side shows
the surviving starboard hull of the ship
(seen on the left here) while the other
section is the 'virtual hull', the missing
port side made for viewing and exhibition
display. In this section of the museum,
visitors experience the feeling of being
aboard the re-created deck levels,
wandering among salvaged objects – from
bronze cannon to musical instruments
– displayed in their original context.
Ship and artefacts are thus united once
more after nearly five hundred years.

With its translucent polymer surfaces
layered by laser using computer-
generated design, this beautiful model
suspends the hull and virtual hull afloat in
space. It was conceived in the workshop of
Wilkinson's firm, in which a small team of
product designers are occupied in keeping
up with the demand for the concept
models that architects at Wilkinson
Eyre like to use throughout the design
stage, not always just as a final flourish.
The models, like this for the Mary Rose
Museum, are therefore not fully detailed,
'but rather an abstraction of the
architectural design,' as Wilkinson points
out, 'blurring the boundaries, like a piece
of artwork'.

Chris Wilkinson and
Jim Eyre, *Bridging Art
and Science*, London,
2001

Peter Davey and Kurt
W. Forster, *Exploring
Boundaries: The
Architecture of
Wilkinson Eyre*, Basel,
2007, pp. 133–39

Eric Parry RA
b. 1952
RA 12 December 2006

30 Finsbury Square, London:
perspective looking northeast, 2002
Pencil, 616 × 764 mm

Eric Parry's Diploma Work drawing, beautiful and intriguing, shows the principal elevation of an office building that he designed overlooking an historic London business square now lined with mainly twentieth-century classical buildings. The design is extremely contemporary, almost like an Op Art piece in its abstract ebb and flow: a balanced composition, which the architect acknowledges then subverts. Parry's use of stone under varying pressures, as if it were post-and-beam construction from the days of ancient Greece, led a friend of his to describe it jokingly as 'high-tech stone age'.

Delicately worked in pencil, Parry's drawing emphasises the static horizontality of the storey levels, broken by the pattern of apertures. Although it is an aesthetic composition, this elevational study is nevertheless based upon the engineered distribution of weight bearing down through the piers. Parry had hoped to integrate an additional break in the tension of the visual grid by wrapping a small section of the stone-frame composition in sculpture of stainless steel balls by Richard Deacon RA, like an interweaving necklace, but this did not receive planning permission.

Parry created this drawing of the final design as the conclusion to a long succession of studies drawn by hand, his preferred method of working. 'There is a bone of a computer drawing underneath it,' he related in conversation with the author, referring to the need to use a computer for working out such engineering aspects as stress and load. But once these factors were in place, Parry took things forward to the next stages by making hand drawings.

Parry's Diploma Work drawing represents one of the many buildings in which the architect and his team at Eric Parry Architects have employed a patterned 'skin'. Appointed in 1987 to create a masterplan for Pembroke College, Cambridge, by 1998 Parry had completed a new Master's Lodge and a building for student accommodation. Sited around pleasant green college courts and cloistered gardens, the exterior has fifteen façades. A geometric grid of windows pierces the cladding of honey-coloured Bath stone; on some elevations large, deeply incised rectangles are each given a different pattern of surfaces and openings, decoratively abstract yet also practical for protection from solar gain. The visual effect, as in the Diploma Work drawing, is of order in flux.

The largest example of Eric Parry's use of a cladding grid is his eighteen-storey office building, 5 Aldermanbury Square in the City of London, which uses a six-metre grid of stainless steel fillets stacked one upon the other. In the end elevations, the rhythm is ruptured, as in the Finsbury Square building, by apertures of varying sizes, with those at the top curved to follow the line of the entasis of the upper storeys.

Parry is also responsible for the comprehensive renewal of the London landmark church of St Martin-in-the-Fields, concluded in 2008, 'a truly epic undertaking' as *Building Design* described it (7 November 2008, p. 12). James Gibbs's baroque church with its great portico and steeple facing Trafalgar Square was completed in 1726. Perry refreshed the interior, which had grown dingy, and returned the ornate stuccowork to white, highlighting that of the east end with touches of gilding. In the pedestrian plaza to the north of the church, he sited a new entrance pavilion, a glass rotunda, giving access to the new subterranean spaces below connected to the crypt: a sequence of church halls, a chapel and a music rehearsal room, lit by a circular light well formed around a sunken court in the plaza.

In his latest project, the refurbishment of the Holburne Museum in Bath, Parry has sensitively combined historic and modern, restoring and adapting the existing Georgian building to high museum standards while adding an extension building at the rear to provide more galleries and a restaurant. The upper storeys of this new building, whose façades are clad in ceramic panels behind glass and then streaked with cobalt and olive ceramic fins, appear to float above the glazed ground floor in another example of Parry's skill at layering space to give a play of light and shadow.

Eric Parry Architects, 1, with contributions by Dalibor Vesely and Wilfried Wang, London, 2002, pp. 178–89

Edward Jones, 'Story in Stone: Eric Parry Architects in Finsbury Square', *Architecture Today*, 136, March 2003, pp. 38–51

Fiona McLachlan, 'Dancing Windows: The Restless Façade', *Architectural Research Quarterly*, 10, 2006, pp. 190–200

Sir David Chipperfield RA
b. 1953
RA 11 December 2007

Neues Museum, Museum Island, Berlin,
Germany: longitudinal section, 2008
(detail opposite, full drawing overleaf)
Print with coloured inks on canvas,
895 × 2190 mm

In 2008, with the imminent opening of his most important project to date, David Chipperfield presented this large sectional drawing to the Royal Academy as his Diploma Work. The view is a slice right through the central length of the Neues Museum. Raking shadows slash the upper parts of the exposed brickwork of the courtyard galleries as light floods in through glass ceilings. Through the centre rise the main lobby and stairs; a pair of dark wooden doors pierces the building's core. Small delicate patterns of frescoes form a sequence on the left.

Chipperfield's rehabilitation, conservation and transformation of the old ruined museum building in Berlin has been cited as one of the most sensitive and painstaking jobs in the long process of architectural reconstruction in Germany following the Second World War. Berlin's Neues Museum had sat derelict since aerial bombardments in the 1940s. Before its destruction, the colourful and decorated interior had comprised a series of historical tableaux associated with the displays and collections of ethnology, Egyptology, plaster casts, prints and etchings. The Neues (New) Museum, completed in 1855 by the architect Frederick August Stüler, was the second of five museums to be built on Museum Island, near the Altes (Old) Museum by Stüler's famous master Karl Friedrich Schinkel.

On the Neues Museum project, Chipperfield worked in conjunction with the conservation architect Julian Harrap, who focused on repair and restoration. In a BBC radio interview Chipperfield acknowledged the delicacy required to handle the building's reconstruction at a moment when Germany was 'moving from memory to history'. Against the wishes of a small band of campaigners who believed that the Neues Museum should be restored as closely as possible to its former glory, Chipperfield chose to follow principled conservation methods within contemporary practice.

Although whole sections of the museum had been completely destroyed, other parts remained, with decoration and surfaces surviving. The art of Chipperfield's reconstruction was in blending the retained original fragments with his interventions. Shattered fragments of wall finishes and ceiling frescoes were recorded in minute detail and then painstakingly conserved millimetre by millimetre, with the repairs given similar but not identical colour tones. In those portions of the building where surfaces had been eradicated, brickwork was left exposed and handled with the same rigorous balance between ruination and reinvigoration.

This architectural presentation drawing conveys the power of historic decay, renewed with freshness and to exacting standards. Created in Chipperfield's Berlin office and then refined in his London office, the image is a combination of media – photogrammetry, computer-generated imagery, line drawing and colour rendering – all digitally edited and then printed out on canvas.

David Chipperfield's architecture has moved progressively towards quiet physical and historical contextualisation since the establishment of his practice in 1984. His early working days with Norman Foster RA and Richard Rogers RA put him in touch with the vision of modern architects who were largely examining the potential of technology in building. But later, teaching at the University of Stuttgart and working in Germany and Italy, Chipperfield became more attuned to finding solutions that are traditional yet reduced to modern essentials that permit conservation. In this balancing act, says the architect: 'We must embrace history and reject it' (*Form Matters*, p. 11).

'David Chipperfield: 1984–2009', *AV Monografias*, 131, May/June 2008, pp. 36–45

David Chipperfield Architects: Form Matters, exh. cat., Design Museum, London, 2009, pp. 132–39

Rik Nys and Martin Reichert (eds), *Neues Museum Berlin: By David Chipperfield Architects in Collaboration with Julian Harrap*, Cologne, 2009

David Chipperfield interviewed on 'Night Waves', BBC Radio 3, 13 October 2009

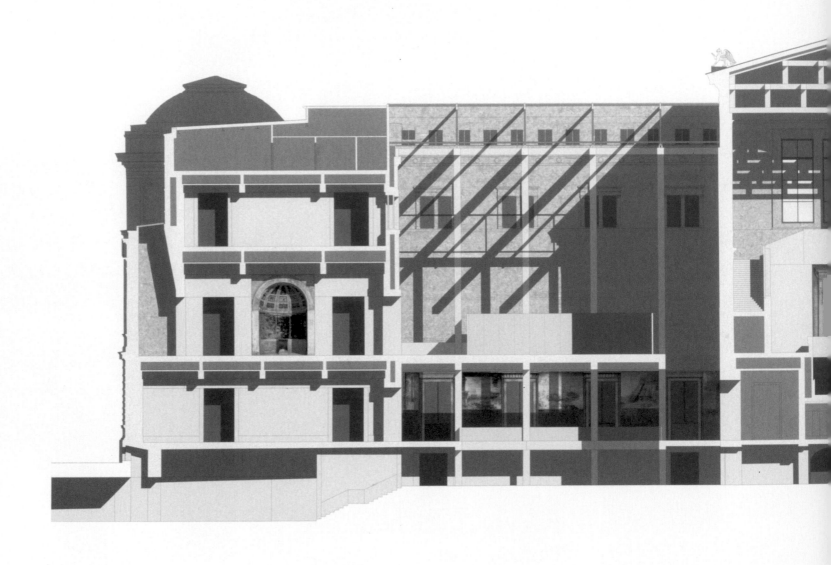

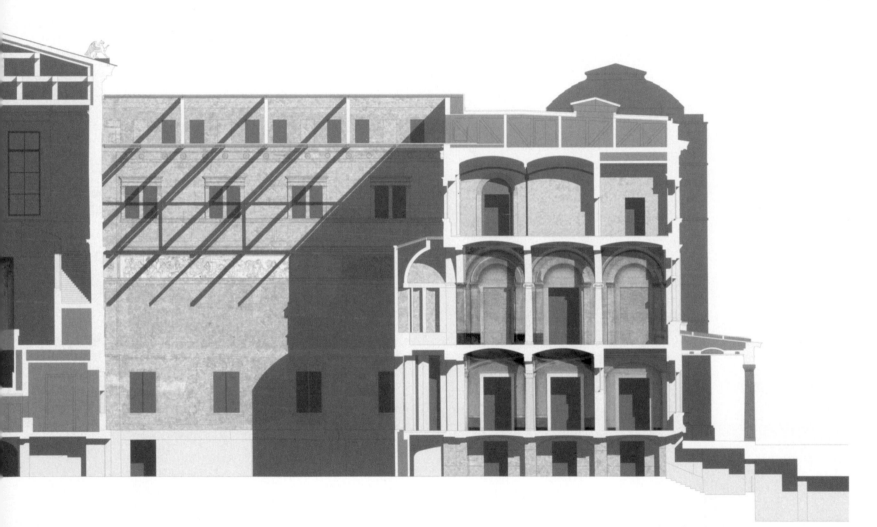

DAVID CHIPPERFIELD
Neues museum Berlin

Spencer de Grey RA
b. 1944
RA 9 December 2008

The Sage Gateshead, Tyne and Wear, 2009
Wood, acrylic, paint and metal,
812 × 912 × 207 mm (case)
Model made by Pipers Fooks, Ashford, Kent

'Of course I didn't tell them I was from Newcastle,' jokes the architect Spencer de Grey. The performance venue, the Sage – designed by Foster + Partners with de Grey as head of design – is in Gateshead, facing Newcastle from across the River Tyne. There is a friendly rivalry between these two northern English cities, and with the Sage Gateshead definitely scored a winning point.

Spencer de Grey grew up in Newcastle. His parents were both highly respected painters: his mother was Flavia Irwin RA, and his father Sir Roger de Grey PRA, who was then teaching at the art school at Durham University. Thus, taking up the job on the Sage Gateshead, says Spencer, 'had a lot of resonance'. So as well as being an act of recollection, presenting an architectural model of the Sage Gateshead as his Diploma Work was also one of continued celebration, because the building, having opened five years previously in 2004, has been an overwhelming success from the start.

'I was looking to tell a story visually,' he says of the model. So, instead of the usual straightforward, miniaturised representation of the building in a single aspect, de Grey created an architectural narrative in a collage of images, letting the story unfold. Study of the model is easiest if one begins at the lower right with the site plan showing the building set on the quayside. The long outline across the top represents the Tyne Bridge.

The lower centre image, the concourse plan of the Sage Gateshead, reveals the three distinct internal spaces: the large hall at the bottom, the rehearsal hall and restaurant area in the centre, and the more intimate, ten-sided smaller hall at the top. The third shape at the bottom left is the roof form, the glistening metallic shell, which so much defines the building in real life: an undulating stainless-steel construction, multi-faceted to catch the light both by day and night. And above, dominating the model, is the large, shallow longitudinal section, cutting through the principal hall and showing the sweep of the roof form and figures of congregating visitors in the public area behind the glazed wall overlooking the river.

The Sage Gateshead model gleams in its silvery finishes and seduces by its detail. Spencer de Grey's intention is clear: to create an architectural drawing in three dimensions. Unlike most models that lie horizontally on a plinth, his is made to be displayed vertically, like a drawing or painting, affixed to the wall. In this way the viewer can appreciate the building at a glance.

The Sage Gateshead is one of many important projects that Spencer de Grey, working with the Foster team, has created since joining Norman Foster RA in 1973. In his portfolio are to be found the Great Court at the British Museum, the Cambridge Law Faculty, Dresden Station and, yet another outstanding music venue, the Dallas Opera House. And, with further resonance, there is the Sackler Wing of Galleries at Burlington House, adding its beautiful light-infused reception space to the home of the Royal Academy, a Foster project undertaken when Spencer's father Sir Roger de Grey was President.

Edward Robbins, 'Spencer de Grey', *Why Architects Draw*, Cambridge, Mass., and London, 1994, pp. 80–101

Architecture Today, 156, March 2005, pp. 54–69

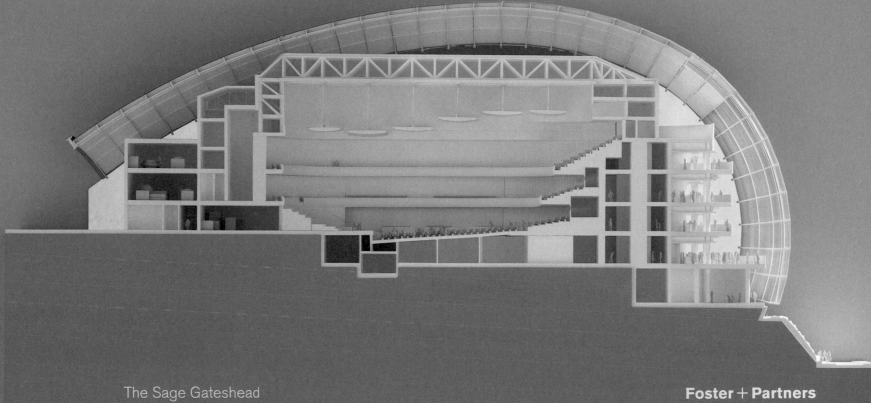

The Sage Gateshead

Foster + Partners

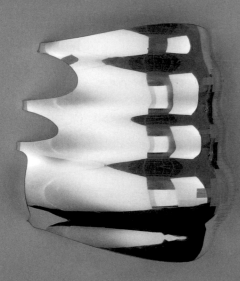

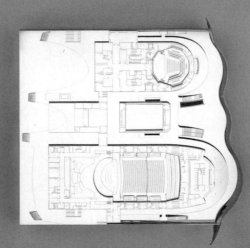

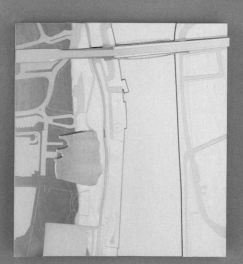

Alan Stanton
Stanton William Architects
b. 1944
RA 9 December 2008

Belgrade Theatre, Coventry, West
Midlands: sketch studies, 2006
Pen with black ink, pencil and coloured
washes on 15 sketchbook pages (2 sizes),
140 x 90 mm and 145 x 100 mm

As part of his Diploma Work, Alan Stanton presented a sequence of studies from his sketchbooks, in which he explored shapes that he and his architectural partner Paul Williams had employed to create their design for additions to the Belgrade Theatre, Coventry, a project completed in 2007. The sequence of fifteen drawings begins with a playful abstraction of overlapping straight lines that quickly coalesce into blocks before finally coming together as the recognisable theatre building. The resolution is as satisfying as watching someone solving a Rubik's Cube puzzle.

This drawing process, Stanton explains, is about 'finding form by pushing and pulling' (interview with the author). Of course, using a computer for design has its advantages – it is a good means for testing physical dimensions for example – but it demands accuracy; models are a means of seeing a design in three dimensions; and photography allows a change of scale and perspective. But when drawing, Stanton feels he is able to keep the development loose, working backwards and forwards, looking for 'accidents'.

The Belgrade Theatre was originally opened in 1958. Designed by Arthur Ling, Coventry's city architect, the theatre takes its name from a gift of timber from the then Yugoslav capital. The building was a symbol of the bombed-out city's post-war reconstruction, a cultural institution to complement Sir Basil Spence's new cathedral (see pp. 140–41). Half a century later, the theatre received Stanton Williams's delicate refurbishment and a much-needed extension.

The sketchbook studies express the architect's search for a means to examine the necessity of 'volume wrapped around movement', of making the principal spaces required of the design interlock through the flow of circulation and that of purpose. As the sketches progress, the low horizontal volume emerges, representing the theatre's new entrance and enlarged foyer, while the great cube and enveloping masses suggest a second auditorium, rooms for rehearsal and dressing and, glowing blue at night, a transparent polycarbonate surface.

Exhibition design first brought Alan Stanton and Paul Williams together in the early 1980s when both were engaged with projects for the Tate Gallery. Stanton Williams was formed in 1985, and at first the architects established a practice in refined interiors. They created a series of London fashion boutiques with Issey Miyake, for example, as well as many blockbuster exhibitions for major London galleries and museums; twenty-nine alone, to date, for the Hayward Gallery. When Sir Terence Conran's new Design Museum opened in 1989 in an old Thameside warehouse, Stanton Williams's cool, white and flexible gallery spaces were heralded as exemplars of the industrial beauty being awoken in the regeneration of London's Docklands.

Stanton speaks about the architectural practice as having been 'built up from small to large' over the next decades, taking its designs 'from inside to outside, creating a sensibility of working interior to exterior'. Many of these projects have involved substantial additions to historic listed buildings, such as Compton Verney, Warwickshire, where they have successfully created a new arts centre. Stanton Williams's next great challenges include a major scientific research institute funded by Lord Sainsbury of Turville for the University of Cambridge and the new University of the Arts campus at King's Cross, London, as well as new museum projects in Berlin and France.

Architects' Journal, 226, 13 December 2007, pp. 30–37

Stanton Williams, London, Lucerne, 2009

Stanton Williams: Volume, London, 2009

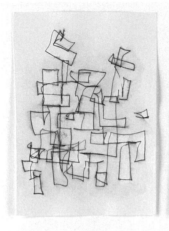

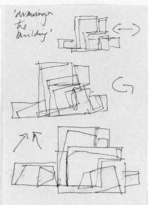

'drawings the building'

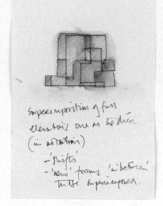

superimposition of full
elevations one on the other
(in no particular)
- 'shifts'
- 'new' forms 'in between'
these superimposed.

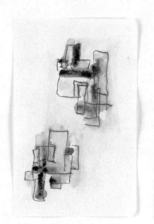

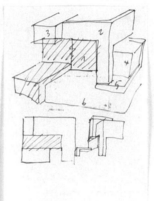

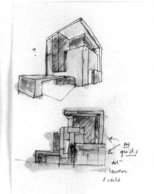

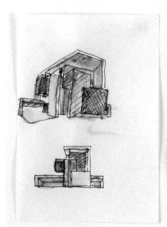

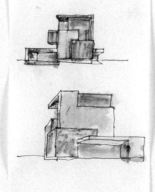

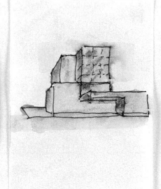

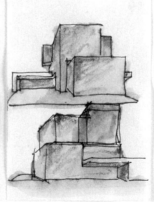

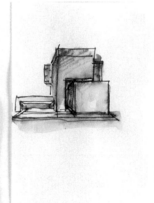

Honorary Royal Academician Architects

In chronological order
by date of election

Eugène Emmanuel Viollet-le-Duc HON RA (1814–1879)
Elected 15 December 1859

Ragnar Östberg HON RA (1866–1945)
Elected 10 June 1930

Cass Gilbert HON RA (1859–1934)
Elected 5 December 1930

Ivar Tengbom HON RA (1878–1968)
Elected 24 April 1947

Walter Gropius HON RA (1883–1969)
Elected 20 April 1967

Pier Luigi Nervi HON RA (1891–1979)
Elected 20 April 1967

José Luis Sert HON RA (1902–1983)
Elected 22 May 1980

Ralph Erskine HON RA (1914–2005)
Elected 17 January 1985

Jørn Utzon HON RA (1918–2008)
Elected 20 May 1985

Ieoh Ming Pei HON RA (b. 1917)
Elected 10 December 1993

Arata Isozaki HON RA (b. 1931)
Elected 23 May 1994

Frank O. Gehry HON RA (b. 1929)
Elected 21 May 1998

Tadao Ando HON RA (b. 1941)
Elected 29 May 2002

Daniel Libeskind HON RA (b. 1946)
Elected 23 May 2003

Renzo Piano HON RA (b. 1937)
Elected 31 May 2007

Associate Royal Academician Architects

In chronological order
by date of election

Edward Stevens ARA (c. 1744–1775)
Elected 27 August 1770

Joseph Bonomi ARA (1739–1808)
Elected 2 November 1789

Joseph Michael Gandy ARA (1771–1843)
Elected 7 November 1803

William Burges ARA (1827–1881)
Elected 28 January 1881

Sir Arthur W. Blomfield ARA (1829–1899)
Elected 17 January 1888

Edward S. Prior ARA (1852–1932)
Elected 20 March 1914

Sir Robert Lorimer ARA (1864–1929)
Elected 22 April 1920

Further Reading

Neil Bingham, 'Architecture at the Royal Academy Schools, 1768 to 1836', in Neil Bingham (ed)., *The Education of the Architect, Proceedings of the 22nd Annual Symposium of the Society of Architectural Historians of Great Britain*, London, 1993, pp. 5-14

Howard Colvin, *A Biographical Dictionary of British Architects 1600-1840*, fourth edition, New Haven and London, 2008

James Fenton, *School of Genius: A History of the Royal Academy of Arts*, London, 2006

Kenneth Garlick and Angus Macintyre (eds), *The Diary of Joseph Farington*, New Haven and London, 1978-98, 16 vols; index volume, Evelyn Newby, 1998

Algernon Graves, *The Royal Academy of Arts: A Complete Dictionary of Contributors and Their Work from Its Foundation in 1769 to 1904*, 8 vols, Wakefield, 1905-06

A. Stuart Gray, *Edwardian Architecture: A Biographical Dictionary*, London, 1985

Holger Hoock, *The King's Artists: The Royal Academy of Arts and the Politics of British Culture, 1760-1830*, Oxford, 2003

Sidney C. Hutchison, *The History of the Royal Academy, 1768-1986*, second edition, London, 1986

Walter Ison, 'Burlington House', *Survey of London*, vols 31 and 32, St James's and Westminster, Part 2, 1963, pp. 390-429

Walter R. M. Lamb, *The Royal Academy: A Short History of Its Foundation and Development*, revised edition, London, 1951

G. D. Leslie, *The Inner Life of the Royal Academy*, London, 1914

Royal Academy of Arts, *Catalogue of the Diploma and Gibson Galleries*, London, 1939

William Sandby, *The History of the Royal Academy of Arts, from Its Foundation in 1768 to the Present Time, with Biographical Notices of All the Members*, 2 vols, London, 1862

Nicholas Savage, 'The "Vice-Roy" of the Academy: Sir William Chambers and the Royal Protection of the Arts', in John Harris and Michael Snodin (eds), *Sir William Chambers, Architect to George III*, New Haven and London, 1996, pp. 193-98

Nicholas Savage, 'Exhibiting Architecture: Strategies of Representation in English Architectural Drawings, 1760-1836', in David H. Solkin (ed.), *Art on the Line: The Royal Academy Exhibitions at Somerset House, 1780-1836*, New Haven and London, 2001, pp. 201-16

David H. Solkin (ed.), *Art on the Line: The Royal Academy Exhibitions at Somerset House, 1780-1836*, New Haven and London, 2001

David Watkin (ed.), *Sir John Soane: The Royal Academy Lectures*, Cambridge, 2000

Photographic Acknowledgements

Index

All references are to page
numbers; those in *italic* type
indicate illustrations